HIDING IN PLAIN SIGHT

THE CONCEALED UNDERWORLD

OF SIBLING ABUSE

SEAN TOREAN MCFADDEN

SEAN TOREAN MCFADDEN
PUBLISHING

Hiding In Plain Sight:

The Concealed Underworld of Sibling Abuse

Copyright © 2021 Sean Torean McFadden

The events within this book span more than thirty years and are recounted to the best of the memoirist's recollection; neither the memoirist nor any of the memoirist's representatives are to be held responsible for any unrecognized or overlooked discrepancy.

The memoirist has tried to recreate events, locales, and conversations from his memories of them. In order to maintain their anonymity in some instances he has changed the names of individuals and places; he may have changed some identifying characteristics and details such as physical properties, occupations, and places of residence.

No part of this book may be reproduced in any form or by any electronic or mechanical means including information storage and retrieval systems, without permission in writing from the author. The only exception is by a reviewer, who may quote short excerpts in a published, professional review. For permission requests, write to the publisher, at "Attention: Permissions Coordinator," at the following email address. SeanToreanMcFadden@gmail.com

Portions of *The Destructive Narcissistic Pattern* by Nina W. Brown are reprinted by permission of Praeger Publishers.

Portions of *Why Is It Always About You?: The Seven Deadly Sins of Narcissism* by Sandy Hotchkiss are reprinted by permission of Free Press.

Portions of *Humanizing the Narcissistic Style* by Stephen M. Johnson are reprinted by permission of W. W. Norton Company.

Portions of *People of the Lie: The Hope for Healing Human Evil* by M. Scott Peck are reprinted by permission of Simon & Schuster.

Portions of *Identifying and Understanding the Narcissistic Personality* by Elsa F. Ronningstam are reprinted by permission of Oxford University Press.

ISBN: 978-1-7367265-0-1 (Trade Paperback)
ISBN: 978-1-7367265-2-5 (Hardcover)
ISBN: 978-1-7367265-1-8 (eBook)

Library of Congress Control Number: 2021916598

First Edition
Printed in the United States of America
www.SeanToreanMcFadden.com

TABLE OF CONTENTS

Disclaimer v
Introduction vii
Prologue ix
   1. Rude Awakening 1
   2. Home, Unsweet Home 13
   3. 1993 and a New Life 23
   4. False Words 33
   5. 1995 47
   6. Preparing My Escape 55
   7. Escape from Dark Territory 69
   8. The Turning Point 97
   9. A Struggle for Self 115
   10. The Fall-Out from My Letter 129
   11. Two Conversations from Hell 151
   12. The Appointment 167
   13. The Depth of Hatred 175
   14. Bad Seeds 185
   15. The Bully 201
   16. A Time of Reckoning 209
   17. The Unredeemable Family 241
   18. July to December 267
   19. The Next Generation 285
   20. A Dichotomy of Evil 301
   21. Signs of Transformations 315
   22. A Generation Ends and The Final Blade 331
   23. Acknowledgments 345
Bibliography and Resources 347

Disclaimer

This book is not intended to be used as a means of advice, professional counseling, or to draw conclusions regarding personality disorders or other forms of character defects. It is also not intended to harm anyone, but rather represents a legitimate public interest in exploring themes of sibling, narcissism, and family-related emotional and psychological abuse.

This book is intended to help others to better their own lives and offers themes for forgiveness, hope, and healing. Any direct or indirect correlation to real people or real events is purely coincidental, although specific behavior described herein is truthful.

Conclusions and analyses are my own based on my personal interpretation and relate directly to actual, published research by scientists and/or doctors in the study of human behavior and its science, and not through professional diagnosis. Finally, timelines are taken out of context or are a creation by the author to enhance the story.

If legal advice or other expert assistance is required, the services of a competent professional person should be sought.

— From a *Declaration of Principles* jointly adopted by a Committee of the American Bar Association and a Committee of Publishers and Associations.

Introduction

All families are imperfect, yet within the expected range of imperfection you may believe that your family is particularly afflicted with a profound dysfunction and that this dysfunction is so severe as to inhibit the happiness and success that every person within that family unit deserves.

Sibling abuse is one of the more controversial areas of domestic violence. Society places great emphasis upon sibling relationships exemplified by the use of terms such as "brotherly and sisterly love" to reflect strong attachments of love and caring, but not all sibling relationships are healthy and well-adjusted. Several studies indicate that sibling abuse occurs in more than sixty percent of families, crossing all racial and socioeconomic lines, making it a common form of domestic violence and an area in need of greater research. For many years, very little research was conducted into the dynamics of sibling abuse, and what researchers do know comes from clinical studies. Parents often ignore it, researchers do not study it in great detail, and many therapists find it a normal element of growing up. However, there is an increasing focus on the fact that, in less than a majority of cases, sibling wars develop into a form of repeated and inescapable abuse.

In the last quarter century, as of this writing, only two national studies that I am aware of and a few specialized books have looked at this phenomenon in detail. I discovered John V. Caffaro, a clinical psychologist in San Diego, who defined sibling abuse as a pattern of repeated violence and intimidation. "Things are chaotic, boundaries are blurred, and supervision is minimal," he said, noting those families do not always look chaotic from the outside. "Sometimes the father is basically out of town and Mom is not a good limit-setter," he says. "In other cases, parents escalate conflicts by playing favorites and ignoring clearly obvious victimizing."

One study determined that, as siblings grow older, their abuse decreases.

I can personally and unequivocally state that this is not always the case.

The word "evil" has been used in this book more than one hundred times. It is not a word I take lightly, nor should you. I struggled immensely with its use and required in-depth soul-searching before determining whether to use it or not. One normally associates evil with demons, possession, dark cults, and the like, and most notably with the devil itself. This book is not about that. It is about premeditated and unbridled betrayal, cruelty, emotional and psychological harm, half-truths, outright lies, and other forms of deception that leave no outward scars. While these, I have concluded, are all weapons in the devil's massive arsenal, because of that there is no question in my mind that with the existence of *human* evil, the devil plays an active role. With that thought in mind, I determined my use of the term in this book was proper.

I respect your right as an unbiased and open-minded reader to draw your own conclusions and to decide for yourself which of my views—if any of them—you wish to keep or discard as you turn each page. I am not a doctor or professional in the field of human behavior or psychiatry, nor am I expert in theology, spiritualism, or God. Having said that, rest assured I have meticulously completed my research and my homework—and then some.

It is my greatest hope that, should any aspects of my life within these pages sound familiar to you from your own experiences, you will learn from *my* experiences, be nourished and strengthened by them, and become strong enough to prevail in healing with truth and a greater sense of self.

Prologue

*"All that is necessary for the triumph of evil...
is for good men to do nothing."*

— EDMUND BURKE

I recall my therapist taking me back to my childhood, to the age of nine or ten, as I was eating my sandwich at the kitchen table. I watched my mother, just having departed my sister's room, lean against the kitchen sink and, with a look of terror, slap herself in the face as hard as she could several times, uttering unintelligible sounds.

I had forgotten about this moment entirely, but after this work with my therapist, the memory of it has remained indelible in my mind over these past several years.

Workplace and school bullying can be intense and carry tragic consequences. Domestic abuse has long been a serious social problem—and it's not always in the physical form. The family abuse that I'm describing in this book is slightly different from these other forms and can be characterized by a long-term corrosion that gradually eats at your soul. The abuse happens over a period of years and even decades. The intensity waxes and wanes; there are sharp attacks followed by periods of relative calm. The perpetrators endeavor to leave no tracks or evidence. The parties involved—both abusers and victims—are bound by family ties that are difficult to break, and so the victim suffers in silence and strives to find a way to keep a semblance of family connection while at the same time keeping the abusers at arm's length.

And, as you will see in my case, some victims have a powerful motive to stay close to an abusive family because of love for one family member who is a normal, loving person, and who does not deserve to be abandoned to the cruel mercies of the others. In my case this person is, namely, my father.

After reading this book one may argue that my personal plight doesn't come close to the deep suffering of those who have been physically victimized by their families. There is incest, physical abuse, and other forms of abuse that leave deep scars emotionally, psychologically, and physically. Every year thousands of women are beaten and even murdered by their husbands or significant others, and let's not forget the abuse of innocent children by those preaching the word of God, many of whom are now in prison where they belong. Beyond the priesthood, there are others associated directly with the church who make the devil laugh, live life in a lie to themselves and to others, and then go to serve God.

In no way do I minimize the pain and suffering of the victims of such people; clearly their suffering is on a far greater scale than my own. It is only my intent to enhance awareness of the abusive creatures who may live within the family structure so that if you recognize yourself in these pages, you may find the strength to endure, to seek professional help to maintain your sense of balance, stability, and structure, and ultimately to transcend a family environment that you did not choose and that is painful to experience.

Rude Awakening

1991

"It is during our darkest moments that we must focus to see the light."

— ARISTOTLE

I had always known there were internal issues with respect to our family structure, but during my years of military service I was never home long enough to personally witness more than the occasional interaction of this nature. For the most part, I only knew what I heard from and the anguish I would see in my brother, Patrick.

Patrick was just ten months younger than me, having been born in 1953 while I was born in 1952. He was short in height and proportionate in weight. His hair was rusty red and straight, and he wore it long enough to cover his ears. His pale but handsome baby face was incapable of growing a full beard or mustache, though he tried in spite of this. I would often tell him to forget about it, and he would smirk in acknowledgment. He had a round and prominent chin; narrow, oval-shaped eyes; an upturned nose; and high cheekbones.

The beginning of our rekindled relationship upon my return home was rewarding, but that would change.

My older sister, Kayleigh, on the other hand, seemed to be in a constant state of anger but never toward me directly; she would be angry in general about things that were displeasing to her or that did not meet her needs. Though I believed that her anger must have a reason, I never saw anything during my visits on military leave to justify anger in my sister, and it was the same on each visit over the years.

It was bewildering.

I have a strong memory of Kayleigh's three days of rage during my wife's first visit to my family home. I met Maureen while I was stationed in Germany. She was the owner of a small crafts shop on the base where I was stationed. She was smart, funny, and had a great personality. We connected while I was browsing through her store looking for Christmas gifts and I nonchalantly asked if she'd like to have dinner one day, to which she delightfully agreed. She was divorced with three children, but that didn't matter. The more we dated, the more I liked her and eventually came to love her. We married two years later.

It was 1986, and we had just been married, so naturally I wanted Maureen to meet my folks. This did not keep Kayleigh from making a nasty first impression. Because of the simple fact that we were staying in her room, she would scream that she had no room and could not breathe. She slammed cupboards and stomped her feet, and other times walked around silently with an eerie look of contempt on her face, her rage unmistakable. She did not throw things, seeing as my elderly parents were present, I assume, but she was capable of it. It was coming to me then that there were deeper issues at play here. I did not know what they were, but it was inevitable that I would find out.

Kayleigh was tall and heavy but not obese; she was big-boned. She had the typical Irish features of a big chin, thin upper lip, and the structural features of her nose were of topographical complexity. Her hooded eyes seemed to cross their pupils in a slight diagonal. Her long and straight jet-black hair seemed out of proportion to her green eyes, and she kept her bushy eyebrows thinned and well-trimmed.

Despite Kayleigh's rage, my mother, who doted on her, expected the rest of us to include her on family outings. This was the first time I saw my mother as my sister's supervisory authority, and left me with an instinctive indicator that she was left out of outings with my brother and his wife in the past. Something wasn't right. On one occasion a couple of months after we'd permanently returned from Europe in 1991, my wife, Maureen, and my brother's wife, Brianna, were sitting on the front stairs of my parents' house, simply conversing.

Brianna was as tall as my sister but thin as a rail in contrast. She was as pale as pale could be, with green-and-hazel eyes set close to her nose. She always wore makeup to minimize her porcelain Irish skin that she felt had to be covered up at any cost. She also had jet-black hair like my sister but with a coppery tint. It flowed to her waist so that she often had to tie it back while cooking or performing anything that would make it a liability.

On this particular day, I was standing on the porch, as were my mother, my wife, and my sister-in-law. It was a quiet, beautiful summer day. My wife and sister-in-law were planning to go out somewhere together and conversing over details.

Suddenly my mother snapped, "Are you going to ask Kayleigh to go with you?"

There was no difficulty translating her tone and message: "You *will* take her with you."

Following a moment's silence, she demanded again, "Are you taking her with you?" Having been met with more silence, her tone became more intense. To my shock, she spat, "Sons of bitches!"

I was stunned into silence. *Did this just really happen?* I thought to myself. I would never have believed it had I not been there.

My mother was not always so hateful in her tone that I remember at that time. She was afflicted with multiple ailments, which I remember started in my teens. She held a job at the post office for a few years, but then multiple surgeries for major arthritis made her a stay-at-home mom for the remainder of her life.

My dad was a loving husband and father who had a calm and relaxed manner about him. Not once did he ever raise his voice; his strength came from his heart, his honesty, and his goodness. Completely devoted to his family, he worked two jobs to support us. He worked as a sales manager for a prominent men's store in Philadelphia and held a second job as a customer service manager. We were not poor but were not well-to-do either. Dad always made sure we had food on the table and the bills were paid. It wasn't until I was in my early teens that he was able to buy the only car he ever owned.

We moved to Philadelphia after my grandfather died, and we remained there for about thirty years. This three-family home was the typical style for this town and was referred to as a "three-decker," a style that was prevalent on the East Coast. These types of homes were relatively close in proximity, separated only by chain-link fences or small driveways. Each level had a rear porch the full length of the house, which was used to air-dry clothes. We did not have a dryer, so this was common for my family.

The backyard was very small and enclosed by a small, wooden fence. The four front stairs led to the main entrance of all three apartments, with the lower-level apartment on the first floor and a stairway off to the side leading to the second and third floors. The front porch was not very big but large enough for a few chairs to enjoy a quiet summer's day.

My family lived on the first floor, and my brother and his girlfriend lived on the second floor. An older woman and her daughter occupied the top floor.

This neighborhood was typical for a major city and had its share of street thugs and crime. It was rundown but not poverty-stricken, though I remember once our home was broken into and we were robbed.

Even so, I have fond memories of this beige-sided, three-family house. I recall as kids my brother, our friends, and I would stand up ten to fifteen baseball cards against a wall not far from the house, side-by-side with a small space between them, and then we'd kneel some five feet away on the curb with a stack of cards in hand. The objective was to "shoot" the baseball cards to knock them down. If you knocked even one down, you got another turn; if you missed, you lost your turn. Whoever knocked the last card down got the prize: all the cards on the sidewalk. Sometimes there were dozens of baseball cards as the prize.

I used to have a shoebox full until many years later my mother accidentally threw them all away. Who knew some would be worth a fortune?

My mother's outburst, unfortunately, was not a one-time occurrence. On a later visit, I was again standing on the front porch leaning against the railing, and Brianna and Maureen were sitting on the top stair again talking about going out for a good time. This time I noticed my mother standing in the living room. It was not that I could actually see her, but the curtains moved and two of the blinds separated as they do when one looks out a window. My wife saw it too. This event added more negativity to Maureen's feelings about my family.

Admittedly we had concerns in our marriage, and this family behavior was not helping. I found myself in a constant state of trying to balance myself and my marriage and to keep a level of awareness and perspective. The struggle for me was trying to understand my family's behavior and to keep peace with my wife and within myself.

It was around the time that Brianna gave birth to my nephew, Patrick Jr., that things changed between my wife and sister-in-law in a highly negative way, one I hadn't experienced before.

Brianna and Maureen initially got along well, but an event transpired in which Brianna felt she was wronged by something my wife said. My nephew was a baby when my wife innocently remarked that he looked like someone we knew, a mutual friend I had grown up with. He actually looked like me and my brother too, for that matter. There was no intent on my wife's part to be insulting, nor would she ever willingly insult anyone. It was a slander of major proportions to my brother's wife, though.

In my efforts to smooth things over, the situation became worse. My brother, Patrick, demanded an apology from my wife. He would tell me on my next two visits that his wife would cry over what Maureen had said, and that if my wife apologized to her, it would be over. I was shocked by both Brianna's overreaction and Patrick's *demand* for an apology.

To appease him I agreed to talk to Maureen, but I knew I would never be able to convince her to render an apology for something Brianna had perceived as an insult. After all, babies look like a lot of people. I did, however, speak with Maureen about Patrick's request for an apology, and Maureen felt she had not said anything with ill intent. I agreed. Over the next two weeks I visited the family alone; my wife was not comfortable coming to the house at all now. Patrick continued to insist my wife apologize as his wife remained upset. This went on for weeks.

Knowing that we would have to visit the family eventually, I felt that appeasing Brianna with an apology might end the nonsense once and for all. I suggested to my wife that she make a call for the sake of peace. Maureen agreed and called my sister-in-law on the phone to render an apology, which she did sincerely, adding that it was an innocent comment meant without ill will toward her or the baby.

That was not good enough for Brianna or Patrick.

Brianna refused to accept the apology and demanded Maureen come to the house to *personally* apologize to her face. This was a shocking development in view of the fact that millions of people apologize by telephone daily and that this is a socially acceptable means of communicating such messages. In response to this completely disproportionate reaction, I became defensive of my wife. *Now, I thought, this is going too far.*

My visits to my family would continue every couple of weeks. Usually I went on a Sunday, and I would go alone. My wife was not comfortable coming for obvious reasons. On the first visit I made after Maureen attempted to apologize on the phone, my brother approached me alone outside near the garage and explained that his wife remained upset. To me it was more like she was making his life hell from something that should have been over. He said, "All that Maureen has to do is come down and apologize." My position was that she *had* apologized, and it was over as far as we were concerned.

The telephone apology should have been acceptable, I said. If it was not, then he had a much bigger problem at home that required his attention to fix. I added that my wife would not bow down to his. There was not much more to say about it, and Patrick did not press the issue.

Another week or two passed, and I visited my parents and my brother again. On this second visit since the failed telephone apology, another opportunity came (perhaps conveniently, now that I think about it) for my brother and me to be alone outside again. He repeated what he had said before: "All she has to do is come down and apologize to her." I was convinced now that there was some level of tension in his life over this issue and that Brianna had been making him miserable, but my position remained that the fight was over. My wife *had* apologized. He insisted that it would be over when my wife came down and apologized again in person.

I disagreed again, and then he was no longer requesting that my wife come down. He said she *had* to come down and apologize personally. I responded, "No, she did apologize."

Suddenly his anger intensified, and a hateful, venomous look came across his face. Referring to my wife, he shouted at me, "She's no fucking good!"

I was shocked into silence. *Did he really just say that?* I thought. *My wife is no good because she won't bow down to his wife?* This would be the first time I would come to see Patrick as an enabler. His wife showed signs of a sadistic ego, although I did not know it then. He had a responsibility to do what was right—namely, to talk sense into her, the one who was actually behaving in a manner that was totally inappropriate. Instead, he made matters worse.

I headed home and had to tell my wife what had transpired. That only caused more turbulence and anger in her. I did not know how to fix this mess.

This particular event brought back memories of a pattern of interaction between Kayleigh and Brianna, in which either one or both of them would state, "I'm not talking to her until she apologizes." It is impossible to count the number of times I heard this; it was so often that now I see it was a normal, sick interaction between them and within the family. Though they lived under the same roof, at times they would not speak for weeks until the other apologized. It was utterly childish and the most ridiculous behavior I had ever witnessed in my entire adult life.

I vowed my wife and I would not be pulled into this drama, but it seemed inescapable and ultimately added more stress to my already strained marriage. Because of Patrick's willingness to be a player in this destructive game, my relationship with him slowly deteriorated too.

My wife could not remain absent from every family birthday or gathering I attended, so eventually, for the sake of peace, we kept to ourselves. My wife did eventually apologize to Brianna in person, but after that, we had to practice restraint, tolerance, and be on our guard whenever we visited my family. They were unpredictable, irrational, and increasingly hostile. It did not take long before we realized we had to be careful what we said within their earshot. The most innocent comment of any sort was likely to ignite the long fuse of a psychological and emotional bomb that, though hastily manufactured, might not explode for weeks.

Whenever I quietly replayed these events in my mind, in an attempt to make sense of them, connecting the proverbial dots was not an easy task. With the exception of my father and of Patrick's children—my niece Michaela and my nephew, Patrick Jr.—it seemed that the very spirit of the family had been nullified by a lack of behavioral boundaries. The adults in my family—specifically my mother, sister, brother, and his wife—had interacted in this way for more than twenty-five years—most of which I had spent away in the military—so that while this behavior was clearly dysfunctional in my eyes, it had become normal to them.

I saw my wife and myself being pulled into it and I had to fight that. It would be many years before I would begin to understand what the underlying causes might be from this and other aberrant behaviors, but for now I only came to realize I had been fighting something I could not see or comprehend.

It was an invisible monster, and it would be as resilient as a malignant tumor.

The events of the first eighteen months after Maureen and I returned from Europe took their toll on our relationship, which was already significantly strained based on differing views of our blended-family interactions especially as related to her children.

My wife was not happy in Philadelphia, and I understood why. I was not either at this point. The inevitable snowball effect had begun with Maureen's first visit, on those three harrowing evenings of my sister's fury because we were staying in her room. Though that event had occurred years earlier, it was the basis of an emotionally charged and psychologically unhealthy environment that already existed long before I returned home.

THE SEPARATION

One summer weekend in 1992, when my wife and I were both at home, we were exchanging words in another unpleasant attempt to communicate. I recall saying, "I can't do this anymore... I have to leave, and I'm filing for divorce." There was no forethought on my part and no anger; it just came out. I think I surprised myself as much as I did her, and I remember the emptiness and that tired, drained feeling. I called my brother and told him what had happened. That same afternoon he drove up the highway in his car as I was driving down the other side in mine, and, passing each other in opposite directions several times, we carried carloads of my personal belongings to my parents' house. I was going home.

The reason I chose to move in with my parents was purely financial. As a result of decisions made during my marriage to Maureen and our divorce, I had a mountain of debt.

Our divorce was amicable. I had no savings, Maureen had the children and needed support, and I had the bills. In order for her to keep a home for the children, I agreed the furniture was hers and gave her most of what we had purchased during our marriage. I took the bills and bought her a car. I was not out for blood, nor was she; that would have been ridiculous and not what we wanted or who we were. With the divorce papers filed, we left the courthouse and had coffee together.

As I attempted to rebuild my life, I had no choice but to live at home with my parents, attempt to pay off our bills while saving money, and work hard to save enough for my own place. It took five long years before I had a comfortable nest egg to move out.

While things between Patrick and I were not great, and I certainly did not like some things I saw in him, I kept the relationship amicable. For my own sanity, though, I distanced myself emotionally from him to some extent. His wife's treatment of my wife and his defense of it—this self-righteous, self-deception of Brianna as a god to be bowed down to—were major red flags. She employed, at least in the case with my wife, intimidation, demands, and hostility to subjugate Maureen, and my brother provided brutal backup. While I did not know what this was in terms of behavior and attitude, I knew the problem was not with my wife.

Having left home at seventeen and returning at thirty-nine, I had no idea what the lives of my family had been like over the intervening years, nor did I know who they were as people other than what I had experienced, which was intermittent though extreme. Before moving in I believed the confusing, abusive behavior was fleeting. I never could have imagined what would soon transpire in my own life, living under the same roof with my mother and sister, nor do I feel I was naïve to think of my homecoming as an opportunity to develop and grow as siblings should, to make up for lost time and reconnect after my absence.

I was happy at the thought of being friends with my brother and sister, but that thought would be erroneous and short-lived.

As I was about to enter a house of so much anguish, I could not know at the time there was something else at play, a force interacting within each of them. It had been part of my family for many years and was not just any force, but a dark one. Concealed by a mask discovered years earlier by those devoted to the study of human behavior, it hid a powerful, negative energy that I would soon experience.

2

Home, Unsweet Home

"It is the endemic result of our culture's material perfectionism. It bridles a very significant proportion of our people and cripples some of our most gifted and giving individuals. Yet, while the culture reinforces it, its breeding ground is the family."

— DR. STEPHEN M. JOHNSON

So, I moved back to the old familiar house where my parents and sister lived. I had fond memories of growing up in this house and had spent most of my childhood there until I left home for the military in the late sixties.

It was not my intent to remain there for an extended period of time. I was getting back on my feet financially from my divorce, and moving home helped. I also thought that it was an opportunity to reacquaint and reconnect myself with my family following the years I was absent.

I believed things would be different with respect to their behavior under these new circumstances. It was the first time we would be living in close quarters for the long term since I had left home. In spite of the experiences my wife and I had had with my family, I still thought being with them now would allow us to interact and grow closer as a family.

My final year in the air force was a milestone I had long awaited. My divorce was pending as I prepared to retire. McGuire Air Force Base, where I was stationed upon my return from Europe, was just under forty miles from the house, and the commute was not very difficult even though the base was in another state.

Unfortunately, the first two weeks in my parents' home were horrendous.

Problems began the day I moved in. It was a repeat from my wife's first visit only on a much larger scale of intensity, and this time I alone was the target.

I was still placing boxes in the basement of my parents' home. My brother and I, using our separate cars, had made several trips to my previous residence on the air force base to get my personal belongings. During the process, my sister had been screaming various phrases openly and with an indignant rage that was hurtful and bewildering. She stomped into the basement, where I was neatly stacking my boxes in an out-of-the-way area.

Within sight yet never looking directly at me, Kayleigh repeatedly shouted deafening phrases: "There's no rooom in here!" "It's cramped in here!" "I can't mooove—I can't breeathe!"

Her dramatic vocal delivery of extending the words served to emphasize her contempt and devaluation of my homecoming. She alternated among these phrases each day for nearly two weeks. Her constant state of rage clearly let me know I was unwelcome. Initially, her discomfort made me think my belongings were in the way enough that I questioned how I had placed them and checked whether my things were really in the way.

I did not have many boxes since I had willingly given Maureen all the furniture and most of the things we had accumulated together. All I really wanted was my life back. None of my boxes were oversized, and they were placed in the basement, stacked neatly on top of each other so that they took up minimal floor space. There was only one other place where I had belongings: the bedroom I had slept in as a small boy, which was out of the way of the family. These were things I needed to have readily available for daily living.

None of my personal belongings were in anyone's way.

Kayleigh fed off her own anger at my homecoming until her contempt toward me was exacerbated beyond understanding or comprehension. Merely verbalizing her anger and hostility was not dramatic enough to make her point. There had to be some physical emphasis to punctuate her outbursts. She slammed doors and kitchen cupboards, and stomped her feet when walking. Though I came to expect such outbursts, it did not make them any less mentally or emotionally draining.

While most sisters are elated and joyful when their brothers return home from military service, mine held me in contempt. I felt bad for Kayleigh as I watched her isolate herself from my life, and her cruelty tested my patience. It was equally bewildering seeing that my mother was not only fully aware of, but encouraged and supported my sister's tantrums through silence.

So was my father silent, but I would not understand why for some time to come. I was all alone in this environment, and I had nowhere else to go.

Kayleigh's consistent and mindless raging mirrored the behavior one would see in a vicious, spoiled child. My thoughts returned to Maureen's first visit to my parents' home six years earlier and the similar treatment she received from my sister.

I wondered now why I had not quite seen or felt what my wife did at the time. What was clearly evident, to my dismay, was that my sister's behavior then and now were the same and occurred for the same reasons.

My wife and I had invaded my sister's territory by staying in her room for our visit, and I was now invading her territory once again by being in the home. It became clear there was a family structure in place in which everyone had an assigned role. This structure was rigid and completely inflexible. I came to understand what I experienced by researching published works by professionals in the field of behavioral science and through therapeutic sessions completed between my business trips over the coming years.

A NEED FOR THERAPY

I was losing sight of myself and I could feel it. Everything about my life, which was at one time peaceful and clear, was now in a state of anxiety, uncertainty, unpredictability, and to some extent fear. I was in need of a support structure to keep me grounded in reality and to keep me connected to myself. I sought a family counselor just weeks after moving back home, though I would not learn about the forces of narcissism until I sought therapeutic interaction. It was during a session in 2004 that the term "narcissism" was used for the first time by my therapist. It not only seemed to fit the situation, it compelled me to learn more.

No formal diagnosis was ever performed on my family members, and the closest I could come to understanding the behavior, including from years past, was initially from Dr. Nina Brown. She brought much to light and seemed to connect several dots in her 1998 book *The Destructive Narcissistic Pattern*, when she wrote, "Psychological boundaries are those that define you as separate and individuated from others and provide the sense of knowing where you begin and others end or where you and others are different. Personal, or territorial, space can also be a psychological boundary."

My sister's behavior during my ex-wife's first visit and my arrival home seemed to meet the criteria for an *invasion of territory*. This was further supported by Dr. Sandy Hotchkiss in her book *Why Is It Always About You?: The Seven Deadly Sins of Narcissism*: "Since Narcissists seek power as a way of pumping themselves up and off-loading shame, we are most likely to encounter the boldest and most ruthless among them wherever there's a piece of turf to be controlled."

Though some blurs of confusion were fading, I never understood why my father seemed oblivious to Kayleigh's behavior. I knew he was unable to hear well, but he seemed to be not so much unaware of her behavior as he was accepting of it as normal.

This was a new environment I had never known before, one of great personal hostility. My father seemed to be the only sane one in the house, yet I also noted a high tolerance in him from the abuse, and it was actually my therapist who pointed that out as a personality trait—one that he saw in me too.

Despite being verbally chastised by my sister and mother, my father would casually move about his business—read the paper, watch television, all the while remaining in a relaxed state as though nothing happened.

I often wondered about that. How could he maintain that kind of control? The inner dynamics in my family were very confusing, and I had many questions for my therapist.

In one of my sessions, Jim, my therapist, opened the palm of one hand fully at forehead level, and in slow motion moved it downward his torso while describing an invisible shield. He said, "Your father found a way to shield himself. He doesn't absorb the bad; it bounces off him. You, on the other hand, take in your sister's personality and likely parts of other family members' and then fight the urge from attack to retaliate. You absorb it and then must resist becoming like them. Resisting the urge to provoke hostility in yourself is a strength, but this is where the conflict in you arises."

For several reasons, I was never able to bring myself to ask my father the deeply personal question about why this was so, although I wanted to on many occasions. A part of me felt he was very aware of it, and I was not certain if he regretted or felt guilty for not doing some part of stopping these behaviors years ago. I did not want to make him feel any negativity on my account, so I decided just to figure it out myself.

Whether he knew he should have been more assertive and made attempts to stop the aggressive behavior of my mother and sister, I will never know. I do not believe at this point it matters, but there is a high probability he would have come under some level of attack if he stood his ground. Knowing what I know now there is the strong likelihood my father was beaten into emotional and psychological submission. It was more than apparent there was a dynamic of "conditioning" going on in the household, and that conditioning took place by overt abuse to the internal world of the family, which was hidden from outsiders.

My mother validated, through her control, everything my brother had told me from years past. He was right; she fiercely guarded my sister and in so doing encouraged my sister's inherently malevolent nature toward everyone.

No sooner had I walked in than I was looking for a way out. I could no longer take Kayleigh's screams of betrayal; my sanity was tested as well as my restraint.

In less than two weeks I was able to obtain a room on the base. According to regulations I was not technically authorized one because my paygrade was above the allowed ceiling, and on-base quarters were for lower-grade personnel. After I explained the situation to my commanding officer, though, he authorized me to stay there for a few months until I found a more permanent place to live.

I went home to gather some of my things and told my mother I was moving onto the base. Sitting at the kitchen table she looked down and quietly said, "You don't have to leave." It was difficult to read her. I could not tell how she was feeling; whether she was sincere or not, but it didn't matter. I had to leave.

Unfortunately, my timing could not have been worse. After just two weeks of living at the base, a military construction project appropriated funds to upgrade and restore several apartment-type structures that were on-base quarters. The building in which I resided was the first to be upgraded. I had to vacate with nowhere to go but back to the house. I explained to my mother that a construction project was beginning and I had to move back home, but was going to find somewhere else and hoped it would not be long.

She looked back at me without speaking, and from the way I just explained myself and what I was planning, she knew I was asking if she planned to correct or stop my sister's behavior toward me. Instead of answering, she gave me a look of bewilderment and innocence, tilting her head slightly and raising her eyebrows as if wondering what my concern really was.

While this happened several times during my sister's rages, on one particular occasion of her raging, my mother actually asked me calmly if something was wrong. It was enough to make you lose your ability to think.

Still financially strapped due to my divorce and working to start my life over, each time I walked through the door of the house, I would put myself in an emotionally defensive position. It became an automatic reaction. It was not a safe home; on the contrary, it was a hotbed of potential violence. Physical violence never occurred, but the possibility was always there. Intense verbal attacks could come at any time without warning.

As the result of years of abuse, my brother and his wife despised my sister, and for making any defensive effort they would be summarily chastised by my mother.

And now she was doing the same to me.

My mother's and sister's unhealthy relationship was not the only problem in the family. As time went on, other things contributed to the family's volatility and would have the same stunning effect on me.

It was a good thing my son, Thomas, lived out west with his mother, and as much as I missed him, it was a blessing he was not exposed to this.

In 1993, I received another awakening. I had been home now for several months. My brother and his wife lived on the third floor of the three-decker. Walking up the back stairs to the top floor to visit, I heard some arguing and yelling, but it was mostly coming from Brianna.

I continued up the stairs believing they would stop when I arrived. Standing at the top platform on the threshold to the kitchen entrance, I saw Patrick and his wife standing in the middle of the kitchen floor in an "up close and personal" position, that is, inches apart and with her finger to his face. I watched her scream with indignant anger, "You don't tell her anything—she's *my* daughter! If you have anything to say to her, you say it to *me* and *I'll* tell her."

They were arguing about Brianna's daughter Erin. She was born some fifteen years before during a previous marriage, but Patrick had raised her from a small girl.

On the surface, this was more than a typical disagreement that couples have when there are stepchildren involved—he was raising her, and when you take a walk around any close-knit neighborhood like this one, you're likely to overhear some sort of family squabble. I was bewildered into silence by Brianna's vehemence that my brother had to go through her to speak to her daughter. It was equally bewildering that they were completely oblivious to my presence, even though I was standing just feet from them. Neither as much as acknowledged me. I watched my brother meekly looking down at her in silence with a hurt puppy look upon his face.

I turned and started back down the stairs to the ground floor feeling sickened. After I told my mother what I saw and heard, she said simply, "She always treats him that way when it comes to her daughter. He can't say anything to her. I feel so bad for him."

I didn't feel bad for him. I was disgusted. Patrick was a grown man. I could not help but wonder where, when, and at what point in his life he had lost so much self-respect that he would accept this and more than that, take it into his family.

If it weren't for my brother and parents, Brianna and her daughter may not have had such a good life, and this was how Brianna demonstrated her gratitude.

I was beginning to see more severe underlying problems in the family, and they were much deeper than I thought. Over the coming months, whenever I spent time with my brother, I never mentioned these things, but I often wanted to ask what had happened in his life while I was away. I was afraid of opening Pandora's box.

I could not feel a positive spirit from him that was based on trust, but I was trying. He had a short fuse, with sometimes impulsive and irrational tendencies to be contradictory that were more reactive in nature. I often had to step back from the potential volatility.

In seeming jest, he would often call his wife "stupid" and laugh jokingly about it in front of others. I saw very little joy in the house, which validated two decades of what I had heard while home on visits in my service years. I sometimes saw his wife glance at him with that "look," silently saying, "That bothered me; you should not have insulted me." I kept a level of emotional and psychological distance not because I wanted to but because I had to.

We were clearly in different places and, indeed, on different planets.

Nevertheless, my largely now superficial relationship with Patrick allowed us to have fun fishing and going out to Flyers and Seventy-Sixers' games. Our two favorite places for the occasional Irish beer and pub fare were McGillin's Olde Ale House or The Bard's Irish Bar. Patrick had an affinity for Guinness. I was never much of a drinker for an Irishman; I just never really cared about it, but now and then I would enjoy a beer or two. One of the best times we had and always looked forward to was the Saint Patrick's Day parade in Philadelphia, one of the largest parades in the nation, which was understandable as Philadelphia is ranked as having one of the United States' largest Irish populations.

In my first year home, even when I was still married and despite the tension, I would go to Center City with Maureen, Patrick, Brianna, and Kayleigh for free summer concerts. Getting along on those nights was easy, but I didn't even attempt deep conversations on meaningful levels. I tried one time with my brother while in the backyard just talking, and although I do not recall the topic, I was stunned when he turned and said, "You know, you're too good for your own good."

I fell silent, temporarily unable to process what he had said. With the passage of years, I still have no recollection of how I responded, and am not certain I did. What I do recall was wondering how someone could be too good for their own good. I thought, *Does that mean good is bad and bad is good, or is being a "little" no good a good thing?*

My question would inevitably be answered.

1993 and a New Life

"The worst of all deceptions is self-deception."

— PLATO

The new year was hours away. Though I had been separated from my wife now for six months, I had not dated or gone out much, but rather threw myself into my work and traveled for business frequently. On New Year's Eve, I decided to take myself out for the night to dance and celebrate.

On the dance floor two minutes before midnight came a tap on my shoulder. There stood this pretty woman, Amy, who smiled at me and asked if I would dance with her for the final moments of the year. I could not resist her pretty smile.

We danced to several songs, and the night ended. She and her girlfriend were leaving. I was hesitant to ask for her number but not sure why. As the days and weeks went by, I found myself thinking about her more and more, and over the coming weeks wondered how I could find her. I placed an ad in the singles section of the city magazine describing the night we met and how, and I asked her to contact me. There was a million-in-one chance she would materialize in a city this big, but a few months later I received a message, a response from the ad, and it was her. Her girlfriend, who was with her on New Year's Eve, noticed it and called her.

From our first date, Amy and I would, over the next eighteen months, become close. Eventually I moved in with her in hopes of a long-term commitment. She was a good woman with a heart of gold. She was thoughtful and kind such that before planned visits to my parents she would ask that I stop at a bakery so she could take pastries to them. She was warm and wonderful; generously giving of herself.

It was both unfortunate and saddening that I would discover how I was not quite ready for a commitment on the level she hoped for and deserved. I had not been divorced long enough and had not fully reconnected with myself.

During our eighteen months together, I never thought much about my divorce from Maureen or my seven years of marriage, or whether I was ready for a commitment so soon. Amy wanted her own family, and I understood that perfectly. I was not in the right space for it emotionally, though, and did not realize it until she expressed her desire and need to get married and start her own family. I felt grief when I saw the look in her eyes, and I was angry with myself that she felt that way.

As I drove from her house that day with my things in the car, I realized I needed to wait longer to meet someone. I spent the next two years without dating but doing things I loved and missed: fishing, driving around Philadelphia and taking rides to the ocean and mountains, and listening to my music.

I was reconnecting with me, and vowed never again to deprive myself of someone who loved me and to make sure I was truly ready the next time.

On some visits to my parents while we were together, though, Amy had heard my brother telling his wife to "shut up" or calling her "stupid" in his feeble, joking fashion, and on other occasions she would hear my sister talking in condescending tones to my parents. She once asked me in the car about it and said she was confused and concerned. She said if she spoke to her parents in that way, they would ask her to leave the house.

Being the wonderful woman that she was, her assessment was thoughtfully compassionate: "Your family isn't happy, Sean."

I kept my thought to myself: *They're so fucking miserable, and not only do they like being miserable, they want everyone around them to be miserable too.*

The truth is my family members were abusive to themselves and to anyone integrated into the family. Everyone was susceptible to the whims of the others, which were exerted randomly and irrationally in order to maintain a bizarre sense of superiority, outright control, and entitlement.

Self-righteousness was deeply ingrained in each of them just as much as their spiteful, selfish behavior. There was absolutely no question my sister was at the center of our family's universe. She was the focus of attention, the favorite, the prodigy and the protected one, the entitled one, able to do as she pleased to whom she pleased with total immunity, and as a result, she controlled every aspect of the environment.

There certainly seemed to be a fit between decades of published research in the field of narcissism and the behavior I was experiencing and witnessing. There was not only a connection, but because I lived it and observed it, even an unqualified conclusion in the absence of a formal diagnosis seemed reasonable.

Observation is reality, and to suggest otherwise would have been to victimize myself with denial. I'm the last person to be an ostrich-type, sticking my head in the sand to avoid the truth.

Having said that, confronting any of my family members on any aspect of their negative behavior would be rewarded with smirks, deflections, projections, anger, and accusations that I was crazy and in need of help, or the behavior would be swept into silence under the psychological rug.

The more I researched the more I became motivated to dig deeper, research more, and read more, and as I did, the more I came to understand and see clearly. Therapeutic discussions reinforced this light of discovery, and the correlations became undeniable.

It was all I had—research and therapeutic sessions.

While I began to feel relief from this newly gained knowledge, I also felt I was grieving from a loss. Although part of me was saddened, I was angry at the same time. There was a high price for this newly gained knowledge.

I developed a deeper understanding of my family's internal dynamics when I read several passages online in a works on narcissism by Dr. David Elkind, an American child psychologist. Introducing the concept of 'instrumental narcissism,' he makes reference to the tendencies of some parents' to view their children as investments, whereby these investments focus on the child or children to form them into a masterpiece; a prodigy, or a genius.

Further to that, parental over-gratification has also been considered another cause of pathological narcissism. Lack of appropriate limits and feedback, combined with direct or indirect evidence of being special, idealized, or overly admired, makes reality attributes secondary and paves the way for grandiosity and entitlement in a child.

Finally, he states that parents who tend to be insecure about their authority, or even go as far as abdicate their authority to a child and thereby tend to be submissive and idealize certain aspects of their child's behavior or attitudes, may contribute to the child's narcissism in which these attributes include entitlement, deceitfulness, blaming, and further permit the child to control one or both parents or the entire family.

Another dot was connected.

My sister-in-law sometimes referred to my sister as the "Queen." She was almost right.

Hidden from the external world, the inner workings of my family were precisely as described. I felt more clarity and understanding.

MAJOR CHANGES

On November 9, 1989, the Berlin Wall had fallen and the Cold War was over. Iraq had been expelled from Kuwait. The Soviets had disintegrated economically with a defeat in Afghanistan, and there was now only one superpower.

The world was changing.

With the Soviet threat essentially extinguished, it was time for me to move on and start a new life and new career in the civilian world. By 1993, I had made the decision not to renew my contract with the air force.

The number of reforms taking place in the air force and across other branches of the armed service in general at this time was a significant factor in my decision to take off my uniform. The end of the Cold War brought many changes, and the most visible was watching each branch open the exit doors to individual service members. Thousands took off uniforms for civilian life. Times were changing at a quick pace, with something significantly different in the air. I felt my time in the ranks had come to an end; my purpose to serve my country had been fulfilled.

More than twenty-four months remained on my contract, which, if I elected to remain, would take me to almost twenty-five years in my service career. While I did not plan on going anywhere just yet, I was seriously considering separating from the military. Fortunately, US Air Force policy allowed me to submit a request to waive the remaining time on my contract if I so elected. I was by now well over the twenty-year service point, the career marker for pension and other retirement benefits to kick in.

I thought of my accomplishments and my achievements from years gone by, the great many people I had met along the way, and the things and places I had seen and experienced, and professionally I knew I was not planning to attempt another promotion.

This was not disturbing. I had achieved six rank grades out of eight and was satisfied. I finally made the decision to request separation, thinking about the stability of civilian life. The air force agreed and approved my request to waive the final two years of my contract, and I officially retired at the end of 1995.

I was on to a new life.

There would be changes in my family too. Crime on the streets in Philadelphia was rising. Over the years of my absence a major change had taken place in my neighborhood, and it was not for the better. My parents decided to sell the house they had lived in for twenty-five years. The plan was to move northwest of Philadelphia but not too far, somewhere peaceful. I'm certain part of the decision was due to my niece and nephew. They were small and needed a safe place to grow and play.

My parents bought a two-family house in a prominent Philadelphia suburb intended for them, my sister, for me while I was still getting on my feet, and for my brother and his family. This neighborhood was quaint and quiet with nicely manicured lawns. Every house was immaculately maintained and had sufficient distance between it and its neighbor to offer a level of privacy.

The front porch of the new house was screened in and extended the full length of the home. An evenly stacked, three-foot-high stone wall, which was eventually replaced with an open post-and-rail fence, lined the front boundary of the house, extending to a driveway on each side of the home so the two families living there would each have their own driveway. A dilapidated single car garage sat alone in the back of the home along with a yard enclosed by a tall, wooden fence.

The rooms in the new house were not very big, but they were comfortable. My room was upstairs and squared with two windows overlooking an office park. There were two businesses across the street housed in the same building with a shared parking lot—a veterinarian and a convenience store.

RETIREMENT

The day came for my official retirement. Wearing my full-dress uniform and ready to depart for McGuire Air Force Base, I asked my brother if he would come as part of the family, to see my ceremony and to be there for my last official day in the air force.

I was thrilled at the thought someone in my family would be part of this great day in my life, but Patrick said he had too much to do. I thought to myself, *It's only for three hours including driving time.* I then asked my sister, and her response was similar. My mother used a walker as the result of long-term physical ailments and my father was in his early eighties. It was understandable they were unable to attend.

The time came to leave, and I drove alone the forty or so minutes to McGuire. With some friends and colleagues, I stood before the great American flag. My final medals were presented, citations were read, gifts were presented to me, and standing straight and tall I made my final salute. Following refreshments, it was time to leave. The event could not have lasted more than an hour; a major milestone that brought me both joy and sadness, and was one of the proudest days of my adult life.

After changing into my jeans and settling down, I met my brother outside in the backyard. As we stood by the dilapidated garage, he said three things in such rapid succession that I was taken aback.

The first was, "I remember when we were kids and I asked you for five dollars and you wouldn't give it to me."

I was too astonished to reply. Immediately following that he said, "When you left, Ma told me to get out of the house. I didn't know what to do or where to go. *You* did that to me." His words were choppy, and he was angry. I felt the pain in him. I remained silent as I processed that as well. The third and final thing he said was, "I spent sixty thousand dollars on cocaine while you were away in the 1980s—*you* made me do that."

I was now in a state of silent and utter confusion. My mind raced to sort out all that he had so abruptly presented. My first thoughts were that I had nothing to do with any of it. As tragic as these things were, none of them were my fault.

It was the first sign of Patrick's refusal to accept any responsibility for decisions he made or to hold those responsible who had truly hurt him. As tragic as it was, it was my mother who had told him to get out, which was the first I had heard of it. I sure as hell did not recall not giving him five dollars more than twenty-five years in the past, and I was just as confused as to how I made him spend his workers' compensation payment on cocaine.

This tragic period in his life on drugs (and with plenty of alcohol consumption) occurred while I was stationed in Europe. I've never had the opportunity to speak with him about it.

It was unfortunate that he did not mention any of the many good things we experienced together as young boys and teens. *He held all this tragic stuff in for two decades,* I thought. It was my first observation of his repressed anger, and his tendency to recall and convey only negative memories concerned me. I was equally concerned that he waited until I retired from the air force while I had been home now for two years.

I distinctly recall the disappointment in him—for me.

Little did I realize these comments were telltale signs of something gone awry, signs of something more terribly wrong.

I wondered what else would come out and when, and asked myself repeatedly what the hell had happened in the family after I had left home. I had no answers and continued to feel threatened in a clearly hostile environment. What Patrick defined to me in all he said was more than anguish, pain, or even anger; there was jealousy, envy, and blame within him.

Brianna continued with confusing persistence for almost a year, expecting that I should consistently apologize to her for the perceived insult by my now ex-wife a year earlier. I grew tired of the subtle sarcasm from her in seeking another apology over the issue week after week, month after month. I finally demanded in anger and disgust, "I'm not apologizing again! It's been almost a year. Get over it!" It was only then she stopped.

But she had to be chastised with forcefulness to do it.

For a year I had appeased her, and living next door I was in the mode of walking on eggshells to keep peace in my own life. I didn't know when some form of verbal attack would come or from whom. It was a totally unpredictable environment.

I had to work hard to avoid being pulled into the pattern of drama and sick interaction Patrick and Brianna shared for so many years, and how they functioned together by feeding off each other's anger and hatred. I was unaware my resistance to the abuse would come with a steep emotional and psychological price.

But I would find out.

4

False Words

"False words are not only evil in themselves, but they infect the soul with evil."

— SOCRATES

One day soon after I moved back home, as I walked through the front door after work, my sister was sitting on the sofa talking on the telephone with her girlfriend. "Fuck 'im! Fuck 'im!" I heard her say in a contemptuous tone, and as she looked toward me, I saw pure venom in her eyes. I remained silent and continued up the stairs to my room. She was speaking just loudly enough to where there was clear intent for me to hear: "You've heard what happens to Vietnam vets! They're abusive! Something is wrong with them."

Now I was thinking, *What is this all about?*

I was never in Vietnam or abusive to anyone, and she knew that. It was obvious I was meant to hear her words, so I stood silently on the upper landing near the stairs where she could not see me, and listened. I had not been home a week at this point, and she was already disparaging me. She was not only disparaging me, but was doing it with outrageous and blatant lies. My accomplishments, achievements, and sacrifices during my military service would make any family proud, and it was not I who was abusive; it was *she* and others in the family.

This was another surprising, new development—a smear campaign that ultimately propagated like cancer.

I did not understand why she would do that. Beyond disparaging me she was destroying any meaningful bond that could have and should have been developing between us as brother and sister, but then she had started that destruction long before the day I separated from my wife and moved back home.

Any level of trust was being utterly destroyed as well. This grown woman was openly making false claims about me. *Who does such things?* I thought.

Little did I realize a major smear campaign against me was already well underway and would become a recurring effort over the coming years, led by my sister and adopted by others in my family. I felt as though I was losing part of myself. Throughout these events, I had to stay focused on maintaining my perspective and my self-awareness.

A NEW PROFESSION

Following my retirement in 1995, I continued to work for the Department of Defense, specifically for the air force as a consultant.

My business travel took me away one week per month for three years, with visits alternating between two Midwestern states. It was demanding work, and the eighty-mile roundtrip commute to work each day was physically demanding. It blended into the already stressful environment in which I was living, yet on the other hand, the drive was also my savior.

THE DRIVEWAY FROM HELL

From the day I first moved back in, Kayleigh and I had agreed that we would share the driveway next to my parents' side of the house. Our agreement was based on my leaving for work earlier in the morning than she because of my commute. Because of that, I parked in front of her. I remember mentioning that if we were both home and she needed to go out, I would gladly move my car. She needed only to ask. It was a logical arrangement—at least at the time it was agreed upon.

Right after I moved in, though, my mother took matters into her own hands. Because I returned home from work before my sister, my mother started the process of reminding me—on a daily basis upon my return home—that my sister was coming home too. The inference was to move my car, but it was never in the driveway because I knew Kayleigh would be coming home. I simply parked on the street in front of the house.

My consistent reminders to my mother that my car was not in the driveway had no effect. It became a daily routine with her, and soon there was no hope she would stop this maddening ritual. For the first few weeks I dismissed it with, "My car is in *front* of the house, Ma—*not* the driveway."

Nevertheless, she continued each day upon my return home with the same comment. I became increasingly frustrated and found my patience challenged beyond measure. It amounted to daily badgering.

At one point, I came to believe it could not be possible that she would forget my daily responses. I thought, *Wasn't she listening?* I often bit my tongue. I also felt resentment toward my sister—not envy or jealousy, but resentment for my mother's badgering in favor of my sister.

From that day forward, I parked across the street. My mother and sister made my car a major issue of unbelievable proportions. Little did I know my mother was positioning me in my family role and conditioning me to be of a lesser status in comparison to my sister.

Where I parked my car was only the first excuse for their behavior. Sure enough, there came something else from my mother and sister, something on a grand scale, both overwhelming and unforgettable. When that day came my sister would cross the threshold from arrogant superiority and outright abuse to violence-provoking hostility, and I would come to curse the day she was born.

The distance from the house to my office was forty miles, or about an hour's drive during early rush hour traffic. As such, my schedule had me up very early—four fifteen in the morning—and leaving the house by five o'clock. I would walk into my office by six o'clock. At the end of the workday, I left the office around two thirty and was home by three thirty.

One morning I left for work an hour later, around the same time as my sister would be leaving. I had finished writing an email and was dressed. I needed only to shave, which perhaps took three minutes, and then I would be on my way.

And yes, for some reason I had foolishly parked my car in the driveway in front of Kayleigh's. I knew I had to move my car for my sister if she needed to leave and I was prepared to do so. She only had to ask, as we agreed.

Just after six o'clock I was lathered and standing in front of the mirror. I kept the bathroom door closed but for an inch to prevent the light from reflecting into the hallway and the room where my parents were sleeping. The only sound was the light gurgle of running hot water in the bathroom sink.

Without warning, an earsplitting *bang!* broke the silence. The bathroom door slammed so hard into the toilet paper dispenser the impact almost broke it off the wall. I literally jumped back from shock and turned to see my sister standing at the threshold of the bathroom door with her coat on and purse slung over her shoulder.

With this look of pure evil, she screamed so loudly and with such ferocious hatred that her eyes were bulging from her head and the veins in her face were clearly visible. Not looking directly at me but straight ahead, she shouted at the top of her lungs, "Sean! I have to go to work! You have to move your fucking car!!" In the background I heard my mother, still in bed, add a nonsensical caveat in support of my sister: "Goddamn computers!" In proclaiming her approval for the outburst, even if she did so with a phrase that made no contextual sense, she let me know that I was in defiance of my sister's sovereignty and rule.

When I think back to that morning, I wonder why my sister chose that option. She could have knocked lightly to say she had to leave—an option available to her and that, one would think, a responsible adult would have chosen. Something I had not yet considered at the time was human warmth and respect in the family.

There was none.

Nor had there been warmth for each other since long before I came home. I would not learn the true nature of my mother and Kayleigh's relationship until years later, but I did know I had to fight being sucked into the drama of the only life they had ever known.

In one of Sandy Hotchkiss's keen insights in her works, *The Seven Deadly Sins of Narcissism*, she states appropriately: "Internally, these individuals remain in a state of psychological fusion with that all-powerful, all-nurturant caregiver, and this becomes the working model for their interactions with others. They treat people as if they exist only to meet their needs, and they have little regard for anyone who can't be used in some way. In a psychological sense, they don't really 'see' anyone else, except when a person can do something for them. . . . [Y]ou will sense that quality of childlike narcissism by the way they relate to the people around them. There will be inevitable violations of boundaries."

I witnessed performances of good behavior that were convincing but not without sarcastic subtleties. The inner working dynamics of our family environment within the home were vehemently concealed from outsiders, just as an outsider does not see what goes on within the confines of a prison environment. The psychological and emotional cruelty, hostile outbursts without warning, and now the potential physical attacks were a reality, harrowing, and progressively getting worse.

Why Kayleigh chose a premeditated attack that crossed the line into purposefully instigating potential violence I could not understand. I did all I could do to seek inner strength and restraint in responding to the viciousness of her attack that morning.

My father, hard of hearing from old age and sound asleep until my sister's rage attack, was awakened and got up from bed. If he could hear her from six feet away in his traumatic hearing condition, I can guarantee the family across the street could hear her. He stood at the bathroom door and asked *me*, shaving cream still covering my face, what was going on, as though I did something wrong and was at fault.

The only thing I could think to say was, "Why can't she be civilized?" Without finishing shaving, I hurriedly dry-toweled my face and left the house immediately. It was in the car that morning driving to work—angrier than I thought I was ever capable of feeling and completely uncharacteristic of me—that it became abundantly clear that remaining in the house with Kayleigh and my mother was no longer an option. I had to plan my escape before they escalated their hostility into something worse.

By this time, it seemed Kayleigh's behavior was designed to specifically achieve that goal: to expel me from the house by making my life so miserable I would leave.

The other problem I faced was based on gender: my mother was old and sick, and my sister was a woman. As a man, I knew that had I even once lost my cool and succumbed to their strategy of provocations, torment, and general abusiveness, or even in a moment of weakness physically threatened my sister, *I* would be viewed by society and the law as an abuser. My sister had already laid the groundwork for that with her girlfriend on the phone that one day. Thus, they would be seen as the victims when, in fact, they were the perpetrators.

I was convinced they were setting me up. But why?

It was clear that resisting her vicious, physical attacks would have only landed me in conflict with the law. I never realized how much inner strength I possessed to restrain myself.

Nagging questions came with no answers. I learned that "baiting" is another term describing narcissistic behavior that is used to antagonize, provoke, and taunt others to garner attention and commit crimes a person would not normally commit. It makes me wonder why one would behave this way if not to be punished or utterly abandoned.

My mother and sister were persecuting and victimizing others while able to convincingly portray themselves as victims.

I had seen clearly visible and undeniable indications that my sister was fully aware that she knew the things she was doing were not right, and she even took sadistic pleasure in them. She was simply indifferent to what she was doing and was often amused by their effect.

It would elude me for years as to how one could act in this manner and not be aware, especially when there was a ferocious effort to deny the behavior and conceal it by playing the victim. Seeing the results of what was transpiring around her—the destruction of the family—had no positive influence to change her behavior.

These were telltale signs I had seen so many times. The most notable was the trademark smirk my sister displayed during and after her attacks in such a way as to convey a meaning of having achieved some great victory. She closed her lips with obvious pressure and forced a smile from ear to ear while flaring her nostrils open as wide as she could, staring at me directly in the eye in a form of defiant victory.

It was the behavior of a spoiled-rotten six-year-old brat.

There was no great effort required to read the look of contempt, condescending arrogance, and pride from her perceived achievement. There was in fact cruelty and great joy in it. The Roman philosopher Seneca once said, "All cruelty springs from weakness," and in this case, he was proven right.

There were more than sufficient indications that my sister was fully aware of what she was doing and simply did not care, and Dr. Nina Brown gracefully and further defines "gloating" as a character trait of the narcissist following "successful" abusive behavior. She writes in her works *The Destructive Narcissistic Pattern*, "Gloating is reminiscent of childhood taunting behavior, and others react to it in much the same way: by being turned off. Being proud of winning or achieving is very different from gloating. Being proud is a personal affirmation of self without devaluing or disparaging the other person. Gloating means you are perceiving yourself as better and disparaging or putting down the other person."

Another term well-defined in my research and with remarkable similarity to my family's structural dynamics, and as much to workplace structures across the country, is the "serial bully."

It is crucial to state that a parent—*any* parent—who makes a claim that, "We, as parents, should do everything for our children," contradicts decades of published research and findings from highly respected scholars in the fields of psychology, parenting, and narcissism. Dozens of professional and scholarly works I read in my research stand by this contradictory position.

Indeed, we should all ensure the safety of our children, emotionally, psychologically, and physically. We should educate our children, give them a good home, and make sacrifices that allow them to enter the real world one day fully armed, equipped, and self-sufficient. This is, without question, the very essence of love. By contrast, even under these conditions of love, constant praise when praising is inappropriate; putting a child on a pedestal; rewarding bad behavior or "looking the other way"; telling a child or alluding continually to the idea that he or she is "so special" or better than others, serves only to develop a sense of entitlement to special treatment, that they should always get what they want when they want it, and is commensurate with developmental malignancy.

From this, the child grows to actually believe they *are* in fact better than anyone else and to have no qualms in conveying it in words or deeds. Unreasonable expectations that their demands and needs be met (while those of others are relegated to irrelevancy) is one of several resulting developmental traits.

Any such parental-mishandling patterns that "over-valuate" a child during stages of their development only serves to inflate the budding ego and nurture a future narcissist.

A blanket statement that "We should do everything for our children," then, should raise eyebrows and many questions. As your child grows to adulthood you will find the answers—hopefully sooner so that you, as a parent, can correct your behavior before it's too late.

THE MURDER OF SOULS

Society accepts the definition of murder only as the killing of another human being in the physical sense, but I would argue that domestic abusers, including sibling abusers, often murder, over long periods of time, their victims' sense of hope and optimism.

This is a death that has no legal punishment.

I felt some level of comfort and healing, though, in reading Dr. Elsa Ronningstam's timely book on narcissism, *Identifying and Understanding the Narcissistic Personality*, which shed great light on the dynamics of what I experienced. Equally, it was of great concern and disturbing to me to learn of the lack of public awareness surrounding the psychopathology of narcissism and that this lack of awareness related to a subsequent lack of funding for research.

Ronningstam writes: "The complex nature of this disorder—high level of functioning, lack of symptoms or consistent behavior signifiers, hidden or denied intrapsychic problems (even when severe), and lack of motivation to seek psychiatric treatment out of shame, pride, or self-aggrandizing denial—have made it difficult to identify people in general psychiatric settings who meet the *DSM* criteria for NPD. Consequently, funding for psychiatric research on NPD has been less publicly urgent, especially compared with the antisocial personality disorder (ASPD) and borderline personality disorder (BPD), for which more obvious human suffering and extensive social and mental health costs have impelled research on their etiology, course, and treatment."

The remarkable accuracy in correlating behavior I experienced with that reported from decades of study and research opened the information channel wider. I found myself reading more, and understanding became a willing process. Whether my mother and sister's behaviour were narcissism, antisocial personality, a combination of both, or another disturbance, I do not know. What I did know were traits characteristic of narcissism were clearly demonstrated even in the absence of a formal, clinical diagnosis.

AN ADMISSION

During the first year of my divorce, in 1993, I stayed in contact with Maureen. Our divorce was amicable, and we remained friends. We would occasionally have lunch together and talk. I would sometimes offer money to help her and the children but could only do that up until the time of Kayleigh's morning outburst kicking in the bathroom door, after which I needed all my funds to help me move out. I admitted to Maureen that she was right in how she felt years ago and I apologized profusely for not seeing what she had.

For my ex-wife's peace of mind, I expressed that not only was my sister the same as she had always been and that both her and my brother blatantly made false allegations against me, but I found Kayleigh's behavior and cruelty were worse than we experienced when we were together. I hoped it would give her closure from her experiences.

What mattered at that moment was to soothe her mind and soul and to try to bring her peace as much as I could. Letting her know I was mistaken was something I owed to her.

The untenable situation at my parents' home and the nearly eighty-mile roundtrip commute to work each day was not helping. While periods of seeming calm sometimes lasted for days in the family, their underlying fueling of anger was always in the air. These brief periods of quietude came in subtle doses, but still there were no boundaries. Everyone was fair game; it was just a matter of time before something or someone exploded.

Personal boundaries in the family did not exist and had not for many years. My sister was fueled by her own negative energy and by my mother's. Trying to communicate with them was fruitless. None of them spoke *to* you; they spoke *at* you. Explosive tirades were the norm. I would often see my sister slumped on the sofa, appearing totally exhausted following a major explosive episode.

HOLIDAY TIME

The holidays would offer some level of superficial sentimentality, as though there was some form of emotional and spiritual acquiescence to the meaning of the holiday, but it felt like when I visited the Korean Demilitarized Zone—a truce period with an eerie silence one cannot describe but can readily feel.

No one was shooting, but the psychological guns were aimed.

Toward the end of 1992 and with Christmas approaching, I was in my bedroom one day with the door closed, wrapping gifts, when a surprisingly soft knock came. It was my sister, who, rather than kicking in the door, asked politely if we could talk. I told her politely in return I was wrapping Christmas presents, which I was. It was my hope she would not attempt to take that private time from me with some verbal tirade. I stopped wrapping to listen intently.

Through the door she said, "I'm sorry for what I said. Can we forget it?"

She was referring to the episode when she had degraded me on the telephone to her girlfriend, and she knew I had overheard.

"I already did," I responded through the closed door, but my response was more from a position of survival than one of true forgiveness. I could have denied her apology and given her a stern lesson in family and humanistic values, but any attempt to either correct her or define the feeling I got from that type of behavior could have resulted in less than desirable consequences. I let it go to keep the peace.

THE LANGUAGE TRAP

My sister's lies and degradation of me to her girlfriend were not accidental. If one can conclude there is willful, positive forethought in demonstrating goodness, there has to equally be willful malice of forethought when devising evil devices. I never understood what was to be gained by it. Moments of superficial reconciliation like this one over the holidays were always short-lived, and I came to see that even language was designed for and used as a weapon.

It was impossible to ascertain if alluring calls with soft tones were designed to throw me off guard, but I would find that out too.

On a Saturday afternoon one summer, my brother and his family were away for the weekend, and my sister and father were not home. My mother was not in good physical condition, so someone had to be home with her. I was upstairs in my room working quietly when my mother called to me.

Her voice was soft and alluring in the sense of a normal tone, and there was no indication of anger or hostility. I walked downstairs, and turning on the last step, I saw her in the hallway closet reaching upward. I thought she needed me to reach something for her. Standing next to her, as I looked into the closet at what she was doing, I asked if I could help her get something. Her soft, alluring tone suddenly changed to seething anger, scolding, and condemnation. The proverbial horns came out, the tail was pointed, and fangs were revealed: "I want to tell you something!" she blasted. "Your father and I talked about this. If he goes first [dies], or if I go first—your father and I talked about this," she repeated, "neither one of us wants to see you shed one tear at our funeral!"

I went back upstairs without another word, slammed my bedroom door, and tried to calm myself. Without question my father was not capable of saying such cruel things. She was lying, and the lie was designed to cause injury.

I came to realize later that even language can be perverted and pathologized, designed to lower a victim's guard through alluring and appealing delivery. One would normally expect loving tones from a mother, but my mother used them as bait. It was the first time I had been lured by a verbal trap intended to be just that: a psychological and emotional vise that hid cruelty and abuse under the initial guise of lovingness.

Following the holidays, a transition to normalcy resumed. I watched the pendulum swing between verbal attacks on both sides of the house, between my sister and my brother and sister-in-law, and I would often get caught in the crossfire.

I spent great amounts of time in my room working at my computer, learning my new defense department job. Throwing myself into my work was the only semblance of reality that existed for me at home. Across the threshold of my bedroom and out in the main house, one entered a twilight zone, an abyss, a battlefield.

I had to preserve my sanity.

1995

"The truth is always the strongest argument."

— SOPHOCLES

Nearly three years had passed since my divorce, near-bankruptcy, and return home. Despite the unrelenting tension, I did my best to achieve some level of normalcy in hopes of reciprocation and positive development—even a friendship of sorts with my siblings, or at least a truce, an emotional and psychological ceasefire.

Something was better than nothing, but my efforts would all prove futile.

Good intentions on my part were not only ineffective, they were viewed with indifference, ignored without reciprocation, made to be bad, disrupted, destroyed, spoiled, taken for granted, or viewed as a weakness to be exploited and worthy of attack.

Death by a thousand, tiny cuts is still death.

A decades-long series of macro- and microaggressions, slights and slurs had built up to the point that they impacted my health, my relationships outside the family, and to the point that I struggled to maintain control versus retaliation.

My patience was tested to the limit, and I had to prevail.

My business trips continued monthly, alternating between a Midwestern and a southwestern state, and at home I continued to walk on eggshells, not knowing when the next attack would come.

One event occurred following my return from a weeklong trip to Texas. As usual, I was having supper with my father. Before my business trip I had painted the fence in front of the house and used all the paint in the can. I did not have time to purchase more before my trip the next day, and decided I would do so upon my return home and finish painting the fence.

At dinner with my father that evening I explained the situation to him. Without warning he pointed his finger upward and proclaimed to my mother, "I don't *need* his money!"

I became silent in my confusion.

I did not understand what that was about or why he had said it. In retrospect, I could only conclude, living at home but being away on business as much as I was, I continued to be the target of smear campaigns. My siblings had done their best to warp my parents' minds so that they believed their older son, with his cushy military retirement benefits and his nice, new DoD contract work, was financially loaded. They might have even suggested to Mother and Dad that I was mooching off them by paying them rent instead of paying for a place by myself. This would all be revealed later to be a big part of their plans for me, but at the time, I had no idea.

Whatever they had said, without me there to counter it, had worked. Following that episode my father would not speak to me for nearly a year.

GRIPE SESSIONS

Throughout the five years I lived at the new house, "meetings" were called to "clear the air" that brought no meaningful results. I learned these had also taken place during the many years I was away in military service. They amounted to nothing more than bitch sessions designed to let certain family members vent rather than to explain how a particular behavior from one affected another personally. There was no introspection or empathy; no understanding of the basic, underlying causes of behaviors; no acceptance of responsibility; no explanations given; and no effort on any of their parts to change their behavior.

This destructive pattern of communicating convinced me to keep my distance.

One of these occasions was most significant and telling. It brought to my attention something new from my sister that was perplexing. In this instance, my brother called a meeting to "discuss" some issues.

The entire family sat around the kitchen table. Each was to have a turn in stating their concerns, and my sister's chief complaints were of course, about me. Nothing was specified. She spoke in vague terms and generalized. There was nothing she said that I could respond to.

Having lived there now for three years I was certain her "list" would be forthcoming. I encouraged her to state precisely what these things were. "Now is the time to get it out. Tell me *exactly* what I do that disturbs you," I said.

She stated that I had a "pattern" of calling her at work and bothering her.

There was one moment of intense aggravation that had not been released, and had been eating at me. I could not contain myself, nor could I keep it repressed.

I responded calmly. "Calling you at work one time in three years does not constitute a pattern. Is there something else?"

Sitting in silence, we waited several moments until finally she stated, "Well, I can't think of anything right now!"

In defense of myself, I asked her how odd it was that she could not think of one thing in three years I did that disturbed her, when her constant, daily complaints were so numerous.

If I were so bad, how could that be? There was nothing for her to say, nor could she quickly fabricate something. It was this type of slander that made meaningful communication with her, much less any resolution, all but impossible. Never accepting personal responsibility for herself, she learned to scapegoat others. It kept the stink off her.

She had no complaints about me.

My father interjected, and looking toward me, he would say one of the most confusing things I ever heard: "Your mother, sister, and I have been together for many years, and there have been no problems." That was all he said.

In the years since I left home at seventeen, there had been nothing *but* problems in the family. What this indicated to me was that the behavior is considered normal.

This was how they lived.

It was the assumption in this statement that I was responsible for the problems in the family that was shocking, despite my sister's openly demonstrated anger all her life and the others' enabling and reciprocity of it. This is what they were used to.

In light of my father's words, I lost my ability to think clearly again and could not find words in my own defense. I was simply drawn into the web of my highly dysfunctional family the day I walked through the door.

At that moment, my sister burst into tears, and I witnessed a bewildering moment in which she portrayed herself a frightened child. "I don't want to be alone!" she wailed. Her words had the usual slight pause between them in their delivery. The word "alone" was emphasized with an extended vocalization, much as one would hear from a three year old crying.

She did not want to be alone, but then for decades had demonstrated behavior that would lead to the very thing she did not want. I felt both compassion and confusion at that moment.

Maintaining my rational thought processing was not an easy task. This was especially true in those moments when I responded in ways when I lost, or was losing, sight of who I was.

THE ORDER OF BUSINESS

The gradual discovery of what had become of my family during my absence was a major disappointment to me. Observing their interactions was bewildering, confusing, and left me feeling negative emotions.

My assigned role as the outsider and invader were treated accordingly.

For those five years living with my mother, sister, brother, and sister-in-law, even when working in my room with the door closed, I would stop to listen intently to the yelling from downstairs to hear what the issue was now—all to anticipate possible evasive action.

There was never any hope for peace.

I'm reminded of an occasion when I was in my bedroom, this time with the door open, on the phone with a girl I had recently started dating. More than once she told me she heard doors slam, loud bangs, and my sister yelling in the background. It was impossible to hide, and explanations of the environment were inevitable. She took it with some humor but realized the seriousness of it all. Oftentimes she would jokingly say, "I can hear your sister is at it again, huh?" and she would chuckle.

Following a phone call with this new woman a few days later, I heard my sister coming up the stairs. She stood at the threshold and must have heard me say goodbye. Without entering the room, she moved her hands up onto her hips with a sense of superiority, tilted her head slightly, and in a condescending tone questioned, "Does *she* know what goes on around here?"

"No," I lied to avoid engaging her. It was an utterly ridiculous question. Of course she knew. She had heard it for herself many times.

How could Kayleigh's behavior and the extent of her raging be hidden? The only things "going on around here" were her outbursts, foot stomping, slamming doors, and the like. In pausing to process this event, it seemed apparent she had an awareness of the behavior, and the focus of her question was on wondering if it had been exposed to the outside world.

This begged the question of why she would not stop if there were concerns that concealment could be breached or compromised. Her main concern was exposure.

Concealment was the strategy designed to maintain a good *image*.

And of course, one must not overlook the possibility that it is the narcissistic person who is so convinced of his or her *entitlement,* that the idea of their activities falling under the harsh glare of judgment by an outsider is simply incomprehensible.

Me, the narcissist, be judged? Impossible!

OVER FIVE YEARS

Some years ago, in an early discussion with my brother, he described one of Kayleigh's similar behaviors and then asked me, "Now, is that normal?" I remember he would say she had no idea what she was doing or how she affected other people. I had my doubts from my own experiences, as there were many indicators of awareness on my sister's part. Her smirks alone, as I previously mentioned, revealed her awareness.

There had to be a consistent supply of chaos, havoc, and disruption in some form or no one was "happy." Even in quiet moments, an air and spirit of turbulence reflected on their faces.

There were never any smiles and certainly no elements of warmth for a very long time.

TIMES OF REFLECTION

In playing over in my mind the cumulative betrayals and all that transpired, I have tried to make some semblance of sense from it all. Envy and jealousy from my brother and territorial issues from my sister were unquestionably underlying motivations. The primary source and instigator of chaos was my mother; entertained immensely by fanning the flames of havoc within the family.

There are certain odd things about my mother that were prevalent and, to me, were undeniable. The venom I had seen upon her face more times than I can count was akin to a demonic look. I use the word "venom" in describing that look of certain hatred with great reservation and following great thought. When she had that look, which came out of nowhere, her eyes were dark and empty; the corners of her mouth twisted downward.

There was something clearly satanic about it—a ghastly, frightening expression.

More than once I stood before a mirror in my own attempts to recreate that look without success. I could not replicate it no matter how many times I tried, and it was apparent that it—whatever *it* was, must simply be *in* one. There were times I thought she was possessed, but I have never been in a qualified position to make that claim.

It was this very same look in her I saw in my childhood that I open in the Prologue—slapping herself in the face some forty-five years earlier with a ghastly look.

One other thing about her was always clearly noticeable and was equally significant to me—her facial skin. Inconsistent with an elderly woman in her eighties and well into her nineties, my mother's facial skin was always taut and smooth. She had no wrinkles. When one encounters an elderly person in their eighties or nineties one sees a very creased and wrinkled face. This was never the case with my mother. She aged in body but not in mind (which was clever), and with respect to her facial skin, she was often complimented on how beautiful her skin was. And it was.

It brought me to thoughts of Dr. Peck, in one of his many works, when he describes this same observation during an exorcism that he participated in.

Taking one demonstration that I've described thus far—just one by itself—I could not conclude reasonably that something was wrong.

People are simply people, and we have our occasional moments, and weaknesses.

On the other hand, a sustained chronological history of inherent malevolence and unabated abuse in various forms constitutes a major dysfunction of—something.

I was thankful my work-related travel kept me away at least one week per month. When not traveling I would leave the house for a drive—for peaceful moments, to visit friends, or to go to the ocean, where its quiet healing powers were soothing.

Remaining in touch with my inner spirit was a priority, lest I forget who I was. I wondered if my siblings' actions were motivated in any way by my success in the military, my military retirement benefits, or even my new job with the Department of Defense, all of which they would only see for its financial rewards.

I became acutely aware of the volatility and the blatantly disproportionate reactions that were enacted without thought. There were severely problematic and disruptive responses to the most minute of issues, including those they fabricated and perceived. Anything a normal person would find innocent could be considered offensive or critical and viewed as an attack, and met with sometimes planned and other times immediate retaliation.

And yet, the worst of their malice had not even really begun.

Preparing My Escape

1996-1997

"No one is hated more than he who speaks the truth."

— PLATO

The year 1996 was no better. I used avoidance as my primary strategy, as much as possible, to negate conflicts and I worked hard to minimize contact.

For three years now, not once had I "lost it" in terms of a hostile reaction, despite intentional provocations, taunting, and outward attacks. I was often out in the evenings to minimize contact as one strategy to stay out of the line of fire. Even so, my home life reached a point where I was beginning to have difficulty concentrating at work.

This macabre relationship—this alliance of shared psychosis (an appropriate terminology), was self-generating—they were feeding and fueling off each other.

In 2005, I came to discover that my mother and sister's relationship, from my research and my observations, that the potential "symbiotic" relationship was present. This is a coupling of two people which is ultimately good for neither.

This psychological use of the word, I found, differs from the use biologists put to "symbiosis," which can be good or bad depending on circumstances.

I started to understand and was able to identify this through the published works of Dr. M. Scott Peck, in which he explains that narcissistic intrusiveness can appear in the form of a symbiotic relationship.

Dr. Stephen M. Johnson's work *Humanizing the Narcissistic Style* also revealed to me that the symbiotic relationship suffers primarily from the failure to resolve the issue of separateness. As time went on, I continued with my research and was seeing a bigger picture and more clearly.

Looking back these many years later, I see now that I never stood a chance, nor in fact did anyone who was in my life and whom I sought to integrate into my life.

Anxiety further complicated the forced suppression of any attempt at my own defense. The more I defended myself the more the attacks came. Teaming up was common and came to be expected. It was becoming hard work to control the impulses they instilled either singularly or from a team effort.

One occasion became too much. I called my mother from work to calmly tell her how I felt about her encouragement of my sister's treatment over the past few years. She started screaming at me with such force I was compelled to move the phone away from my ear.

I had already come to know that their rage served to manipulate me to succumb and to prevent my defense. It lent credence to the adage that some believe: "The louder one yells, the more *right* one must be."

During my mother's phone tirade, my sister-in-law was next door. She heard her shouting and came over. Taking the phone, she told me that I was upsetting my mother.

It was the same old story: hypersensitivity and then a hyper-response. Across normal skin, a gentle touch can be comforting. The same gentle touch applied to a gaping wound will make a person howl in pain. You soon learn to avoid *all* contact, lest the hypersensitive person howl in pain even when the contact is completely benign.

Another common theme for many years came from me expressing frustration at my sister's behavior. The theme I was given from my brother and his wife on many occasions was to keep quiet, let it go, and "Do it for Ma."

Accept the premise that the person who feels the greatest pain deserves a free pass. You cannot help but to touch the gaping wound and therefore, it is your duty to endure the subsequent howling. For wanting even the smallest scrap of love and normalcy within the family, and because I attempted to foster some semblance of a family, I was selfish and on the attack.

PERSONAL BOUNDARIES (OR LACK THEREOF)

An outright disregard for personal boundaries marked the house as a major battlefield. My brother and sister, though bitter enemies were allied against a mutual enemy. The ancient proverb "The enemy of my enemy is my friend" seems to ring true. While they were vicious to each other, they protected each other when it came to me.

My life would be so much better, at least in their minds, if I gave up my personal boundaries and was consistently compliant while maintaining blind obedience.

Hell would freeze over before I ever let that happen. I was already living in its searing heat, so I knew hell wasn't freezing over any time soon.

One afternoon in April I came home from work and went into the kitchen before going upstairs to my room and greeted my mother, sitting at the kitchen table.

My sister, following her return home from work, was also in the kitchen and standing at the sink. In her usual demanding and condescending tone, she blurted out, "I have a bone to pick with you, Mister!" My mother chuckled in seeming humor.

My immediate response, as calmly and composed as I could, was that she had no bones to pick with me, adding sarcastically that I was neither her husband nor her boyfriend.

My mother was now laughing at the entire interaction. My sister's concern was that I should clean the house a little more often, and though the substance of what she was saying was not unreasonable, her tone and choice of words conveyed the authority she believed she had over me. These types of interactions, in which the substance was trivial but the tone was demeaning, occurred constantly.

Throughout 1996 my father remained distant from me, and I still had no idea why. There were times when I would speak to him and he would either walk away or not respond at all. It was clear to me their major smear campaign was continuing in my absence.

In any event, I made an effort to defuse things with my sister, although by now I knew it would not make a difference. I still had to try and keep some peace by showing my mother I loved my sister, or as a minimum by appearing to be friendly. My life with them in those days was always about two things: my sanity and my survival.

In one effort I made to diffuse matters, I invited my sister to Atlantic City since she liked to go to the casinos there. Though I am not a gambler, I thought a weekend away—or even one good day—would add some peace and quiet to the household. I did it to show my mother that I harbored no hard feelings and to keep my sister's abuse at bay. I thought it would make some difference in minimizing the abuse.

My goal was to spend time with her and somehow not touch that open, gaping wound.

Plans were made a week in advance. It was a late summer afternoon the day before we left. My sister was sitting on the sofa in the living room watching television when I walked downstairs from my room just to confirm our departure time the following morning. "Hi, just checking. Are we on schedule to leave at nine in the morning?" I asked.

I stood looking at her and waited for a response so I could plan my wake-up time the next day.

Instead, she asked me what was going on with my father and me. My parents were sitting on the front porch in their chairs, which were positioned on each side of the open living room window six feet or so away from where my sister was sitting. The weather was comfortable, and the front door was open with the screen door in place. My brother and his wife were not home at the time.

I explained casually what she already knew; that I had no idea what had happened on that night some eight months previous, and it was still bothering me that he was not speaking to me. I also reminded her that she was aware I had attempted to talk with him to no avail, and asked if she knew anything about it. I was confused by her sudden query when she knew of my many attempts. Without warning and no indicators, she raged in such a manner that I thought surely neighbors would call the police.

She held this look of seething hatred that came out of nowhere while screaming: "You *willll* sort this out! You *willll* fix this! Do you hear me? *Do you hear meee?*"

I had to muster all of my strength to maintain my composure.

It was another unexpected and extreme verbal attack that came without provocation. I tried to remain calm, but she had gotten to me. I told her I was not taking her anywhere and that she could go to Atlantic City by herself.

Since I already had a few open wounds myself, she found one of them and stuck her finger right into it. I had lost control, and now I had become an abuser by unloading the dreaded C-word on her, which surprised even me.

I knew I had to leave the house permanently before something more terrible happened. I had to constantly monitor myself, my reactions, and what was going on around me.

What I really had to do was to hold on to the man I was, and that was a constant.

There were several other occasions throughout the five years living at home in which I attempted to defuse the environment through kindness and thoughtfulness, although with reluctance and always to no avail. If anything, these attempts only served to trigger more attacks.

For example, I not only offered to take my sister to Atlantic City to gamble for a day that went down in flames, but I also offered to, and did, build her a résumé, which she did not have (nor did my brother). But it was another failed attempt at making her attitude less hostile and the environment more peaceful by doing something nice. I thought it would help.

When I finished it, there was no positive change in the behavior and not even as much as an expression of thanks. It felt as though she was entitled to such things and demanded good treatment. During this same period, my mother continued in her behavior toward me. It had become evident long ago that it was who she was.

Phone calls were another thing I came to dread, and I learned to be quick on the draw in answering it when I could. When my mother answered a call for me, whether a friend or even my boss on one occasion, she would walk to the stairs with the portable phone and scream up to me, "Pick up the phone!" Everyone could hear this incredibly crude tone of voice.

That initial bathroom door kick-in seemed to be looming again on several occasions, but one in particular came the closest. I was shaving once again before work, but I learned my lesson well from the first event. From now on, I kept the bathroom door open.

My sister was trotting up and down the stairs in quick steps, making several trips to her room and mumbling in a low tone that was inaudible. I could not make out what she was saying, but thought she had to use the bathroom. I asked on one of her passes.

She did not respond and acted as if I was not there; simply continuing on her way. Her nonverbal communication was unmistakable. She was pissed off.

I continued shaving and heard her come out of her room this time with heavier feet, and I asked again if she needed to come into the bathroom. Again, she continued downstairs without responding. I finished shaving hurriedly and was thankful there had been no outbursts.

Before I left for work, I asked why she did not respond. "I was late for work, that's all!" she said. Nothing more was said.

The holidays were upon us again in December. This was another empty period when there should have been joy. Brief periods of quiet in the household were a pattern during the holidays, and I came to dislike Christmas in the years I lived there because they were so fake.

Going back to my military days, there were plenty of times when I had wished I could go home for the holidays, but it turned out to be a happier time than I would find at home. Even far away in solitude on major holidays offered peace that I did not have with my family.

As things would turn out, 1997 held no hope for a positive change in my sister's behavior either; instead, each passing year brought with it a progressive intensity.

A NEW REVELATION

After the turn of the new year, I visited my brother to discuss the family when during this discussion, he informed me that when our mother was growing up her brother locked all the doors of the house they lived in, and proceeded to chase her and beat her in and out of every room. My mother's aunt had to literally break down the door to save her.

I had no previous knowledge of this, and I had been home now for several years.

The story held a ring of truth it seemed, if not only because there was no question something happened to her that she took into her adult life and into her relationship with my father; something that had infested everyone around her with despair.

Whatever happened to her in her childhood, she never sought help, although I am aware in those years none was truly available. Whether her mother or father was narcissistic, I do not know. Whether her brother had an inclination toward violence or was perhaps favored by their father or mother, who pitted one child against the other as my mother did, I do not know. Whether she provoked him as my sister did to me, I also did not know.

Those questions would never be answered.

What I did know was that something was terribly wrong. I knew that sometimes it's one or both parents who either consciously or unconsciously feed discord among siblings by carrying into their parenting unresolved issues among their own brothers and sisters.

There are also parents who play one child against the other to maintain some perverted form of control. My mother created an environment in which she was the puppet master pulling the strings. It had been working for so many years that the pattern was hard for them to break.

Perhaps because I had left home at seventeen and was not present to be infected—it didn't work on me, and I was paying the price.

What I also knew was that, clearly, whatever it was in my mother, it was evil. In giving some thought to the disconcerting news that my mother experienced this trauma, I was equally curious as to why her brother would make the obviously conscious decision, before beginning his physical abuse that day, to make certain she could not get away. It seems to me in a moment of such deep and immediate anger, one would strike out rather than think of such premeditation.

THE ESCAPE PLAN

The turn of the new year into 1997 was key to what I can appropriately describe as my "escape." I had been working and secretly planning my move for several months. Thinking back to that time I do not know how I avoided succumbing to the violence they provoked and intentionally bred. I knew only that I had to look deep within me so many times to maintain the strength I needed for self-control.

I'm reminded of one night at the end of January when in my room working. Downstairs in the living room my sister was watching the Golden Globe Awards. My old and dear friend Bob, whom I had met in the service overseas many years ago, called; he was feeling melancholy because his mother's health was deteriorating and he had recently widened the doors in her house to accommodate her wheelchair. His father was also not in the best of health.

He asked if I wanted to go out for a short time and said he would come by and pick me up. He was in need of a friend. He was also very aware of my sister's rages, having heard her on many occasions, and knew everything that transpired in my family, how they interacted and treated each other and me.

It was a bitter, cold night. With my coat on I waited inside by the front door and watched out the window for when he pulled up. After ten minutes or so my sister asked in a condescending tone, "Are you waiting for someone?"

I politely told her Bob was coming by to pick me up. I could not help but to sarcastically add, "Hope that's not a problem for you."

I had parried her jab. Now I was going to pay the price.

She got up off the sofa and looked at me and said, "I didn't know he was coming by," in a condescending tone as though I was required to inform her that he was coming over.

"He's not coming in. He's just picking me up. I'm watching for him," I said calmly.

She blasted again, "I don't care *what* he does!"

With that I turned and in a low voice said, "I know."

Angrily, she responded, "Oh please! It's too late, and I don't want to hear it!"

At that point, I went outside and waited on the front porch. It was another perfectly innocent and harmless situation used to manufacture misery and tension. She was letting me know she had a right to know what I did and with whom, and that I was required to tell her. She was fully in charge of my life and had a right to know everything I was doing.

It was also her way of getting in the last word.

It was her *modus operandi* to start a scene and then give herself immunity by forcing me into silence either verbally or someone walking away. More importantly, I would come to see that her being critical regarding everything about me, everything I said, everything I did, everyone in my life, my life's achievements, literally everything—was weaponized and designed to subjugate me.

Some days later, an elderly woman who lived on the second floor of my parents' previous home passed away. She had always been good to me, and I attended her funeral services. At the calling I saw and spoke with her granddaughter, whom I had not seen since I was a small boy. She had been a friend of the family for decades. She asked if I would pass a message from her cousin on to my sister, and I agreed.

By some chance, I did not see my sister that night.

The following morning my sister was sitting on the sofa watching television when I walked downstairs. I was standing in the living room and began to relay the message to my sister, also asking if she had the cousin's phone number.

She interrupted me with a disgusted look on her face and without warning screamed at me, "No! Why?"

I snapped back, "Don't talk to me that way. I'm trying to relay a message to you!"

She snapped back, saying, "*Don't* talk to *me* that way!"

How could a simple thing like delivering a message be so fraught with emotional risk?

I departed my parents' side of the house feeling frustrated. I went out the back door and into my brother's house, and told him what happened. He responded only by announcing that he had a recent diagnosis of a health condition, without being specific, and that he no longer wanted to know anything regarding what went on in my parents' side of the house.

The day was coming for which I had worked all these years. After diligently paying my debts and saving, I was at a point where my bills from my divorce were paid and I had sufficient money saved to sign a lease for an apartment that would begin in early spring. My new residence was in New Jersey and closer to my office on McGuire Air Force Base.

I decided to give my family only a day's notice, believing that had they known I was leaving in advance, it would have fueled greater and more constant rages to get their last attacks in. It was clear I had to keep my personal life to myself even when it came to the most innocent of things.

At the dinner table on a Friday in late February, I made the announcement to my mother. She kept eating dinner and did not respond. While I could not read her silence it did not matter, nor did I care. The important thing was to make my escape.

Later that same evening my sister was in her car driving. She passed me going in the opposite direction on a small main road and saw me. I recall a clearly unmistakable look of what I felt was surprise on her face, probably because my mother told her I was moving out.

I had seen this particular look so many times before; it was similar to what one sees in a child who has been caught with their hand in the proverbial cookie jar. She emitted the energy and spirit of guilt even from a distance in passing.

My brother, on the other hand, would simply smirk when he knew he was caught in a guilty situation. He dismissed the awareness as, "Oh that? That bothered you? That was nothing!" This position was always one of arrogance and defensive as in the message, "I did not say or do anything bad; you just took it that way." Knowing it was another of his false allegations that betrayed me, the real and true translation was: "Yes, I know what I did or said, but I relegate it to my right to denial by telling you your feelings are wrong or don't matter and there's absolutely nothing you can do about it. Now we shall forget it and move on."

In this way, he also remained the victor. But that was only in his mind.

My brother, his wife, my sister, and my mother sent each other similar messages with condescending arrogance. They were so used to betraying and lying to each other that they mistakenly assumed I would be a willing player in their sick interaction and tolerate it as they did, accept it, and make their web of hatred part of my life.

The constant smirks relayed joy that would bring my attention to their blatant lack of empathy and remorse and significant traits of narcissism. In contrast to my sister and brother, my mother used a verbalized tirade to "whip you into place" by force and with self-righteousness.

The results were always meant to achieve a triumph or victory and to solidify their positions in the household. In dealing on any level with the adults in my family, with the exception of my father, I was always prepared for one thing: they were always right and I were always wrong and should I disagree, I was personally attacking them and there should be a battle. It was what their lives had always been and what they were used to.

They hated life and liveliness as much as they hated the "light" (truth). As for myself, they underestimated my strength, the depth of my spirit and awareness, my need to grow, my sense of justice, and my will to resolve and survive.

That I looked the other way for years was not a sign of weakness, as they erroneously believe, but of my strength. The longer I remained away from the constant anger and hate, the more I began to think clearly. Leaving my family's house was a cure.

And so, I reached a point after five years where I was able to comfortably depart from the tyranny and living hell that my family called "home."

I had achieved physical freedom. I never realized or gave thought to what would transpire in their behavior after my permanent departure from the house. Before I left, I provided my family with my phone number and a post office box address for mail. I did not tell them the physical address of my new apartment.

Even so, although I was no longer present, the attacks continued with differing methods of employment and the smear campaign continued and intensified.

There was an eerie calm that came over the environment following the announcement of my departure. The rages stopped; the outbursts stopped; the anger all but ceased. While on the one hand, it seemed they were victorious in expelling the "enemy," on the other hand I felt great relief that the reign of terror was over.

At least, that's what I thought at the time.

Escape from Dark Territory

"Whoso rewardeth evil for good, evil shall not depart from his house."

— PROVERBS 17:13

Continued frequent business trips left my free time at a premium, and getting settled into my new place took longer than expected. What I wanted at this point, and had been completely unable to do while living with my family in what I came to refer to as Dark Territory, was to meet a woman and develop a meaningful commitment.

In 1997—and for the first time in my life—I was one of several people who were let go at work. I viewed it as an opportunity to apply for a position in another program that I really wanted and knew was coming open. This new position was in the defense business, but programmatic circumstances would not allow me to start just yet.

The wait would be six months. Until I was called to start in this new position, I decided to take a long overdue sabbatical from working. In the interim, I enrolled in a six-month accelerated course in advanced project management at the local university three nights a week.

A NEW BEGINNING

The new position would last approximately fifteen to twenty years from start to finish. It was my hope to make this position both my final career job and to see the program through to the end. Doing my small part to help keep citizens safe was a source of pride for me and came with great personal rewards. My profession in the defense industry has been a passion since I was seventeen and remains a passion to this day.

I maintained my relationship with my family with weekend visits to see my parents and found myself traveling even more extensively for work. Travel became so much a part of the job requirement that I found myself on the road more than home.

It would be this way for more than a decade.

Despite the difficulties I had with Patrick and his wife, when I learned he was nearing the end of his position at work, my thoughts took me directly to the possibility of his getting a position on my team, which was in the process of a buildup. I casually asked him if he had a résumé and discovered he did not. At that time, our relationship was such that we could go still go out and enjoy time together, though I had a longstanding, deep mistrust of him from some of his past behavior and from the fact that his thinking was clearly defective on many fronts.

I tried hard to maintain a relationship with him. In fact, though I'd moved out and thankfully no longer had to live under the same roof as my family, I tried hard to maintain relationships with all of them for the many ensuing years, no matter how hateful their behavior toward me became, all for the love of my father. I could withstand their cruelty if it meant I could spend time with my kind and selfless father, and to give him a little bit of the family he so desperately needed.

There had been other times I thought of the possibility of my brother working together with me like we did during our teens. Essentially, I felt I could help him land a secure and well-paying job and we could have some fun working together and traveling together from time to time.

While I knew he had few academic skills, I wanted better for him. The most I could do was to submit his résumé and hope he would be seen for the qualifications I felt he possessed. I did have some influence with those who knew me, and based on my recommendation, it was a distinct possibility he would be hired.

My coworkers are the most gracious, devoted human beings on the planet, and I am personally grateful to be part of their lives. Patrick would have enjoyed working with them too. The job held significant national importance with travel, and the pay would have made him comfortable. With a fifteen- to twenty-year program, longevity was possible, and I saw his job change as a great opportunity with many great benefits.

The program was just beginning and testing was still in progress. Highly complex processes were in development to field the new systems, as well as a long-range schedule. Site surveys started, and my travel was picking up.

Bringing Patrick on board would not have been far off, and since several of the guys on the team lived out of state and worked remotely from home, it was something we could have likely worked out for him too. His initial travel would have been minimal just to get him familiar with the systems and processes.

I asked for his performance reports and other background material, which he provided, and I had more than enough information to build a good résumé for my brother. He mentioned that he might need these documents back if something else developed, so I agreed to make copies and return the originals.

It was almost a month and countless iterations before I was satisfied with the final product. I wrote Patrick's résumé based not only on the documentation he provided, but appropriately toward the construction skills required in this new program. The construction aspect was within the realm of his past work experience, so it was my hope to get him on a site overseeing and reporting daily on progress.

It was an opportunity of great proportions for him. He appeared to be receptive to the notion, but I recall no noticeable level of anticipation or excitement in him when I handed him the final product on résumé paper I bought.

The program was not quite at the phase where we were assigning locations to people yet, so I held his résumé until we were ready. I just needed him to be patient.

The intensity of my work requirements started to pick up even more. I found myself away on business to Washington, DC; California; Indiana; Florida; and four trips to Michigan that year alone. I was also given sole responsibility to lead the management effort for four other locations: two within the Department of Defense, which had one location each in Indiana and Michigan, and two other locations requiring close coordination with another federal agency in Washington State and New Hampshire.

It was the Michigan location that would be my greatest challenge.

The government accelerated the Michigan location's timeline. A normal schedule requires a forty-eight-month process, four years, but I had less than two years to complete this assignment. Although it was started and then put on hold over a major winter storm that delayed the schedule by eight months, I was in high gear.

From May to December 2001, I averaged twelve-hour workdays five days a week, planning the installation design of this new system.

My visits to my family over the next couple of years would become even more limited based on my travel. I was only able to visit once a month and at times once every two months. The Michigan location would take me away for most of 2001 to 2003, including through winters.

I recall a major blizzard in October 2002 that found me driving ten miles to a town post office in the Lower Peninsula of Michigan to get three family birthday cards in the mail. Fortunately, it was the only time I found myself in that kind of wintry situation. When it snows in the northern areas of the Lower Peninsula with subzero temperatures, it is not something you forget anytime soon. Lake-effect snowstorms are unbelievably horrendous.

This assignment would find me in the Great Lakes region approximately twenty-six times within a period of eighteen months, totaling more than six months on the site. Trips to the area lasted from one week to three weeks, and eventually I was there every month of the year. My joke with the hotel staff was that I was there so often I should run for mayor. The people in this town were absolutely fantastic to work with and to know.

I have always been fond of nature and the beauty of the earth, but I would forget neither the blistering cold winters nor the comfortable summer days.

Fall complemented the beauty of northern Michigan. Hunting and fishing were prevalent in this area surrounded by woods and wildlife. I would often see deer in their quiet beauty peering through snow-capped bushes or between pine trees more than one hundred feet tall, and an occasional family of rabbits running at full speed through the brush would bring a smile to my face. Blue jays, robins, woodpeckers, and the great American bald eagle would make their way in and out of the construction site, adding a final touch of serenity to long, hard days.

But there was also potential danger during the two-week hunting season. As the project leader, I was called to the Mayor's office one morning without notice for a meeting regarding the safety of my crew on the site. He was a short, middle-aged, well-dressed man with graying hair and a friendly face. Reaching out to shake my hand, he said with a smile, "I know you're busy, so I won't keep you, but I wanted to warn you about hunting season near where you're working. Tell your people for the next two weeks not to hang a white hanky from their back pocket, and instruct them to wear bright colors."

Two weeks wasn't that long to be extra cautious; then once again enjoyment of the peaceful, quiet beauty would return.

Despite my frequent physical absences from home and extensive travel requirements, I continued to remain the target in my family. While overt hostility had been drastically reduced since I was not physically present, I would still come to experience subtle and not-so-subtle acts of aggression in which I continued to be progressively devalued.

There were times I would lie on my hotel bed and reflect on my family and my life, especially my homecoming. Between my sister's unwelcoming hostility upon my return and my mother's tolerance and encouragement of it, I found myself oscillating between anger and compassion—compassion for the fact that their hatred detracted from their own happiness.

Coming home had been one of the major disappointments of my adult life. It was heartbreaking to see what had become of my brother and my sister, what they had done to their lives and to the family.

2002

I was away for most of 2002 with short breaks to return home that were sometimes for several weeks or on the rare occasion for a couple of months. I would visit my family this year only on a Saturday or Sunday for an hour when I was able to get home on a brief break.

In November, I had a phone call with my brother. It was another one of those events that were difficult to comprehend and left me speechless. I was traveling to a pending work location in northern Oregon, where I was conducting a survey and participating in local meetings. This location was assigned to me because my son, Thomas, lived in the area, having moved from the southwest several years before. The team manager was good in that way: personal issues were considered when assigning locations to the team.

While relaxing in my hotel room after my long plane ride and the thirty-five-mile drive to see my son, I called my brother to say hello and to chat.

My travel left little time for visits; my cell phone was the best way to reach me, and the family always knew that.

My brother answered in a tone that instantly put me in a defensive mode. I assume his caller ID had identified me. He answered my call by asking, "What's up?" but his tone was indifferent and uncaring; there was no joy or pleasantness and no real greeting on his part. His position was more, "What the fuck do you want?"—not anger but indifference to my call.

Giving him the benefit of the doubt as I often did (perhaps too many times), I felt he may have had things on his mind or may have been having a bad day. Nevertheless, I attempted to prompt an explanation. I said, "I don't know what you mean by that, 'What's up.' I just called to say hello and see what's going on. I'm on my way to see Thomas, and I'll be here working for a week." In a self-righteous tone he said, "Well, isn't that *special*."

It was so off the wall that I felt confused and somewhat irked. I felt it appropriate to ask, but not sure why I chose these words, "What, are you always right?"

His response was matter-of-fact: "Yeah, I am."

At that moment, I lost my sense of clarity as I had on a few occasions in the past. This time it was not based just on his choice of words but on the tone in which he said them. I fell silent momentarily, processing what he said and how, and found myself incapable of thinking clearly.

I felt a pang of anger from all those previous times I had fallen silent when his words confused me, and this time I just did not want to talk to him any longer.

I pressed the "end call" button without a goodbye.

I was happily on my way to see my son for the first time in two years, and I had to stay focused on my work. *Patrick was not going to take that away from me*, I thought. It was another bewildering interaction, and the joy that I had been feeling moments earlier as I was dialing his number vanished. Even the joy I was feeling because I was about to see my son after a long absence and a seven-hour flight was replaced by negative pangs in my stomach.

A NEW RELATIONSHIP AND OLD FAMILY PATTERNS, 2002

Early in 2002, I was fortunate to meet a wonderful woman. Colleen was recently separated and going through a divorce, although emotionally she had been free for several years. She was vibrant and happy, had a character and personality that glowed, and was always laughing and smiling. We met on a dating site for professionals, she being a successful real estate agent and me being an engineer.

God knows how hard it was to find a dating site that was reputable with all the negativity and horror stories one heard about them, especially in the early days of the internet. I tried the single dance thing, the speed dating thing, and a few paid matchmaking agencies to no avail.

The more time we shared together, the more I liked her. I was drawn to her spirit, her goodness and her aliveness; she had a good soul and a great heart. She had three children and was a very loving mother who taught her children values and provided them the emotional and mental balance needed to foster normal development. I admired her for that.

Colleen had a good-hearted personality that seemed to make things bounce off her, but she was also sensitive, very feminine, and had class.

Despite the difficulties of her divorce and her less than amicable ex-husband-to-be, Colleen remained happy, and she came to love me—and I her. She was supportive of my frequent travel during that time and appreciated hearing about my work. She always made me feel good that way and even came with me on several occasions on business trips. We visited my parents together, and she attended family birthday celebrations.

On one business trip to the Pacific Northwest, she met my son Thomas.

Due to my persistent naïveté (you would think I would have learned by now!), I did not realize that she was soon to be in the crosshairs of my family in ways similar to my ex-wife, and would generate more family drama.

THE WEDDING

Colleen had been with me on several family visits, but there were times when, as a mother of three, she could not make a visit. On one solo visit, my brother's wife, Brianna, told me that her daughter Erin was getting married sooner than planned and that I was invited. Patrick was visibly upset by the accelerated wedding timeline.

I told her I was not sure what my work-related travel schedule would be in the coming months, but if I could make it I certainly would. I sent my schedule via email to my brother so they would know, but with a caveat that my schedule was fluid and could change without notice.

Other developments transpired over the coming weeks of which I was unaware, and on another visit several weeks later, Patrick and Brianna were even more visibly upset. Erin had told them that her future in-laws were making all the wedding arrangements, and that my brother and his wife would not be deeply involved.

Patrick and Brianna were understandably not happy to be shut out of the wedding plans. Eventually, my brother and his wife were given the job of sending out invitations, but Erin had made it very clear the parents of her husband-to-be were handling the major details.

On another visit several weeks later, Brianna coldly informed me that I could come to the wedding but that I could not bring a guest. She informed me that she did not make the rule; the groom's parents had, and there were no exceptions. It was explained to me that even an adult family member who was unmarried, regardless of which side of the family they were on, would not be able to bring a guest. One had to be married to get a plus-one.

I found it odd and bizarre and had never heard of such a requirement for a wedding. I was surprised and had to ask why. Brianna responded by repeating what she had said moments earlier: the decision was not hers. Brianna said it was for "financial reasons" that unmarried people could not bring a guest.

I thought there was a simple enough solution: I would pay Colleen's way.

I offered to pay two hundred and fifty dollars to cover for Colleen. Brianna's response was, "No, the rules are the rules," even though I explained that money was not an issue and saw the opportunity to offer to pay for Colleen. Again, she said, "No!" firmly and without hesitation. "The rules were made and they apply to everyone," she added.

Still dumbfounded because the rule was so unbelievable, I turned to my brother and asked him to simply ask Erin if she would be willing to have Colleen attend with me if I paid for her to go. I saw no harm in asking the question since it was just that, a question. He apparently saw no harm in it either and said he would ask her.

I would never have expected the consequences of asking the question or I would have avoided asking him altogether. It was two weeks later, on another visit, that an inevitable blowup would come out of nowhere. Despite longer absences between visits, Patrick and Brianna continued to blame me for the problems in their family. These accusations were becoming more ridiculous with infantile and unjustified hostility. Their thinking and reasoning abilities were aberrant, ridiculous, and defective as much as they were confusing.

The step-daughter, Erin, apparently became incessantly angry with them for asking my question—highly explosive, in fact.

Briana said that my "interference" was the cause of a confrontation. Her behavior and reaction toward them had nothing to do with me.

My brother then added calmly, "I'll *never* do anything for you again!"

I was shocked by this revelation.

I explained that I did not understand and mentioned it was a normal and reasonable request to ask to bring a guest to a wedding; I could not understand why their daughter would become upset at them for asking, especially since I had offered to pay. With as much composure as I could muster, I mentioned I was not responsible for Erin's behavior toward them and that her reaction following the query was certainly not my fault or Colleen's.

A short time later I walked over to the kitchen sink. My brother and his wife were at the kitchen table, still visibly angry and seemingly hurt. Brianna kept the unfortunate event with her daughter on the surface and directed the blame toward me.

While tapping the tip of her index finger on the table, she remarked arrogantly, "You're responsible for all the problems in this family."

Why is an accusation that is so ludicrous also so hurtful? Because you cannot easily separate intellect from emotion. Understanding does not equal acceptance. "No, I'm not," I said. Patrick sat there meekly in silence, which constituted agreement with Brianna.

How could I possibly be responsible for all the problems in their family?

They needed a scapegoat to soothe the turbulence, and it was easier to hold me accountable for their daughter's reaction.

Perhaps we should blame a rape victim for their rape or an innocent murder victim for the scumbag that took his or her life, I thought to myself. *We should always blame the victim.*

Apparently not convinced that I had gotten the message, Brianna repeated the statement again while tapping the tip of her index finger on the table.

This second time she tapped her finger was to emphasize her contemptuous position. It reiterated the destructive behavior and poisonous attitude I had witnessed and come to expect from them over the past thirteen years.

I knew that I was in the presence of evil.

There is one thing I want to add at this point regarding evil. In her 2007 book, *Evil Genes,* Dr. Barbara Oakley, whose work focuses on the complex relationship between neuroscience and social behavior, describes advances in the study of the human brain to determine whether evil people are born with evil genes, essentially whether being evil comes from nature or nurture.

I believe it's a mixture of the two. Scientists have discovered a gene through brain scans for people who commit acts of evil consistently. However, you can over-wean a child to the point that they become self-inflated thereby planting seeds of narcissism. By contrast, you can abuse a child by not responding to their needs, which makes them turn within themselves for comfort. In other words, that someone may be born with a gene that will deploy evil later on.

Narcissism is created through parental mishandling, or by those around you. It infects everyone around it.

From a psychological perspective, scientists use terms such as personality disorders, mental health disorders, character disorders, and an array of other terms to refer to those who commit heinous acts of cruelty and evil in some form against others. They relate these aberrances to specifically identified traits of a "mental" disorder. That would mean the *mind*.

Christian theologians relate evil to Satan living in the *mind*, while viewing God and acts of love, kindness, and all things good as residing in the *heart*. In other words, the Devil, who does his work through people, lives in the mind while God lives in the heart.

In sharing these two perspectives, I am by no means suggesting that all people with mental illness are evil. It is cruel in and of itself to call people with mental illness, who, because of and in spite of their illness, are good and decent people who struggle to live a good life. The question is if someone is *sane* and commits evil or *insane* and does it. As I see it, there are mentally healthy people who are capable of evil acts as well as mentally ill people. Sometimes, as in the specific case of my family, there appears to be a confluence of mental illness and evil.

It was still not enough for my brother's wife to blame me for all the problems in their family. At that moment, referring to Colleen, Brianna remarked, "She's in your life, not mine!" Would the converse of this twisted logic be true? I imagine Brianna would not assert that she herself was only in my *brother's* life and not in *mine*. I never made the distinction or separation despite my brother marrying and bringing her into his nuclear family.

It seems all the responsibility for negative events from the past, dating back many years, including problems with my former wife, Maureen, were bestowed upon me, and my family was much worse in their behavior now than they were thirteen years earlier. I was now coming to feel the very sight of my family made me nauseous, disgusted, and repulsed to the point where I could not stand to be in the same room with them. This long-term pattern of scapegoating came to the forefront of my mind at that moment, and I was getting angry.

It was another of those bewildering moments in this persistent script of defective thinking, irresponsibility for their own troubles, and an outright failure to place responsibility where it belonged—on themselves. It was still unclear to me as to what the behavior was from a clinical standpoint, and I did not have enough knowledge to even begin to define it. There was no label or name available to me that would allow me to deal with what I was beginning to identify only as abusive behavior. One thing was for certain, however, and that is that I had long been assigned as the family scapegoat and a dumping ground for their problems, their guilt, and their shame.

The feeling came over me in the coming moments of an awareness that I needed to continue to control my defensive impulses. Usually, I would just walk away or dismiss their abnormal comments, as I had for many years, but I found it increasingly difficult and was beginning to feel I had had enough. I could feel myself wanting to lash out, and I had to consciously control that impulse. I did not want to fall into the trap of becoming the aggressor.

The only remedy was distance.

The negative feelings they inspired in me were strong enough for me to realize it was time to cut my visits even shorter, knowing the longer I remained, the more the abusive emotional and psychological attacks would continue. I saw no end to it. I was also coming to realize their ruthlessness. They were weak, inferior people, totally oblivious to reality and completely irresponsible, and their provocations and displaced blame would only escalate matters.

The years of blame for things I had nothing to do with only complicated and intensified my feelings. As I drove home, my mind again replayed that day many years back when I watched Brianna pointing her finger inches from Patrick's face, and with acute anger demanding he go through her when he wished to speak to her daughter.

It was Patrick's lack of self-respect that brought this particular evil to me, to the family and my life, and to those who were in my life.

An excerpt from his best-selling book, *People of the Lie*, psychiatrist Dr. M. Scott Peck writes, "A predominate characteristic, however, of the behavior of those I call evil, is scapegoating. Because in their hearts they consider themselves above reproach, they must lash out at anyone who does reproach them. They sacrifice others to preserve their self-image of perfection."

My family resented me, I believe, for the life I had made for myself, for the man I had become, and the people in my life were equally targeted—guilt by association. We were all bad in their eyes. I believe the truth is that I represented what their lives were not, and I was coming to understand this decade-plus duration of blaming, and why they believed and vehemently defended their own lies. The long-term pattern of aggression, anger, and hostility was beginning to make some sense. Shame, envy, and jealousy seemed to be significant, underlying factors in their behavior as well.

With the exception of my father and Patrick's two children, Michaela and Patrick Jr., whom he had with Brianna, not one family member could or was willing to commit to the family in a loving way. I know now the likelihood that "malignant entitlement," as I have read in my research, was a prevalent personality trait at work in them.

DISASSOCIATION AND REASSIGNMENT

What I did not understand or realize at the time, or for many years, were the internal dynamics taking place in my family members.

I found it necessary to keep myself in constant check, primarily by keeping foremost in mind who I was and by keeping my visits short. It came to be that when I walked through the door, I felt a part of myself being left behind.

I knew they blamed me for Erin's behavior from a simple and innocent query, and the blame-game strategy had always been prevalent. What I did not know was the name of the process that was taking place—"disassociation and reassignment."

They disowned Erin's behavior toward them and reassigned it to me (and to Colleen). By *projecting* her behavior onto me, they relieved her step-daughter of behavioral responsibility and I remained the scapegoat. In other words, because it was on my behalf the question was asked, I became responsible for Erin's behavior and the resulting conflict.

In essence, I *made* Erin act in the manner she did.

I had a reasonable expectation that my brother would remonstrate his wife, since his stepdaughter's behavior had nothing to do with me and was, by any objective standard, out of line. Instead, he sat quietly as his wife spewed her venomous and twisted blame toward me.

Following the second finger-tapping session, I departed for home again shaking my head in disbelief. I felt it becoming more difficult to dismiss and cast aside as I had these many years.

I was reaching my level of tolerance.

I recall my therapist once said that my level of tolerance for abuse was high. Perhaps he was right, but then again, is self-control not a good thing? What I believed then as much as I believe today is that it is dysfunctional behavior to remain in an abusive or otherwise toxic relationship. Everyone has a limit and can take just so much abuse.

RECIPROCITY AND COMMITMENT

It is perhaps appropriate to mention the aspects of reciprocity and commitment essential to all meaningful relationships, including family and the best of friendships. All normal people are aware of these.

Take holidays, for example. To Brianna and her daughter, I presented gifts at Christmas and on birthdays, although I was under absolutely no obligation to do so. I had welcomed Brianna into my home when she and my sister visited me and Maureen in Europe—another reason I had felt comfortable asking if I could pay to take my significant other to Erin's wedding.

I offered and shared my food when she visited, used my personal vacation time for her weeklong visit to take her sightseeing, and she slept in my home.

There was absolutely no cost to her—because she was family.

It was from her relationship to my brother that I would not deny her these things from me, and in essence, it was one of those family-benefiting acts of kindness on my part and my wife's with the aim of fostering closeness for the benefit of family. It was the right thing to do, and Maureen and I felt good doing it.

Reciprocity feeds meaningfulness. It is natural, normal, and essential for human interaction and relationships that have value. But from none of my family was there any capacity for reciprocation or commitment on any level for the betterment of the group as a whole in any way, shape, or form.

What they were given, in their view, was an entitlement to receive with no need or expectation to give back in kind or on some meaningful level.

MY LOVING SON

You may be wondering why I have not yet spoken of where my son, Thomas, fit into the family structure during the fifteen years since my return home. The short answer is that he did not, nor, in their view and behavior, was he meant to.

The long answer is put forth in the pages of this book.

I knew it was up to me for him to know my niece and nephew, Michaela and Patrick Jr.; they represented the next generation of family, and it was imperative to preserve the future generation. Someone had to accept the responsibility to attempt to bond them in friendship, strength, and love for each other.

It had been more than fifteen years since my son had seen my family; my niece and nephew had been babies when he last saw them. The circumstances of my professional life prevented more visits to a large extent, but there are obviously other more significant reasons, as you have read.

As a father, I could not place my son's emotional and mental stability at risk by exposing him to the same abuse that I experienced. While a part of me believes they would have put on a good "face" (called *masking* in psychiatric terms) for Thomas, I had no idea what overt negative elements he would potentially or actually face.

My abusive welcome home from my sister, the extreme hostility, blind fury, those five long and tormented years I lived at home after my divorce, and my mother's tolerance of and encouragement of it all, as well as the lies—and I was a son and brother!—I was not willing to risk for my son. I could not find one benefit of doubt no matter how I struggled in my search.

A RARE ZODIACAL ELEMENT

It is interesting to note one curious and significant aspect in my family: my mother, my son, and my nephew, Patrick Jr., all share the same birth month, separated by years. Their specific birth dates are relatively close.

While I never forgot my nephew or my mother on their birthdays, on not one of my son's birthdays did any of my family members send him a gift or card. Nor did anyone as much as ask about him.

Later, my mother did make repeated requests for me to provide her with his address so that she could send him a card. I will talk more about that, but due to my unresponsiveness, she even went to my father and had him ask me. The circumstances behind it I viewed as superficial, and I was distrusting of their underlying motives. I ultimately told them to give any cards for him to me and I would ensure he received them. I could not permit them to have complete freedom to contact him without going through me.

In 2003, I realized my niece and nephew were getting older and my parents were aging and in ill health, so I decided to risk having my son meet them. I felt it was something that was important for them all despite the circumstances—that my parents see their first grandchild after these many years and that my son see them before they passed on.

On birthday celebrations in the family throughout this year, I asked my son to call my mother and speak with her. I would let him know what time I would be at the house, and he would call his grandmother. Since he was unaware of family birthday gatherings, I coordinated with him. After so many years I realized how awkward the call might be for them, but I felt that gradually connecting them through phone calls would allow a level of comfort before bringing him to see them and to meet his cousins.

It also meant, however, that he would then meet my sister, my brother, and his wife. I was horrified by this thought, for fear of their coldness and how he would likely be treated, which would most certainly push me over the edge.

ABUSE BY PROXY

What was equally significant was that, in my having been away for so long and so many times from my travel, they could still find a way, in their minds, of blaming me for that which I had absolutely no responsibility over. It was not unreasonable to assume they would also vent their hatred toward my innocent son simply because and for no other reason than he was my son.

A NEW TARGET, OLD STYLE

Memories of what Maureen had suffered at my family's hands instilled nagging feelings within me that Colleen would be targeted as well. I had already seen signs of that. On a visit with my brother and his wife, there was a brief discussion about Colleen, during which Brianna surprisingly remarked, "I don't know why you think we don't like her. We don't know where you got that from."

She was referring to my last visit, several weeks earlier, when she had said that Colleen was in my life, not hers. Yet by any rational standard Colleen was in my life and therefore, by her association with me, was in Patrick's and Brianna's life too.

By claiming she did not know why I thought she and my brother did not like Colleen was backtracking. It was in essence a manipulative lie, and manipulating others through falsehoods is a psychopathic trait. It was especially ridiculous to think that I could not see through her bullshit. Gaslighting was alive and well in my family. I discuss this insidious tactic of abuse in more detail in Chapter 11.

It was clearly an attempt to either make me believe their previous position was without effect, or that what transpired in my last visit never happened, or indeed, she was planting the seed to "set up" Colleen—again.

It was a very shallow attempt to either invalidate or deny what Brianna had said before. When I received the invitation to Erin's wedding, I declined and returned the RSVP card. On an interesting note, I entered one entry incorrectly before making the appropriate correction. It was just an error on a form that anyone could make. My brother called me a week later and asked me several times why I had filled it out wrong.

It was ridiculous. He apparently felt as though it was some intentional criticism or offense.

Months passed with no visits. I needed time to reconnect with myself. Later that year, on a Sunday afternoon in August, Colleen and I ventured a visit. During this visit, in her usual vibrantly happy and non-threatening manner, Colleen commented to my niece, Michaela, "You look like you really poured yourself in those jeans." Perhaps it was an inappropriate comment to a teenager, but Colleen nevertheless was complimentary to Michaela on her looks. Michaela did not appear to be upset, nor did anyone else. Colleen was herself slender and attractive, and she also wore tight jeans and looked good in them.

After our departure sometime later, a feeling of immense relief came in that we escaped without overt conflict, but that would inevitably come.

Two weeks later I visited my parents alone before leaving on another business trip. I went next door to visit my brother and his wife, and saw Patrick sitting at the table while Brianna was picking up around the kitchen. There did not appear to be anything wrong.

Without warning, Brianna angrily looked at me and spat, "Colleen hurt Michaela's feelings by what she said that day, and she owes Michaela an apology! Michaela wanted to say something to her, but she didn't!"

I was taken aback by this sudden outburst and was momentarily silent as I processed it. I responded calmly, "Colleen is a great woman. If Michaela wanted to talk to Colleen about something, she could have. Colleen would never hurt anyone's feelings intentionally, and she's easy to talk to." Brianna responded angrily, "Colleen wears tight pants too. She had no right to say anything to Michaela!"

I responded, "Yes she does wear them. That's why it was not an insult. Colleen complimented her. It was not meant as an insult. They both look good in tight jeans, and to Colleen it was not insulting." To diffuse the anger I added, "I will mention your concern to her."

I was livid and departed wondering why someone did not explain to my niece, who was sixteen at the time, that the statement had an underlying complimentary element. Perhaps my niece was simply too young to understand the comment's meaning and that it was delivered in a jovial way.

My mind was racing. Later that day I spoke with Colleen and told her what had transpired.

She was upset at the thought that my niece felt insulted. Colleen and I spoke at length, and we both came to the conclusion that no one had explained to Michaela that the comment was complimentary and not insulting. Colleen said the next time she went to the house she would call my niece aside and explain to her what she meant. As it turned out, that day would never come.

THANKSGIVING DAY

The end of 2003 was approaching. While at my parents waiting for dinner to be ready, my brother mentioned he was probably going to be laid off next year. The thought again about him working with me came to mind—why, I do not know. I recalled the extensive time and energy I had put into building his résumé for that purpose.

The thought was quickly overwhelmed by the red flags flying high from what I had experienced, and I realized that I no longer cared. More importantly, he had not demonstrated the proper character traits for such a position. He could not be trusted.

Dinner was uneventful but for tension in the air, which was always prevalent.

CHRISTMAS EVE, 2003

This was the day the proverbial shit hit the fan and another reign of terror waged by my mother, sister, brother, and his wife began. It would last for more than six years.

I had gone—alone—to Christmas dinner at my parents' house. Visiting my brother's side of the house before dinner, I was generally relaxed although the trademark air of hatred and distrust saturated the environment.

While I could not stand to be in the same room with them, I had to maintain some semblance of peace for the sake of my father. As I was sitting watching television trying to be invisible, my brother sat down next to me on the sofa, leaned over and whispered in my ear, "You and Colleen tore this family apart. You're going to pay for it."

Then he got up and walked away, ensuring he got in the last word.

It reminded me of my retirement day, when Patrick blamed me for not giving him five dollars when we were kids, for my mother expelling him from the house when he turned eighteen, and for his spending sixty thousand dollars from workers' compensation on drugs. The scenario was similar in another way as well: no one was around to hear it.

This is called "plausible deniability." If no one heard it, he did not say it.

I maintained self-control, but I was angry and it was intense. I internalized my feelings and channeled them so as not to haul back with my fist. It was another moment of stunned silence as I processed what was just said. I departed quietly to my parents' house.

The bizarre and misplaced blame continued to fill me with anger. Dinner went well with no further incidents, but my anger remained internalized, and I had to search for inner control to keep from lashing out in Colleen's and my defense.

I did not remain long, and after Christmas Eve dinner I departed to share a special time with Colleen. I was fighting the urge to call my brother and tell him he better accept responsibility for the problems in his life and his family, and especially that it was not Colleen's or my fault if his stepdaughter was angry with them for asking a simple, innocent question. I felt I could not look the other way again just to keep peace, but once again, I did.

I returned to my parents' house on Christmas Day and as with all past Christmases, the gift-giving ritual was superficial and lacking real joy. The feeling in the air was void of anything but tension.

Prior to the planned dinnertime my mother announced we were eating a little later than expected today. The reason given was that the night before, on Christmas Eve, Brianna had asked if we could eat later since Erin and her nephew were stopping by to exchange gifts but could not stay for dinner. My brother's wife did not want her time with her daughter to cause her to miss dinner. My mother agreed.

It came over me that I, as the one who was away in the family, and had been for so long, was given no consideration regarding any plans I may have had to divide my time between my family and my significant other. It was difficult enough to balance my personal life with my extensive work travel schedule, let alone family time.

I was angry that my brother's stepdaughter—biologically unrelated to the family—would take precedence over me at least in consideration of asking if the delay would disrupt my plans.

Although it was apparent, I was still questioning, as I had been for years since I returned, where it was exactly that I fit into the family. I recall having to bite my tongue and keep the peace, but it was difficult.

"Unfortunately, this change has disrupted my plan to share time with Colleen," I said. I explained the situation and announced that with the sudden change in schedule, and not having the opportunity to re-coordinate the day with Colleen, I had to leave before dinner.

The collective response, in so many words, was, "Oh, that's too bad. Sorry you can't stay." My sister prepared food in containers for me to take, and I departed. I remember feeling angry that no one in my immediate family saw the need to ask if my plans would be affected, or even if I had any. At that time, I had no knowledge or awareness that it was simply something none of them were capable of envisioning. This is not to say I felt the expectation of special privileges—far from it—but I was the one who was away, and I was their son.

As I drove off, I was angry but in control of my feelings, although I racked it up as one more event in which all of the other past experiences came to the forefront of my mind and accumulated in me as one massive conglomeration of negativity.

The day after Christmas, my mother called and asked me what the problem was. I told her I wanted to spend time with her and my father, balance a personal life and my travel schedule, and that holiday dinner with them was as important to me as my personal relationship with Colleen.

I was compelled to tell her what Patrick had said on Christmas Eve day, and explained that Colleen and I were not the cause of any problems between Brianna and Erin.

I added that the sudden change in plans on Christmas Day to accommodate my brother's stepdaughter gave me no room to keep to my own schedule for the day, and told her Brianna's daughter and her nephew should be of lesser consideration because "I am your son, and I am the one who was away." As our discussion ended, I softened it by saying there was no problem and I was just expressing how I felt.

But it was far from over.

At the beginning of 2004, Colleen and I agreed that it was important to us for my niece to understand the truth about Colleen's comment, especially since her mother and her father, who by now had elevated it to a higher level, had a responsibility to explain it but had failed to do so. This failure served no other purpose than to allow my niece to believe Colleen insulted her, and I came to see that it was intentional on their parts. If she had been insulted, the family would close ranks on the outsider to protect her.

Colleen and I also agreed my niece would perhaps hear the phrase many times in her life and that it was important for her development that she realize it was not an insult. Because Colleen was upset, I told her I would drive to the house that night and talk to my brother about it as a first step. It was a step in explaining to him that Colleen did not insult my niece, although it was frustrating that I had to do this.

I called Patrick and told him I was coming down and needed to talk to him. When I arrived in front of the house, he entered my car, and without hesitation the first thing he said was, "Brianna doesn't want to know anything!" I dismissed it and did not respond. I was not concerned with nor did I care about what she wanted to know or not know.

I drove around the corner, and we talked about the incident. I told him it was apparent Michaela did not know the truth about Colleen's comment. I mentioned it was important to explain the nature of the comment to my niece, that Colleen did not have any intent to insult her. I also let him know Colleen and I both felt bad that Michaela may have been led to believe she was insulted, adding that Michaela did not appear to be upset that day.

I stated, "We just need her to know the truth, that Colleen didn't say it with intent to be insulting." Without hesitation, he blasted back in overt anger, "Michaela *doesn't* have to know!"

I disagreed and asked why he felt it was good to let Michaela believe something that simply was not true.

He blew that off as "stupid" and wouldn't acknowledge that they had perpetuated bad feelings in my niece by allowing the perceived insult to exist. He added, "I know Brianna can be unreasonable," but nor did he attempt to resolve the situation.

I did not respond to that even though I could have opened an entirely new discussion on her "unreasonableness." It was apparent they either intentionally *allowed* my niece to believe Colleen insulted her, thus allowing her to believe the lie and creating negative feelings in my niece for Colleen and toward me, or that my niece feeling insulted had been *instilled* in her by my brother and his wife badgering her about it (i.e., brainwashing). Based on their behavior and character, that was a more likely scenario. My concern was they were intentionally ruining a possible friendship and relationship Colleen could have had with my niece by poisoning my niece's mind.

A third possibility was that Patrick and Brianna simply made up the whole thing and that Michaela wasn't upset at all. Realizing it was a waste of time, I ended the conversation abruptly and told Patrick I had to go. I drove around the corner and dropped him off at the house.

When I returned home to Colleen, I explained what transpired. She became quiet. I explained my brother said his stepdaughter did not have to know the true intent and meaning of her comment about Michaela's jeans.

Colleen looked away momentarily in thought. Finally, she was compelled to ask me questions, and her questions prompted me to go into detail about past family behavior.

A door I had kept closed with her was now open.

To the best of my ability, I had shielded her from the behavior of my family—that is, I did not explain the issues that I had experienced since my return home. Perhaps that was a mistake. I was compelled by her questions. I explained past events regarding my ex-wife and other good people in my life who came to visit and had eventually become uncomfortable seeing my family.

Colleen realized she had been "set up" to have her relationship with my niece destroyed, and came to the realization that she had little in common with my family. She did not trust them—any of them—and could not believe them in any sense now.

This, as I was afraid would happen, put a strain on our relationship just as it had with their behavior toward my ex-wife, Maureen. A short time later Colleen's eyes welled with tears, and she said she did not think she could possibly connect in a meaningful way with my family.

She added that it was best we chart a separate course and wished me well through her trembling lips. My attempts to convince her that all would work out in time and be OK were not fruitful. She solemnly walked me to the door, taking my hand in hers, turned and hugged me. Opening the door, her fingers gently slipped through mine as I stepped out.

My family did it again.

In a later conversation with my brother, I let him know that I had explained to Colleen the conversation he and I had sitting in my car and that it prompted questions from her that made me reveal past events of their behavior. I added that Colleen would no longer come back to visit since she could not trust them or believe them. I further added that Colleen was a good parent and mother, and would never let her children believe a lie.

He responded, "Now that you've told her we all suck, remember the story about people who live in glass houses." It was another confusing and amazingly defective position. I recall thinking, *Yes, you do suck, and so does Brianna, but I never used those words to Colleen.* I imagine he wanted me to support his and his wife's decision to lie to my niece.

That was not a possibility.

Now it was becoming even more increasingly clear that my brother was destroying my relationship with the children, although I did not know the extent of his focus until much later. I cannot fathom a father saying, in any context, that his children do not have to know the truth, especially when its concealment would be detrimental to the family as a whole—unless, that is, someone is the designated target and there are underlying motives to isolate that target.

There seemed to be a focused effort to get me out of the way, and for purely self-serving reasons. Colleen—like my ex-wife, Maureen, and others the family had met—is a great human being and woman. She felt the same as the others had, and after our breakup I realized that my family's objectives, starting from my return, had been to isolate and ostracize me from any healthy relationship. I would come to know the reasons later.

The Turning Point

2004

"The words 'image,' 'appearance,' and 'outwardly' are crucial to understanding the morality of the evil. While they seem to lack any motivation to be good, they intensely desire to appear good. Their 'goodness' is all on a level of pretense. It is, in effect, a lie. This is why they are the 'people of the lie.'"

— DR. M. SCOTT PECK

The year 2004 was a year of validation. The more I studied and researched, the more I understood the abuse and its inevitable, progressive intensity. While I dealt with the abuse through therapeutic discussions, it was the defective views and thought processing, the lies and betrayal that I had to really work through.

The more I correlated my family's behavior with published findings, the more dots were connected and the more rapidly I felt the roots of intolerance growing within me. Advancing my level of awareness and understanding through this newly gained knowledge was both a blessing and a curse.

On the one hand, as a blessing, the knowledge I gained was of tremendous benefit in helping me realize on a greater scale the lies, deceptions, and manipulations I had withstood. As a curse, I came to realize a high degree of these same defective character traits existed outside of my family, including in people I knew and trusted, people I considered friends. My mind wandered to instances in which I would feel some level of confusion, accompanied by a feeling of caution, because of things people said that were contrary to a moral value system, and to instances of dishonesty that I had dismissed at those times as ridiculous or senior moments.

My thoughts were primarily that, on the one hand, it is dysfunctional behavior to enter into or remain in any abusive or toxic relationship; and on the other hand, it is impossible to establish a meaningful relationship with anyone who is programmed to be an abuser and whose purpose is to destroy liveliness and joy in others, as well as in relationships—their own as well as others.

I concluded that there were more counterfeit people—human clones, mediocre, and below average, roaming the planet than I ever had reason to give any thought to until now.

But they put up a good front.

During the first week of the new year, I wrote two emails to my brother detailing my chief complaints with the family. I reached a point where I had been stifled and oppressed for too long, and I was no longer able to tolerate it.

In their eyes, I had no voice, but I did—they just did not want to hear it. Mine did not count; theirs did. My tone was not in anger; for the truth, I knew, reveals itself quietly and with great power.

Rather than return an email, my brother left a voice message stating simply, for the second time, that I should "keep in mind who lives in a glass house." He added that if I really wanted to have dinner with my parents I should have stayed on Christmas Day. It was a bewildering comment and reflected a complete disregard for me. Whether he liked it or not, his stepdaughter should not have taken precedence over me.

In a vain attempt to "get through" the confusion of his saying it was I who lived in a glass house, I returned the call and said some angry things. It took only seconds for me to realize the fruitlessness and childishness of this interaction I was being pulled into. I called back and left another message saying we needed a truce and asked him to meet me for lunch so we could talk.

I waited several days with no response to my effort at reconciliation. I finally called his house to talk with him, and Brianna answered. She said that Patrick was not home, and before I could leave a message with her, she hung up.

I finally received an email from him simply stating, "We can talk about the weather and we can talk about sports. Family is not a good topic—it's not healthy."

Yet it had been Patrick who, on Christmas Eve day, had sanctimoniously taken a seat next to me to inform me that Colleen and I had ruined the family. It had obviously not been a painfully unhealthy subject then.

This reminded me of my mother's similar pattern of manipulation, using her health issues to justify avoidance, primarily when it came to another member of the family expressing themselves or to gaining or keeping control.

This tactic was designed to give them the first and last word.

It also ultimately amounted to decades spent denying core issues that accelerated the intensely negative feelings we had for each other. Nothing had ever been resolved during "clear the air" sessions they held over a period of more than twenty-five years. It was confusing and ridiculous behavior. How could a solution be attained without honestly communicating core issues, acknowledging their impact, and making an effort to change the behavior?

In recalling what I would hear from my brother during my brief visits home from military service, I realized that what I was personally experiencing was no different from what he had experienced, except that I was resistant to being pulled into the nightmare web that he had chosen to merge with. He was weak then and even weaker today.

I struggled to keep myself from being sucked into the whirlwind turbulence that made up their daily lives, a life they had always known. From his refusal to openly communicate the issues, I felt a sudden urge, compelling and deep in me, that perhaps it was time for me to go to the new house and to remove my personal belongings from the attic where they were stored.

I do not know why, but I had a nagging feeling it was critical that I remove my belongings completely from my parents' house. I contacted a moving company for an estimate, and because it was winter, I planned for an early spring move.

Two weeks passed with silence on my brother's part as I waited for a response to my offer for lunch. My brother's silence was broken when I received a letter dated two days earlier.

Little did I know it would be the beginning of an even more intense tirade of destructive behavior that would tear apart my relationship with him and break the foundation of the family even more. His letter would give new meaning to the term "twisted logic."

His letter stated he understood that I held a deep-seated hatred for him and his family and asked why I bother with people I hate. He attempted to inject guilt in me for any pain my parents felt, and he said everything was my fault, that what I was doing to them was horrendous. He believed his family was in danger from me. He went on to say a multitude of erratic things that he actually believed: that I lived in the past, lied to Colleen, attacked my mother, frightened his children, and that he had no time for my games.

It was a reversal of roles that left me totally dumbfounded.

Everything that came from them was profoundly bewildering, extremely confusing, and clearly was about *them* versus *me*. How can anyone perform a specific behavior and then attribute this very same behavior to someone who does not demonstrate it?

While I waited for and anticipated a reply to my offer for lunch, this letter was his response. It became necessary to read over several times, with each paragraph requiring careful dissection and evaluation to attempt to identify the defective thinking behind it. *Where is he getting his version of reality?* I thought. I have never been a hateful man and was confused as to how he came to this unrealistic conclusion. The hatefulness came from him, his wife, my mother, and my sister.

I had tolerated the past years of abuse and released as much as possible any negative feelings through therapeutic sessions and devotion to my work, although I did have on occasion a knee-jerk reaction. I had always controlled myself through Patrick's, Brianna's, Kayleigh's, and my mother's actions, but I did not always stay quiet.

I was never retaliatory or revengeful, but rather adjusted my own internal dynamics to be on guard as much as possible. I often felt as though I was losing myself, and his letter caught me psychologically off guard, which happened often from my interactions with the family.

His letter isn't about me; it's about him, I thought over and over with great clarity.

There was irony in his reference to me as "...living in the past." It is an unavoidable and fruitless effort to *not* live in the past, from the sole perspective that the family environment of the past was and continued to be a consistent and prevalently recurring part of the daily *present*.

I started to realize their behavior was so abhorrently normal to them that they saw nothing wrong with it, and, in fact, any indication of goodness was viewed as bad. Was it possible that from decades of betrayal by my sister and mother Patrick had developed a vision that this behavior was actually good and normal?

For many years the only change in their behavior had been a noticeable, progressive worsening. The more times I read over his letter, the more confused I became.

I was facing a massive distortion of their reality from a concerted, major campaign to reconstruct events, and they wanted me to believe it. It was *they themselves* who placed his family and the family in general in jeopardy.

Patrick had always blamed me for everything wrong in his life, including his personal choices and decisions while I was away from home and that I had known nothing about.

There was absolutely nothing I could see in his letter that I could respond to on a humane or meaningful level. Based on the venomous lies he spewed, I had no choice but to remain silent and keep my distance.

The passage of a few weeks found my anxiety and confusion diminishing, I think primarily because I had a temporary absence from the behavior, but my guard remained high whenever I thought of visiting my family. My niece Michaela's birthday was coming up fairly soon, and I took my time, as I always did, in choosing a heartfelt card that conveyed my love. I enclosed money and mailed it. Several days after mailing it, my card to her was returned with a post office stamp that read "Refused," and was signed by my brother's wife, Brianna. It would be utterly ridiculous to assume my brother was not aware of that.

Now they were involving the children in their folly, which raised the stakes to an even higher level. My only option was to send an email to my niece, which I did, explaining my card had been returned and to let her know I did not forget her birthday. I added that I would give her the card the next time I came to visit and sent all my love in closing.

I received no response from her. My instincts, again, were telling me it was not unreasonable that my brother and his wife were now focused on poisoning my relationship with my niece. The proof of that, which again told me my instincts were correct, would come later, in a call I received from her.

I was beginning to also feel, at this point, that I was beyond the point of no return. I contacted my life insurance company and changed beneficiaries, removing my brother as part beneficiary. I also revised my will. My brother had been intentionally destroying his relationship with me and now was turning to my relationship with my niece and nephew from some delusion that I had repeatedly offended him and put his family in jeopardy while he and his wife employed a strategy with my sister and mother to betray *me* at every turn.

I was not going to reward him for bad behavior. The return of my niece's birthday card was the catalyst for far-reaching effects on my relationship with my brother.

I was feeling inclined now to immediately remove all of my personal belongings from the house and with more determination and speed. Stemming from a general sense of escalating hostility, I immediately signed a lease agreement for local storage space.

In the meantime, I was given responsibility for twenty additional locations in the United States that were scheduled for defense technology upgrades located in nineteen different states. My travel requirements would be enormous. I had to remain focused on my work.

In February while on a business trip to Johnstown, Pennsylvania, I checked my voice messages at home to find one that surprised me.

My brother had left me this voice message two days earlier.

He said, "Yeah, it's me. Um, lookit, you wanna try and settle things, um, before it's too late for Ma and Dad, that's fine by me, but has to be in a, you know, a normal manner. So it's your choice; just let me know."

On hearing his message, I felt conflicted: angry at his clumsy attempt at reconciliation and slightly hopeful because of the tone of sincerity in his voice. Yet at the end of the day, I did not believe him. I was still angry that he involved my niece in the manner he did, in an obvious attempt to turn her against me.

I wondered how he could completely disregard what he had recently said and done as though nothing had happened.

I would come to discover that Patrick's effort at reconciliation was a ploy to set a trap for me. It would be my mother this time who was his willing weapon of choice.

SETTING THE TRAP

It was the last day of the Leap Month—February 2004—when my mother called and left me a voice message. Her tone was loving and genuine as one would expect from a mother. She asked me to call her and when I did, she explained there was something she wanted to "do with the house" and wanted to talk to me about it. This message came two days following my brother's voice message wanting to "reconcile." I had a nagging feeling they were related somehow, and while I could not make a connection, the hairs on the back of my neck stood up.

I called my mother that evening and asked if something was wrong with the house. In my mind, I was thinking perhaps work needed to be performed in the attic where my personal belongings were located, making them effectively in the way. It was the only thing that made sense at the time. She said nothing was wrong per se, but she was reluctant to go into any detail.

This caused me further suspicion.

To my probing with additional questions, she responded simply, "We just want to do something with it, and I thought we'd talk to you." I asked her if she could tell me on the phone, and she said she did not know how to explain it.

That raised a major red flag since she had always been very articulate.

I asked her again if there were a problem with the house, and she said, "A little bit," then abruptly said, "Well, not a problem, but we just want to do something with it." She was clearly being evasive, and in an attempt to get at the truthful answer, I said that, if there was nothing wrong with the house, what was it that she wanted to talk about? Then I added that I did not understand. She said, "Because you're not living here, so, if you want your share or whatever, I don't know—we have to talk about it."

Now I understood although she was talking in circles. The topic was her and my father's will and the inheritance. I asked if the following

Sunday at one o'clock in the afternoon was a good day and time, and she responded, "Yeah," but there was something creepy in the way she said it. It was difficult to describe—a connotation of deception, an air of something sinister. What I do know for certain is that my instincts were awoken, which I trust completely, and telling me to be cautious with something that was definitely not right.

The following day was Monday, the first day of March. I contacted a moving company and made arrangements to transport my things the following Tuesday. The remainder of the week was uneventful and quiet with respect to phone calls and voice messages.

On Sunday, I arrived at my parents' house ten minutes before the meeting. I naturally assumed that, since the subject pertained to the house and the will, it would be a family meeting. My sister was sitting at her computer in the small room between the kitchen and living room. She had a stern, cold look as she sat silently typing at her computer. The coldness on her face raised another internal warning of something pending.

A part of me was waiting for the proverbial pounce. My father and mother sat at the kitchen table quietly. My brother was not present and I thought he would be along shortly.

The silence was broken when my mother suddenly turned to me and blasted with ferocious screaming and that demonic look, "I called you down here so you don't think I'm doing anything behind your back! We're changing the will to put the house in your brother's and sister's names, and we're taking you off as having one third. When your father and I are gone, your brother and sister will take out a mortgage equivalent to one-third of the value of the house and buy you out."

She had that venomous look of seething hatred on her face again that I had seen several times before. She said she was doing it to "keep peace in the family because of problems between you and your brother. *You* are responsible for causing family problems with your brother." Within a span of seconds, I went from calm to furious.

My instincts were correct.

Her phone call a week earlier was a setup as I suspected. Using the house and the will as a means of punishing me for my brother's transgressions was the ultimate act of betrayal. The decision had already been made, though she allowed me to believe a family discussion would take place. Without a doubt, my brother and sister were behind it.

While I was and had always been a convenient target, it was not until they succeeded in conspiring with my mother to betray me using the house and the will.

Patrick and Kayleigh revealed their true selves and true motive.

It was not until that successful conspiracy with my mother, after these many years since my return, that my brother revealed decades of repressed aggression, malicious envy, vengefulness, and jealousy seething within him. He had employed every tactic and strategy available to conceal all of it.

Not being satisfied with stabbing me in the back, my mother then began to belittle me. I knew that once an attack started there was no stopping it unless I physically walked away. Her defense of my brother and his wife, focusing on me as the perpetrator of family problems, was an unbelievable lie. I reminded her that I was not only incapable of initiating problems but only visited the house once every couple of months.

It made no difference.

My mind was in a blur, and I was in a fit from the success of her deception. I had trusted her, and she set me up to face her hatred and to stab me in the back again.

Then her attack turned to my son, Thomas.

Pointing her finger at me, my mother screamed that for years she called my son's mother, Marie, to obtain his clothes size to send him clothes as gifts for his birthday. She continued that on his seventeenth birthday, Marie was not home, and my son answered the phone. When she asked Thomas for his clothes size to send him clothes for his birthday, he responded by telling her not to worry because "I don't like the clothes you send and give them to my brother."

I was flabbergasted. My son would never say that, and even if for some crazy reason he had, it was no reason to deny his existence for twelve years, which was precisely what she had done. Among the adult members in my family there was a persistent and severe hypersensitivity to criticism—*any* perceived criticism—although they were quite adept at dishing out the abuse even to the point of lying and deception.

In my son's defense, I told her even if that were true, he was seventeen at the time and was a kid, and that today he was a grown man. I explained that not all seventeen-year-olds are adept at values, and that I did not believe her nevertheless—he loved his grandmother.

I added that when I was seventeen and just a kid myself, I was too young to sign my own name to join the military service, and that my nephew Patrick Jr. was nearly seventeen and a kid too young to make his own decisions as well. I demanded to know why she felt my son was a grown man at seventeen, when my nephew and I were not.

She simply repeated, harshly and adamantly, "He was a grown man!" spewing her hatred once again with that venomous look on her face. As we turned to discuss my brother's and his wife's behavior, my sister interjected in their defense, "They're not here to defend themselves," and my thought was, *Where was I when you all sat around the table talking about me in order to come to a decision about changing the will? Where was I to defend myself?*

There was no consideration that I was not there during the discussions that amounted to betrayal, including the strategy used to secure my presence there that Sunday, but in their minds Patrick and Brianna's absence on this day removed them from culpability. Not in my mind: it was planned that way. My brother's absence was preplanned so he could say he had nothing to do with it, but my mother gave them away with her false justification for changing their will because of my causing problems with my brother and thus his family.

My mother further directed to me that people have the ability to say, "I'm sorry." She was referring to me and expecting me to apologize to those to whom I did wrong. This would have pulled me into their normalcy of not speaking to someone until an apology came. I refused.

I made a quick exit from the house, having been pushed over the edge.

Following this, I knew it was time to tell my son what had been going on in the family during these years, which I had kept from him. I also made a decision that they, in conformance with their wishes through their hateful behavior, would never see my son again if I had anything to say about it. Thomas was now thirty years of age, not seventeen, and was a grown man.

I returned home and was still furious. I called my mother to tell her nothing would change just because she was changing the will. She responded with another outburst of rage: "So does that mean you're going to cause more problems?" It always seemed they would drown me out with rage, which I felt was ingrained in some belief that the louder they yelled, the more right they were, and again I thus had no voice.

I slammed the phone down.

The next morning at work, a Monday in early March, I changed my voice mail from the usual personal greeting to the generic system message that said, "The member you are calling is not available." I also decided not to announce in revised business travel voice greetings when I would be out of town, which I did for each planned trip.

My mother's, brother's, and sister's alliance and their traitorous antics had now compelled me to cut off all ties with them.

Over the next week I received six "hang-ups" at work. This was highly unusual, since in my line of business no one would call without a reason and a message was always left. In the four years that I had held this position, not once had I received a hang-up.

I did not have caller ID to determine who called, and so while at work I had to remain vigilant and in a defensive posture.

The following Monday morning, I called the moving company and told them that my requirements had accelerated and that I needed to make the move first thing the next morning. They said they could perform the service.

At three thirty that same day I called my mother from my cell phone on my way home from work and cordially asked how she and my father were feeling. I spoke in a nonthreatening tone and told her about my upcoming work travel, and the reported snowstorm coming over the next two days. I also mentioned I would be getting my personal belongings from the attic and would remove them "in a few weeks."

I did not let her know that I had hired the movers to meet me early the next morning to make the move. There could be no advance notice; I also could not give them time to usurp my plans or to implement some other form of abuse. I could not give my brother or anyone else time to rummage through my belongings and take anything; they had proved themselves to be dishonest, and dishonest people are often thieves. I needed to make a quick, clean break.

At eight o'clock on Tuesday morning I met the movers at my parents' home. Mom and Dad were surprised when I told them I was there to move my things out. I showed up without notice to ensure avoidance of preplanned hostility on anyone's part. There were no problems, and I remember feeling relieved my things were out. I offered to pay the three movers an additional one hundred dollars cash each if they could get my things out and loaded on the truck in less than an hour. They performed the task in forty-five minutes, and we were on our way.

On Wednesday, I received another hang-up call at work. Because the voice message system did not provide the calling number and I did not have caller ID, I immediately requested a desk telephone with caller ID capability. It was installed the following day.

The remainder of March was uneventful and quiet, with no further calls of this nature.

It was a reprieve.

APRIL

Up until the first week of April there was no communication with anyone in my family. I was at an impasse with myself in discerning what there was to communicate in any meaningful way. The silence also brought an eerie sense in me. An attack of some form could come at any time for any reason or no reason. Conspiring was a key element in their scheming and baiting. In addition, with my absence from the house, I could not discern what, if anything, they were up to.

While another part of me felt a great sense of relief with the silence, it was for my father I seemed to have the most thoughts, and I felt his pain from the betrayal to him and to me from those who surrounded him. I missed him as much as my niece and nephew.

Easter Sunday was uneventful, and the peace and quiet were good. I called my parents to wish them a Happy Easter, and it was a brief call. I thought about my father that day and the kids. Things had changed within me, and I was now in a different space—emotionally distant.

I was devoid of any feeling of family. It was an emptiness that I cannot really describe other than to say it was an oscillation between sadness and relief.

Their recent, planned setup had manifested itself as the final, well-honed psychological knife. The remnants of what I was able to tolerate had been reached.

On a Thursday morning in mid-April, at around six o'clock, a call was made to my work phone. It was odd in that I never received calls that early in the morning. The caller ID revealed it was my brother's cell phone. No message was left, and I remember thinking I was glad I had removed my voice mail's personalized greeting. I presumed that they would now need to exercise caution in leaving a voice message, not knowing if the number was still mine or now belonged to someone else.

I remained silent and focused on my work and my personal life. Through mid-April there was no contact on my part to my family, and no further contact was made on their part to me to the best of my knowledge—that is to say, several caller ID displays of "Private Caller," "Out of Area," and "Unavailable" appeared on several calls, but I would never know the who made them.

THE NO CONTACT RULE: A SURVIVAL STRATEGY

As you have come to see at this point, and will see again in these pages, my efforts to communicate were fruitless, and their efforts were traps. These instances wore out my energy, filled me with frustration, and affected my mental and emotional state—not to mention the physical elements on the body created by stress. You may see my conscious decisions to not return phone calls or otherwise engage from seemingly sincere efforts on their parts to communicate with me as my stubbornness. Far be that from the truth.

My efforts to be heard and to understand the anguish they had caused without concern left me no alternative but to step back—as difficult as it was.

At some point, and you will know when it comes to you, you finally have to say, "No more." It is your voice, without words, heard as loud and clear as though you were screaming it.

Once you stop engaging with the insanity of a toxic person, your head begins to clear; you start to feel a sense of relief. I did.

On a Tuesday morning in mid-April, the silence was broken when my brother called my home and left a voice mail explaining that he wanted to have things the way they used to be. He encouraged me to do my part to resolve family issues.

I found myself more bewildered with each "sincere" attempt at reconciliation. I kept drawing analogies in my mind, the most prevalent being that if a man beats his wife for years and she leaves or ends up in the hospital, he tells her he wants things "to be the way they were" and to get back together.

I found it hard to believe that Patrick did not realize, or chose to ignore, that for me, "the way we were" was horrifying. I have heard this as a common theme among abusers who finally cross the line. I was not about to go back to "the way we were." That would mean continuing to look the other way and that was no longer a possibility. When asking myself what there was to go back to, I had to quickly dispel any thought of it for the sake of my own survival and my mental and emotional well-being.

My return home was still vivid in my mind. Patrick had been no brother to me or uncle to my son since the day I had retired from active military service; in fact, he had made his jealousy, envy, blame, and hatred quite clear.

To the casual observer these three phone calls that had been made to me since April 8—one by my mother and two from my brother—would seem to represent a sincere effort to contact me. But how sincere were they? They each had my cell phone number and could reach me immediately, but they had opted to call my home at times they knew I was likely to not be home.

My proverbial wall remained high and fortified.

Patrick called again a week later and was flustered by my lack of response, and again expressed his desire to get things back on a good track.

I was too angry to speak with him and was mortified that after the three recent attacks he could see nothing wrong. It was already more than abundantly clear that they were capable of anything, and I could not go back to the house without great caution. It was easier to stay away, and I felt no dishonor, shame, or guilt as a result of my avoidance.

I was finally accepting the destructive nature of their behavior, but that did not mean I would be part of it or allow it in my life. I was also beginning to accept the realization more and more that they were each, in fact, demonstrating what I believed and researched was narcissism.

On the last day of April my mother called with a voice message asking how I was and to come down or call. Thoughts of that alluring voice brought up another pending psychological and emotional knife, but I felt forced to maintain a fortified survival position, and the only way I knew how to stop the abuse and betrayals was by avoidance.

I had no choice but to implement a "no-contact rule."

It was more of the progressive and cunning strategies they implemented; they were not accidental, as though they could say, "Well, sometimes people say and do things they don't mean," which was a theme I heard often from my sister.

My responsiveness to my mother's alluring voice on three occasions thus far was not naïveté on my part, but rather my inherent belief that she was representing what a good mother should be: soothing, loving, kind, and warm, someone who represented strength, justice, and fairness. But she was none of these.

There was also no visible indication of remorse. It occurred to me that the timing of my brother's call which was in late April to "reconcile" followed by my mother's alluring call three days later was actually a sign of malevolence.

In the many years since I had returned home, my brother had never behaved in the manner he did following the day I was written out of the will, but his negative actions would not end any time soon either.

The return of my niece's card was in and of itself an overreaction of aberrant proportions, and his letter with its paranoid delusions that I was some kind of threat made it virtually impossible for me to enter his house again. Thoughts of him made me nauseous.

The instinctive warning from my internal radar was unmistakable: I was listening and paying very close attention.

I had no idea at the time it would be to my great advantage to transfer his voice messages from tape to transcription and also digital recordings. They would be pieces to a puzzle that was of enormous complexity, very disturbing, and clearly visible—one that I needed to preserve because they represented the truth about my family's behavior and the severity of their abuse, which would loom even darker and with more intensity as time went on.

9

A Struggle for Self

2004

"Wrong does not cease to be wrong because the majority share in it."

— LEO TOLSTOY

The month of May I had hoped would be quieter, but the silence was broken when I received a call on a Monday and a voice mail at home from my brother. The call came late in the morning and, as usual, when he knew I would not be at home to accept the call. My cell phone has always been and continues to be the best way to reach me, and my family knows this. As such, I could not see any genuine efforts made to contact me despite the seeming efforts.

He was audibly frustrated, scolding me for failure to resolve the issues and that it was on me, and how I had mistreated my parents. He attempted to inject the standard guilt trip over my parents' aging and ill health. Without any acknowledgment of the abuse toward me, the call was more of the same and kept me distant.

I felt bad for the grief I knew my father was feeling, and from that alone I was angry. But there was an even deeper issue at hand if my brother in fact thought his speech would prompt in me genuine feelings to get in my car and drive to the house as though nothing had happened.

I queried an attorney on certain aspects of the law due to my brother's letter in January, the betrayals that followed, the recent and persistent phone calls, and now the guilt-trip tactic.

Something was terribly wrong, for the extreme and persistent behavior triggered a survival instinct in me. My attorney advised me to do what I was already doing, saving every voice message and letter I received from my family, and discussed the possibility of a restraining order against my brother. That same Monday I contacted the local police department to ask about the procedures to do so.

While I was not at the point of actually pursuing a restraining order, I wanted more information. The past years of abuse I had cast aside as much as I could, but this recent behavior I viewed as evidence of escalating hostility.

The police told me I could go before a judge and explain why I needed a restraining order and that, if it was an emergency, I could go directly to the police station. I did not see an emergency yet, but I knew what to do if it came to that. I could see nothing good coming from closing my eyes and sweeping it all under the psychological rug.

My inner struggle at that time was that Mother's Day was the coming Sunday and less than a week away. I had to look deep within myself to try and come to terms with whether I should or should not send my mother a card. She had made it impossible for me to see my father, and her fan club (my brother, his wife, and my sister) were major contributors to this action.

A part of me felt pity for my mother despite what she had done for years to me and what I had seen her do to the others.

My mother was somehow severely disturbed. It was clear as day. While I was in an emotional whirlwind and felt pity and some level of compassion, I struggled to keep that in mind. No one could be as cruel as she without being so. I made additional visits to my therapist during these two months in an effort to maintain balance, and these visits were of invaluable assistance. It was during a session in 2004 that my therapist used the term "narcissism" for the first time and compelled in me a need to learn more.

The first book I read was *Humanizing the Narcissistic Style* by Dr. Stephen M. Johnson. Although his book is written in professional psychological jargon, I was able to extract sufficient knowledge from his findings to keep my attention. I found a seeming direct correlation between his description of narcissistic behavior and the behavior of my family.

It was the second book I read, however, that was the eye-opener, the most chilling, and that fortified my defensive position: *Malignant Self-Love: Narcissism Revisited* by Dr. Sam Vaknin, a man certified in counseling techniques, a doctorate in philosophy, and a certified financial analyst. After reading this book, I felt a need to actually sit and speak with a behavioral scientist with intimate knowledge of narcissism.

Not knowing where to begin, I turned again to the information superhighway and found a doctor in the local General Hospital outpatient psychiatry department who was both a physician and a forensic psychiatrist. I thought that if there was anyone who could help me understand, then it was Dr. Peter Baker.

I contacted his office on a Tuesday and left a voice message requesting a consultation, offering a brief synopsis of what I suspected was narcissism in my family. Later that evening the doctor's secretary called me, and arrangements were made for me to come in the following week and speak with him.

Other than during visits to my therapist, I had kept all that transpired to myself, and I felt a great sense of relief that someone would listen and be able to help more in my understanding. Unfortunately, a short no-notice business trip for two weeks prevented my visit, and I would have to arrange another appointment some weeks later.

My brother called that evening and left a voice message sounding desperate. He insisted that I needed to call and resolve the issues. He was extremely frustrated that I chose to have no contact with the family and said that I needed to make contact "before it's too late."

While there was a great sense of urgency in his voice and tone, I was unable to discern whether it was anger-based, but certainly he was in a state of great anxiety.

I thought about calling in hopes of diffusing him, and that perhaps a "friendly" call would pacify him to a point of not harassing me—that is, putting him at ease would help him back off.

The next morning, I arrived at work at my usual time of seven o'clock. Two emails were in my work inbox: one from my brother and one from my sister. They both revealed seeming desperation that I had to talk to them before it was too late and my parents passed on. Patrick added that the letter he had sent in January was written in the heat of the moment.

The next day, Thursday, was uneventful, and I felt relief that no emails or voice mails were left for me. Between Patrick's messages and work, I was stressed out.

He still had not returned my call.

It took great effort to debate whether there would be any fruitful outcome in sending a Mother's Day card. I also debated making another call to Patrick, and decided to try again. I left a brief and polite voice message saying I was home and asking him to call me later.

That night we spoke for forty-five minutes. I remained calm, reasonable, and truthful throughout the discussion while he downplayed the significance of his January letter and its contents, then dismissed it as "nothing" to the point of stating he was stupid in writing it and he was not the "smartest guy in the world."

He was skillfully evasive when it came to the comments and questions I posed regarding specific events and things said and done that put him and his wife in an unfavorable light. It was denial on a grand scale. As had always transpired in the past, the discussion led nowhere.

The next day, my brother called again and left another message that resumed his past behavior—a turnaround back to the same familiar pattern of denial and projection, shame and blame. Questioning my vision, insight, and ability to see through the manipulation made me see just how ignorant he was, or how ignorant he thought I was.

After work one Monday in mid-May, I checked my post office box for the first time in a week and found an odd-looking envelope—odd in that it had my name and address typed on a label but had no return address. The postmark showed the zip code within the Philadelphia area to be in the immediate area where my sister worked, and my sense was that this anonymous envelope was from her. I opened the envelope that night and found an unsigned sheet of bond paper with one typed line: "At the end of the day, the only real people that are left is family."

Attached was a newspaper clipping with the headline "Faulting others is faulty." Ironically, the article described family members finding fault and criticism in other family members— clearly referring to *me* finding faults in *them*. This anonymous message conveyed that I should not complain about their treatment, but rather be accepting and give them constant immunity.

I was in disbelief that whoever sent this could possibly feel this article was appropriate. Whoever sent it had clumsily attempted to conceal their identity; clearly it had to be either my brother or sister. The anonymity alone voided the very meaning of the article, and instead I felt as if I were being stalked. How could someone conceal themselves while conveying a purported message of sincerity?

The forensic psychologist returned my call the same evening I received the envelope, and in twenty minutes, I offered background information detailing the behavior that had been consistent for many years and had led to destructive turmoil in the family.

He offered to help if I felt his professional expertise was necessary and advised me to keep my physical distance, to avoid going to the house on the basis of my brother's January letter, which I knew was a problem. He said it was unfortunate that I could not see my father as much, and recognized the fact that I may not have the opportunity to say goodbye to him. He offered the name and phone number of a colleague who was capable of providing support if I needed it.

My mother called my home on a Tuesday morning in mid-May and left a voice message asking me how I was and thanking me for the Mother's Day card. I saw no meaningful reason to return her call. I was still angry from her betrayal and her conspiracy with my siblings.

Following that call, my brother called again. I mentioned I was on a long-distance business teleconference, which I was.

A few days later, another voice message from my brother was waiting for me upon my return home from work. He was clearly frustrated by my silence.

Recently, I had been thinking of writing a letter, long as it may be, and specifying behaviors that had caused turmoil in the family, strained their relationships with me to the point of destructiveness, and hurt others in some way. I found it more and more of a struggle to stay calm and focused with each incoming voice message, and now the recent anonymous letter (from Kayleigh, I thought) compelled me to respond with something that would, in my view, help to "open their eyes."

My brother did not seem to realize that it was not simply the past six months that had brought the situation to this point, but rather the past thirteen years during which I had ignored or forgiven their abuse. Everything that transpired beginning in January with his letter, the return of my niece's birthday card a few weeks later, in March with my mother's lie and cunning strategy to get me to the house, to changing the will as a "punitive" measure, the recent anonymous letter, and now these phone calls, were all cumulatively relevant.

The alliance they shared and their decision to become my tormentors using cunning tactics, antagonizing, taunting, and provoking behaviors as weapons of choice served no other purpose than to destroy me—which failed.

It was what they were used to, having behaved similarly toward each other for decades while I was away in military service.

I decided that a voice message to my brother would test the waters. On a Tuesday in May I called and left a voice message informing him that I had received his call and that I needed to step back from their abusive behavior—the anger, denial, manipulation, projections of their behavior onto me, and their guilt trips.

I was tired of looking the other way, and was empty, drained, and feeling too many negative elements from their abuse. Without making a conscious decision to do so, instead of trying to gain closeness, which was always either thwarted or spoiled in some way, I had been sending my life in a different direction.

They simply did not see any wrong in their behavior despite the obvious results, and why they were not learning from their behavior was bewildering.

The days progressed with silence; there were no nasty or harassing phone calls, which was a relief. While I needed peace, I found myself checking my voice mails at home daily, anticipating that another proverbial and inevitable axe would fall.

It did the evening before Dad's birthday. I called him early to wish him a happy birthday, but there was no answer. I was certain that at that hour he would be awake and someone would be home. I considered the possibility that something may have happened. I knew my mother carried the portable phone, and usually she answered.

I had other thoughts, too, that were appropriate for my mother. Spite was a normal aspect of her personality, and my number showed on their caller ID. It was not unrealistic to assume she or my sister would ensure my call to my father before his birthday would go unanswered. If they were in the house, my brother or his wife might do the same.

It was not beyond any of them to block my call to my father and then tell him, "Your son never called you on your birthday." I reasonably suspected this from my brother and his wife returning my niece's birthday card to me.

After waiting a short time, I called again but used my calling card, which I often use to save minutes on my cell phone while away on travel.

After a few rings my mother answered. I was friendly and cordial, but she was cool and seemed surprised that it was me, which solidified my initial thoughts that not answering my call was intentional. When I asked if I could talk to my father, she said, "Sure" in a cold tone. It was evident she did not want me to. I spoke with my father and had a meaningful exchange as it normally was.

During this call he said, "There was no cake." I asked him what he meant, and he said he had had no birthday cake that day. I asked him why there was no cake and he said, "I don't know, that's how it is," meaning that on his ninety-first birthday the family had no cake for him. I was furious but kept it to myself. He added that maybe tomorrow night they would have a cake for him, but I sensed he was rationalizing and I could hear he was saddened.

We ended the call after ten minutes, and I decided that tomorrow, as busy as I was in the field installing this new defensive system, I would make calls and find a bakery or store and try to have a cake delivered to him.

I made several attempts to find a bakery or other establishment that could make and deliver a birthday cake on short notice to my father but without success. Several supermarkets in his hometown were unable to make a delivery, and I had run out of options.

Upon my return home from work another letter was in my mailbox, sent again from the zip code within Philadelphia where my sister worked. My address was handwritten as was the return address—my parents' house.

Inside was a typed letter from Kayleigh. She started by stating she was sick of all of the fighting that started when I came home, accusing me of cruelty toward my mother and exonerating her own behavior. She accused me of playing the blame game, said how spiteful I was, and stated how many times they had tried to "talk" to me. Throughout her letter roles and behaviors were reversed; it was I, she claimed, who was cruel and mean. Of course, the guilt trip and shaming were always major behavioral aspects of her interactions with me. She added that when my parents died in pain, it would be my fault; my doing.

It was psychological warfare in its purest form.

It was also apparent my sister was not aware of my brother's letter from January—at least by all appearances. Her letter focused entirely on me as the culprit and did not acknowledge her own behavioral pattern.

As often as it was bewildering, they actually believed that they made honest attempts to patch things up. Apparently, they believed I could not see through the lies.

The behavior continued on its consistent rail. If she felt her letter would prompt me to believe there could be any level of communicating to "work things out," I failed to see the logic.

One part of her letter in particular caused me to question her perception of reality; she wrote that I always brought all of my girlfriends over, and they (the family) were supposed to entertain them and pretend to be kind while having to endure their looks.

For over a decade, since my return home, there had been only three women in my life, separated by years, all of whom I took to meet my parents. Her reference to "all" my girlfriends is baseless since that implies there had been many. The fact is I kept the issues away from these few good women as much as I could. None of them were capable of what my sister claimed; my family having to endure their "looks" was another lie.

Secondly, if she acknowledged the truth versus her own interpretation of it, she would have seen it was not in my best interest to tell *anyone* in my life about anything regarding her behavior or the behavior of other members of the family. It would be potentially destructive to my relationships, since the only women I am drawn to possess a value system of high morals and are family-oriented. They would not be drawn to the drama and would never willingly set foot in my family's home if they knew beforehand of the antics that went on there. My sister's assertion of "who knows what you told them" was groundless. However, while I never volunteered information, when questions came, I would give an honest answer.

Following my receipt of this letter, I still felt a nagging need to try and "get through to them." The most effective way I could deduce to do this was to provide a chronological history, in writing, in hopes they would see their behavior and that some faint ray of hope would appear.

I asked my therapist about writing a letter. He was adamantly opposed to it and suggested it could worsen the situation. "Typically," he said, "if you confront evil with its evil and reveal proof, it rages and becomes vindictive and revengeful. You must understand evil hates itself and cannot stand in the light of truth about what it is or what it does."

He indicated that revealing truth to certain dysfunctional personalities, especially narcissistic ones, could lead to elevated levels of anger and hostility. Nevertheless, despite his opposition and the reasons, which I understood, I started to write. It would not be a letter that could be written overnight, and would eventually take six weeks with countless revisions.

In late June I was on a plane back to Mississippi for a major eleven-day business trip. I found myself over these eleven days obsessively checking voice mails at home, sometimes three or four times a day. I was aware of this habit, but my family's behavior infected my mental state and brought no peace. Fortunately, the first week of the month was quiet.

With Father's Day coming, I mailed my father a card, but this time I attached a return receipt. With past problems of my mail not being received—too many, and unlikely always from inefficiency of the post office as my mother claimed—I saw no alternative.

On a Friday in early July, after this relatively short but exhausting business trip, I returned home. While every day during the previous ten days I had checked my voice messages at home to find none, there was one waiting from my brother upon my return that he had left that very morning. While his chosen words can be construed as reasonable, his tone was more in line with patronizing superiority, spite, and belligerence.

Though he informed me that my niece graduated the following day and a party for her was planned for the following weekend, he did not tell me where the graduation ceremony would take place, at what time, or provide me with any details about where her party would be. He only stated, "If you want to come, you come; if you don't want to come, you don't come. Again, like everything else, the choice is yours and yours alone to make."

It was unbelievable that, in his mind, the state of affairs was attributed to *my* choices.

High school graduations are major events that require much planning. Patrick gave me less than a day's notice of my niece's graduation when he must have known for at least a month. Regardless, the context of his message and tone of voice made it all but impossible for me to accept even if he did provide specifics.

The less than a day's notice did nothing to help. My brother thus orchestrated the conditions that resulted in me missing my niece's graduation and party. It would be easy for him to express to her that I did not care for her or love her, "facts" justified by my absence and by his claim he had personally informed me.

If printed invitations had been sent out, I was also not a recipient. I never received one.

After painstaking weeks of writing the letter, which in its final form was more than a dozen pages, it was complete and in final review. I mailed it on a Monday morning in June. It was my sincere hope the contents would permit some level of awareness to filter in and that a genuine understanding of the "big picture" would prevail. I also hoped for some indication of empathic capacity and processing, and from that a genuine and sincere attempt for introspection and reconciliation on meaningful levels.

In essence, I was holding up a mirror to reflect back to them their hardcore cruelty. I incorporated a chronological order to the letter to reveal the long-term behavioral pattern that was at the crux of our family's culture and foundational structure. For additional emphasis, I incorporated paraphrases from their letters to me in bold print and included two attachments, my brother's letter from January and a copy of the returned birthday card to my niece.

I stated that a response was not desired or necessary so that we may pursue a face-to-face discussion that was actually meaningful.

The result was not what I expected. Admittedly, I anticipated the proverbial "light to come on" and within a brief time to receive a phone call of understanding and sincere desire to acknowledge responsibility for the pain and anguish they had caused to so many people, and a vow to change for the better.

Kayleigh's response discounted every provision of my letter, negating and defending their behavior and maintaining that I was to blame.

My therapist was right. It was not to be.

Kayleigh stated that I was so wrong and she wants things to be right. Of course, that would mean so long as I was in compliance with their demands; submitted my will to them; gave up my personal identity and my separateness from the family; and agreed to be controlled, betrayed, and backstabbed—all to feed more into their continued abuse.

It was evident that they knowingly refused to acknowledge key points of my concerns that placed highlights on their abuse, behavior that had created the unavoidable and irretrievable family breakdown in the first place.

But they knew what they were doing, when they were doing it.

On a Wednesday at three o'clock in the afternoon, the day after Patrick received my letter, my brother left a voice message informing me that he had received my package but would not open it, saying that it was not worth the paper it was written on.

His refusal to read the letter meant simply that my concerns, which were truthful, and as always were not a factor for acknowledgment or consideration. He held the same position as my sister and mother, and as always, I had no voice.

But I was determined to have my voice heard, and that would mean raising the bar.

The Fall-Out from My Letter
2004

"Sometimes people don't want to hear the truth because they don't want their illusions destroyed."

— FRIEDRICH NIETZSCHE

As presented before and as revealed by excerpts in this book from qualified practitioners, shame-dumping and guilt trips are common strategies for narcissists. I did nothing to hurt my mother and father and attribute any upset they experienced to my sister and brother's raging reaction to my letter and to their behavior in general. That is what upset them and always upset everyone: *their* behavior and abuse.

From my research, I discovered one of the first telltale signs of narcissism is the tendency to blame every mistake, failure, or mishap on other people.

I can only deduce Patrick's refusal to read my letter was due to the painful truth it contained, and that it was too intolerable for him to bear such great self-inflicted shame.

All indications are that my sister did read it, and knowing her explosive, uncontrolled rages, I concluded that she must have erupted in another outburst, which upset my parents. Of course, my brother blamed me in the same manner that I was blamed for his stepdaughter's behavior. It was not my letter that upset my parents; it was Kayleigh's and Patrick's reaction to the truth. This was a common dilemma I faced. I was responsible not just for their problems, but for their behavior as well.

I *made* them react in the way they did.

Since I had controlled myself in the face of their constant lies and betrayals over many years, I was certain there would be a positive outcome to stating my concerns, which they would have refused to hear and denied in person had I elected to have another face-to-face "clear the air" session.

My therapist correctly assessed that it was not a good idea to write a letter, but on the other hand, I was able to gain some sense of relief because of the additional insight it provided into how their distorted minds functioned.

In addition, my letter afforded another opportunity they consistently denied me: my right to my voice, my right to be heard, and my resistance to their behavior and treatment.

The remainder of the month was silent until the July Fourth holiday when I received a letter from my sister. She merely provided additional insight to her sense of entitlement to do as she pleased, her lack of respect for family members, lack of remorse, and lack of personal boundaries. As was usually the case, she had to get in the last word.

JULY

I called my parents several times in early July to see how they were. In one call I spoke about the upcoming Saturday and asked how my father felt about going out to dinner. He asked me to call him on Friday and said that it depended on my sister's plans so as not to leave my mother alone.

A few days later, I called my father again regarding dinner to which he agreed, and I mentioned I would meet him outside in front of the house. It was best, at this point, that I not go inside. I did not emphasize that the hostility of the environment had to be avoided, and I did not bring up anything negative. He said he would be outside waiting for me at four thirty.

During dinner he surprised me by stating he was concerned that I "hated" my mother. I explained I did not know where that came from, although I know it was likely from my brother, sister, or my mother herself. I told him I did not hate her and did not know how that had come to be determined. I had to prevent myself from telling him she was the hateful one.

I discussed concerns I had, and felt he opened a door to a place where I could express myself at least to some extent while being careful not to hurt his feelings. I explained my brother's letter from January, the return of my niece's card, the use of the will as a weapon in March, and my mother's feigned invitation to a "family discussion."

I went into the details of my efforts to foster a positive family environment through my gifts to my brother's stepdaughter for thirteen years, and the resulting lack of reciprocation. He said his concern was not with my brother and sister and me, but between my mother and me. He asked me to call my mother and talk to her. I agreed.

Our dinner was enjoyable for the brief time we had. I felt good responding to his concern regarding my mother, but I did not want to elaborate and upset him more than the betrayals already had. My family members had already broken his heart. I took him to the house and walked him up the stairs, reiterating that I would call my mother and kissing him goodbye.

The second Monday in July was an emotionally trying day. As my father had asked of me, I called my mother in the morning. She was cool toward me, yet I remained as cheerful as I could be and cordial. I mentioned my father's concern he had expressed at dinner Saturday, and told her I did not hate her.

She focused on the portion of my letter to my brother and sister that said I felt she stabbed me in the back and made untrue statements about me. She was in denial of her behavior and of the tactics she employed in luring me to the house in March, in scheming with my brother and sister, and she wanted me to accept her denial and evasiveness as truth. My numerous efforts failed to convince her that, despite expressing what I perceived clearly as her deception, it did not equate to hating her.

She responded, "I will think what I want, and you think what you want!" Out of nowhere, and to my surprise and dismay, she brought up my son and said again as she previously did that, at the age of seventeen, he was a grown man and knew better than to give away to his stepbrother clothes she had sent him. I was in a moment of stunned silence while trying to process how she could have perceived this as a continued "injury" for more than ten years now.

Communicating with my mother when she was in this aggressive-defensive position was impossible. I could not help but think again at that point that it was actually best for my son that she not be part of his life.

One point of particular interest was explaining my brother's letter from January to her and in telling her what it said. I read from the letter verbatim, specifically stating that he said I was capable of causing harm to his family.

It was my hope she would see this as a ridiculous assertion, knowing well that I was not hostile and that hostility and the potential for violence were always generated by her and other family members. As I listened, she twisted his words into a meaning completely opposite of the one I had perceived.

The excerpt was just one sentence and was not difficult to comprehend. I gave her the benefit of the doubt and repeated the sentence again verbatim. She again reinterpreted the words in a way that reversed their meaning. I found myself reading it to her verbatim a third and final time, and she still twisted the words and meaning, regurgitating it back to me before I realized what she was doing: she was sowing confusion and frustration in me with her own version and expecting me to believe it.

I had to tell her I needed to protect myself and my interests, and it was my brother who demonstrated a capability for premeditated and unnecessary hostility. I simply told her I could not enter his house again under the conditions of his letter, adding that her protection of them and her outright lying were not helping matters.

Several times during this call, I told her I loved her and appreciated all she did for me to lessen the tension, but this was to no avail. There was no reciprocation, and she remained cold. I stated I accepted the situation for what it was and told her I had to go.

She gave no acknowledgments of the truth on any of these matters, and before the call ended, she disavowed my son's existence for the fourth time before handing the phone to my father. He asked about my travel and if I would call him again. I told him I would. The call to my mother was another exercise in futility, which fueled more anger in the family through her re-creation of the facts.

The same day at two thirty, Patrick called and left another voice message saying he was sending me a letter, and if I wanted to read it, I could read it, and if I didn't, then I shouldn't. He added that I could put it with my collection but suggested, in a demanding tone, that I read it.

It was interesting to note that he refused to read my letter to him in June, which he openly indicated he would not read because "it's not worth the paper it's printed on," and now he sent a message that could be translated into: "What you have to say is not of interest to me and you have no voice; and it is what I have to say that matters."

Suffice it to say, in my experience at being his scapegoat for so long (and exercising restraint and looking the other way), this one-sided communication was not uncommon. As was often the case, I saw nothing of any real value to respond to. The behavior continued to force me to keep my distance and not engage.

One hour following his voice message, he called and left another message telling me he had just spoken to my mother, and that he concluded I was out of my fucking mind.

It seemed it did not take long following my phone call with my mother for her to share with my brother her rendition of our earlier discussion. It was the pathetic ritual of twisted truth and outright lying to each other through which my mother continued to sow the seeds of chaos, anger, and hatred between family members.

Manipulators thoroughly enjoy viewing the chaos they create in the lives of their victims. It's when they do their best work.

This was precisely what I witnessed in their manipulations: starting fires between others in the family, holding themselves immune, then sitting back to watch the chaos they had created.

Less than ten minutes later, Patrick called a third time and left a message telling me that for someone who's supposed to be so smart, I was pretty fucking dumb.

His tone was again arrogant and contemptuous. His belief in my mother's rendition of our discussion again left nothing to respond to; it was his letter and the one sentence in particular that I had read verbatim.

If the thought processing and behavior were not so evil, it would almost be entertaining.

On a Thursday in mid-July, anticipating the next wave of abusive phone calls regardless of where I was on business, I frequently checked my home voice mail. The passage of two days of silence came as a relief.

The silence was broken when my brother left another voice message reminding me of what "I did to him" and telling me he always told me to leave him alone.

I could not help but wonder if he was truly out of *his* mind. One of the most surprising aspects of his behavior following my mother's betrayal with the will was that in the previous years he had been bad, but not *this* bad. He falsely believed, and rather stupidly, that with my mother on his side he had power over me and was invincible.

I had to remain emotionally removed from it all. Engaging would be a grave mistake. I had already figured out they were baiting me, and it was not going to work further. They should have realized that by then.

It is equally clear that it was my mother who was stirring things up and causing strife. Her willing deceptions added accelerant to any fire. She had mastered the perceptions and responses of everyone in the family, and there was no one who could make the truthful connection after all these years as to what exactly it was that she was doing with the exception of myself. They were like mindless puppets on a string because such a lifestyle was normal to them. It was even more troubling that not one of them was sick of the turmoil. They needed it and seemed to thrive on it.

Two uneventful weeks passed, and at the end of the month I flew to Louisiana on a very brief business trip. While in Dallas awaiting my connection, I bought a postcard for my parents, filled it out, and dropped it in the airport mailbox, although I was not certain they would receive it since my mail to them at times got "lost." I could not let that prevent me from sending them postcards from my travels to let them know I was thinking of them.

After checking in at my hotel and settling in, I called my home voice mail to see if any messages had come in. It remained a conscious habit and would become almost a daily ritual for months. It was an effect I noticed was now within myself, expecting and anticipating their harassment. This, I had learned, was part of the psychologically abusive effects toxic people have, and I had to be on my guard not to let it consume me.

The second half of July was quiet. I debated returning Patrick's letter unopened in order to send the strongest message that I would no longer tolerate his behavior of unfounded blame and his other abusive strategies. Ultimately, and being fully aware of his explosive patterns with relentless harangues, collusions, and a smear campaign with other family members, I decided to continue with my "no-contact rule" until such time as I sensed a change in their behavior.

As Patrick had so snidely suggested, I kept the letter with my collection of others.

August was a quiet month until one morning while at work, for the first time in several weeks, I received two hang-up calls. The caller waited until a voice message was required at the beep, and then the hang-up came. As I mentioned previously, I do not normally receive hang-up calls in my line of work. The remainder of the day was uneventful until I returned home to find a voice mail from my brother telling me my parents were not getting younger, that they had tried vainly to communicate with me, and that I consistently rebuked everything they'd done to resolve the matters.

Persistent verbalized hesitations of "ah" and "um" indicated he was thinking much too hard to form his thoughts. Since truth and honesty flow freely, his excessive verbal hesitations reminded me of his dishonesty. I was too angry to speak with him regardless of the apparent sincerity in his tone, which could not be trusted.

Since the time of my letter in June asking him to stop, he had left eight voice messages, all of which were manipulative, contained subtle threats, name-calling, swearing, blame, distortions, contempt, and unquestionable hatred in delivery.

He continued to use my parent's age and ill health as a manipulative means to inject guilt into me.

The threshold for the opening of a dialogue can be very low. It doesn't take much. But will I stick my head into the lion's den without some reassurance that the lion will not bite off my head? No. I couldn't do it, and I don't know who would.

AUGUST

August had been another extremely hectic business travel month, and as always, I sent postcards to my parents. This month I was continuously on business with consecutive trips to Mississippi; Louisiana; Utah; and finally, back to Michigan.

I called my parents one day early in the month and spoke with my mother. I asked if she had received my postcards and she said she believed she received one. I mentioned that I sent four—one each from Mississippi, Louisiana, Utah, and Michigan.

She reiterated she only received one, and I had my own thoughts as to how three postcards out of four did not make it home.

That evening I called my father. He mentioned he had scheduled a doctor's appointment because he had been getting dizzy. This was the first I had heard of it. My brother of course never mentioned it in all of his many voice mails.

It reminded me of the time when my mother fell and hit her head and my brother had called me two days later to inform me. When questioned as to why he waited two days to let me know, his response was, "Because it was nothing." It would seem to me that when any elderly or sick person, especially a parent, falls and hits their head, it is in fact a big thing.

After the call ended, I decided to send future postcards in envelopes, certified mail, with a return receipt.

I debated changing my phone number but then realized I would give the new number to my father, which would make it accessible to my brother and would render change meaningless.

I also had more frequent thoughts to request a restraining order to get Patrick to stop his continual harassment.

I departed on another business trip to Louisiana for the week—my fifth business trip in seven weeks—and I was exhausted. Waiting in Dallas for my connecting flight, I called my parents to see how they were, again with no answer.

Arriving in Louisiana, I checked into my hotel and filled out a postcard and sent it by certified mail. *We'll see if it gets lost this time,* I thought. It was impossible to give my mother or siblings the benefit of doubt in view of how many postcards had been "lost" at this point. I had a passing thought that mail tampering is a felony, but then again, my family had demonstrated that they thought they were above the law.

I arrived home early on a Thursday in late August and by coincidence ran into a mail carrier. I approached him and asked what the procedure would be if I chose to request an inquiry into mail theft. He explained a similar situation he knew of that involved checks and said I should contact the postmaster general in the town my family lived in to initiate an investigation. He added that it was his opinion that it was unlikely three out of four postcards, each sent from a different state, could become lost.

I agreed. The remainder of August was uneventful, but inner tension remained.

SEPTEMBER

In my effort to gain further understanding of the interactions within my family, I joined an internet support group dedicated to narcissistic personality disorder (NPD). There I found a wealth of knowledge on behavior that was strikingly similar to what I experienced with my family. I also realized the general feelings people in the group had were similar to my own.

I posted a message on the NPD Group Support Forum requesting if anyone knew a city attorney knowledgeable in NPD from whom I could seek guidance and whom I could possibly retain as an attorney if needed. Unfortunately, there were no positive responses, although some general feedback was helpful.

I called my parents that same night. My sister answered, and once she heard my voice, she adopted a subtly hostile and arrogant tone. I asked if Dad was there, and she said, "No! He goes to bed early, actually!" She then added, "But if you want, I can try!" I told her not to wake him up and that I would call tomorrow. She hung up without a word before I could say anything further. *Spiteful bitch,* I thought to myself.

On a Tuesday in mid-September, while at work, I stepped outside where I had good cell reception and called my parents. My father answered and said there were major problems in the house and that there was talk about stopping my phone calls to him and my mother entirely. I was furious. I told him no one had the right to stop my calls. I was not certain if this talk came from my sister or mother; both were spiteful and capable of increasing the severity of the issues.

As I thought about what could have brought this on, I considered that there was a distinct possibility this was my sister's work-around to my postcards getting through by certified mail, but I could not be certain. She had been hostile the night before, and clearly this would be another form of control, an effort to continue ostracizing me from the family.

My father seemed to be defensive of her, which was troubling. I had to explain that he saw only what they wanted him to see and knew only what they wanted him to know. He said, "You say they lie, they say you lie. I don't know what to think. They say they tried to talk to you, but you do not want to talk to them."

I could feel his confusion and hear his sadness. I assume since my brother used those exact words to me in several of his voice messages, he had told my father the same thing with my father merely repeating the words.

The fact is there was nothing to talk about with my brother or my sister since their behavior was not conducive to meaningful discussion, nor had they tried to talk to me.

My father had not seen anything or known of the voice mails or their letters, and I could not defend myself since I was not there. They were discrediting me through lies while concealing their behavior from my father, and it was pissing me off.

My father mentioned that I said in my letter, referring to the one I sent to Kayleigh and Patrick in June, that, "Mother has a place reserved in hell." It was *not* what I had written, I told him; it was what my sister *told* him I had written. Her intentional reinterpretation to him of my statement that "Dad has a place reserved in heaven" meant my mother had a place reserved in hell was unbelievable. It was an opportunity for her to twist something to breed more bad feelings in my father and disrupt my relationship with him. While she could interpret it any way she wanted, or have an opinion, it was not what I said.

Why she would mindlessly hurt my parents with cruel and despicable recreations of truth was incomprehensible. There was no remorse, guilt, or conscience in her or my brother—even when they saw what they were doing to the family.

Any event that provided them with an opening to spew their venomous lies was opportune. Kayleigh and Patrick's only objective at this point was to destroy me; if other family members were hurt in the process, they were considered collateral damage.

I conveyed to my father that in my letters to both my brother and sister I clearly requested that if anything happened to either of my parents, I was to be notified. My father said that, because of what he was told (by my sister, evidently), my mother said what she had once felt for me was dead. He mentioned he would ask my sister to permit him to read the letter, and I indicated that was precisely what I asked her to do in the letter, but she had refused (lest the truth be told).

He then said she would let him if he asked. I listened as my father turned at that moment to relay to my mother that I had never said what my sister claimed. In the background my mother yelled loudly, "He doesn't want to know when I die. He's a fucking liar!"

It was incomprehensible what my sister was doing.

The truth is that if my mother read that and saw it (the truth), she would choose to ignore it and believe what my sister said. Nevertheless, my sister's behavior was geared toward destroying any relationship I could have with my father and mother.

My father and I went over some of the things in my letter several times. I found myself repeating my words often because his hearing simply did not allow him to comprehend, but I was not disturbed by it; he needed to understand the truth. It was disappointing that he seemed to have more faith in what my sister told him than what I said, especially knowing well what her behavior was like.

I knew if he questioned my sister, the "special one" in any dispute, it would result in my mother's wrath. This made things even more complicated and frustrating. Regardless, I was not there to defend myself, nor did I believe it would do any good even had I gone down to "talk." They were predators, as they proved themselves to be so many times, and their alliance ensured they were always right.

Dad also said his anniversary was coming up, and that any card I sent might be returned. I repeated that no one had the right to refuse my cards to him or my mother, or interfere in my relationship with them. He said I should do what I had to do as long as it was the right way. I told him the environment was too hostile, but he did not seem to understand the word "hostile" due to his difficulty hearing, despite my repeating the word several times.

I was saddened and angered by my mother, brother, and sister when finally, he said, "All I want is for my family to be together."

The ones closest to him had made that all but impossible.

I found myself in a game of spy and counterspy, trying to anticipate what my mother or sister's next betrayal would be and mentally preparing to counter it. I thought that if my sister let my father read my letter, she may first reconstruct it to the precise wording she wanted it to have. If she did that and my father believed her words came from me, it would destroy his love for me.

That was not beyond the realm of possibility. In the final moments of that call, my father added, "If this is the way it has to be, you stay there and they stay here. You should find a good woman to take care of you, cook for you, and get married."

My father was always deep in his love and affection. I finally mentioned to him that in ten years there had been three women in my life who were worthy and whom I had brought home— all good, decent women, and all left in tears.

It was time for me to return to my office, so we ended the call at that point.

How incredibly sad he sounded, and all I could do was contain my anger. In this universe of torment, there was no higher pain for me than knowing my father, a decent and loving man, father, and husband, was trapped in this terrible environment and caught in a life that offered neither joy nor the rewards of a family he wanted and deserved. They were all without remorse and without conscience, to put my loving father through such heartbreak and anxiety.

Upon my return home from work I called Dr. Baker again, the psychiatric specialist at Philadelphia General. I left my number requesting he contact me. I was feeling some anxiety from the recent event of my father's upset.

I felt the need to actually talk to someone and to avoid leaving another voice message. At three forty-five I called again and spoke to a woman named Kelley, briefly explaining I was hoping to connect with a doctor knowledgeable in disorders. I needed to know *exactly* what I was dealing with. She provided the number for the group referral and a number for the intake program, where she felt I would be successful.

In the morning, I again called Dr. Baker and left a voice message requesting he reach out to me. Two minutes later he returned my call. I explained briefly that I had returned home from twenty-three years of military service, and that after thirteen years of aberrant, bizarre, and extremely disruptive and destructive behavior in my two siblings, my brother's wife, and my mother, that by reading published, professional research findings I had recently come to believe that most of my family members exhibited behavior on the far end of the narcissistic personality disorder or some other form of disturbance.

I indicated it would be helpful if he could direct me to someone who was well versed in behavioral science. He referred me to three hospitals: The Department of Psychiatry and Human Behavior at Jefferson Hospital in Philadelphia; Belmont Behavioral Health Hospital, also in Philadelphia; and New York-Presbyterian Hospital. These were the three most renowned behavioral hospitals in the region. He further suggested I should make an inquiry about dialectical behavioral therapy (DBT).

I called my therapist and asked if I could see him for a session on short notice. I needed to channel my anger and the sadness I felt in my father. After informing him of the recent events at home, he agreed to see me that afternoon. He was well aware of what transpired in my family.

The stress from the past day had been intense. In thinking about my letter, I again found myself playing Spy-Counterspy and regretting that I did not sign each of the pages of my June letter and/or have each page notarized. *How ridiculous,* I thought, *to have to do such a thing in order to protect myself from dishonest people in my family.*

I realized that, when it came to defending myself against their lies, I would need to maintain clear and convincing evidence that had to be thoroughly authenticated. This was a ferocious battle in the psychological and emotional sense, and I was not about to let them win—although in many respects they had already lost, whether they realized it or not.

Later that day I sat in my therapist's waiting room and decided to check my home voice messages, which I had been doing daily now for some time in anticipation of more verbal attacks. There were two messages from my brother, left just a few moments before I was to see the doctor.

The first sounded recited rather than impromptu, and my sense was that he had written or typed out what he planned to say and was reading from it. It was also more organized and structured than his typical, illogical speech patterns. I noted his voice was low as if he was making the effort to not be heard, and his tone was arrogant and self-righteous.

How dare I blame him for anything, the message said, and how could my advisor—Mickey Mouse in his view—come to any such conclusion. He added that I consistently insulted them, and that I belonged in Hollywood with my fantasies. He now blamed Colleen for causing all the problems in his family, and he again disowned and reassigned his behavior onto me.

It was utterly amazing how he could be insulting to others but did not possess the capacity to accept any criticism, and perceived anything that did not agree with his or his wife's immature and sadistic egos as a personal insult.

It was equally bewildering to ascertain how he concluded Colleen (or anyone outside the family, for that matter) had the power to tear them apart. All families are destroyed from *within* their own environment, and no one outside a family possesses that kind of power.

They were their own chief victims as much as they were victimizers.

I thought back to when he openly proclaimed to me his daughter didn't have to know the truth that one night in my car, and felt disgust with his complete lack of respect for his daughter. By concealing the truth, he ruthlessly maintained a lie in the mind of my niece that Colleen had insulted her, thereby implementing the destruction of any relationship between my partner and my niece.

My family was destined to be decimated from within. My brother's hostility and his efforts to make me suffer were the reasons I severed my relationship with him, and my mother's and sister's alliance with that behavior were other reasons I would not come to the house.

Since my letter in June and my voice message in July, Patrick had left eighteen aberrant and harassing voice messages. He simply refused to respect my wishes, my rights or boundaries, and instead demonstrated uncontrolled behavioral patterns of false accusations and fabrications.

Of particular interest was his voice message in mid-September when he talked again about his January letter and made mention of it several times, yet in our forty-minute phone call in May, he said he wrote the letter in "the heat of the moment," that he did not mean it, and I should forget it and throw it away as he had done.

In other words, he oscillated from one position to the next by validating it and stating it described my behavior (what I came to learn was their *projection*). It was a mentally and emotionally draining experience to witness this pendulum swinging in his mind.

Just as unbelievable was the assertion on his part that I did not come to the house because I was "ashamed." His shame-dumping was a major behavioral hallmark, essentially disowning his own shameful behavior and projecting it onto me. My sister and mother did the same thing.

I was ashamed only of what he and my family represented, and that he bore the family name was a source of extreme shame to me. It was my father's name and he is honorable.

After I explained to my father there was underlying jealousy in my brother and sister, my father must have relayed that to my brother, for Patrick's first call that day I sat at my therapist's office was not sufficient. He had to make a second voice mail to deliver impromptu and joyful arrogance, saying simply he was not jealous of me, and that I had nothing he would ever need or want. His delivery contained vocalized pauses between each word, followed by a ridiculously childish and unintelligible sound that punctuated his condescending pride. I wouldn't connect this particular call and his "pride" with anything specific until after my mother passed away.

My therapist mentioned that I should consider attending group or family therapy, and I thought it was a good idea at the time, although I mentioned that, since my brother and sister did not feel they had any issues and I was obviously the one with the "problem," they would likely refuse. He agreed but suggested I make the effort.

My no-notice session ended after thirty minutes.

I contacted the Department of Psychiatry and Human Behavior at Jefferson Hospital and left a voice mail at the referral number, and shortly received a call from a woman in the referral office. She mentioned the name of a doctor who was considered a renowned expert in this area, and said he was booked until October. She referred me to a social worker who administered groups and worked with this very doctor. I called her immediately and left a message.

In checking the Jefferson Hospital website, I found a link for family workshops. There was one later in the month for borderline personality disorder (BPD) held by the area expert. From my research, I learned that BPD and narcissism were in the same family of personality disorders, and I decided it would be beneficial to attend the workshop, learn more firsthand, and hopefully personally meet the doctor.

I felt there may have been other developmental or awareness programs that could assist me in building greater emotional and psychological self-preservation barriers while learning more about the battle of minds I was involved in. I also thought it would be a great idea, based on my father's suggestion, to seek family counseling for my brother, sister, and me—that was, if I could convince them to attend sessions with me under the doctor's guidance.

In evaluating my sister's position on resolving the issues, I felt that, since they were so "sincere and genuine," they surely would not hesitate, especially since they actually believed their behavior was good and justified. My gut instinct warned me this suggestion would present its own challenges, though.

I did not know just how right I would be.

I called my parents on Friday afternoon. My mother answered, and we spoke for a few minutes cordially, and then I spoke with my father. I let him know I felt he had had a good idea the other day when we spoke of group/family therapy, and said I would go the next week to talk to someone. I asked him to talk with Patrick and Kayleigh to see if they would agree to attend. I also told him the doctor would have to be the right doctor—a special doctor, a family therapist—and that the three of us could share in the cost over time. It was my intent to attend regularly with them and hammer this all out.

At least, it was my belief we would. What was I thinking!

He agreed and again said all he wanted was for his family to be together, which again was saddening. I couldn't do this alone. His broken heart was more hurtful to me than the behavior of my siblings, my mother, and my brother's wife. Unfortunately, my father did not understand the depth of the behavioral issues that had plagued his family for decades, issues that I was just now beginning to understand myself.

I received a call the following Monday from the doctor's assistant, and I explained briefly the situation and particularly the behavior of my family, as well as the current environment. She understood the severity and scheduled an appointment with the doctor but said it would not be for two more months—late in the summer.

The family workshop was an overview of BPD hosted by the doctor and his assistant. After the session, the doctor and assistant were quickly surrounded by other attendees whom, I assume, had loved ones under his care. They were more of a priority than I was, so I departed the meeting place thinking I would see him at the appointment.

I made the appointment for mid-October at Jefferson Hospital, one of the top psychiatric hospitals in the country, with one of the world's most renowned behavioral scientists specializing in family therapy.

I mailed a package that contained relevant information describing every instance of their behavior, and I called my father to tell him about the appointment and, more importantly, that General Hospital had referred me to a doctor at Jefferson.

Because my sister and brother insisted to him that I was the one lying, I let him know the doctor we would be seeing could not be lied to and would know who was lying. I was going to give him the name of the doctor, place, and time, but he said I should talk with my sister and give the information to her. I also told him I would pay for the first visit. He said he would tell my sister to expect my call.

I called my sister and told her about the appointment. She sounded fine with it.

Her tone was civilized, and then, without warning, she became angry and said with condescending arrogance, "You know it didn't even *have* to come to this!" I simply reiterated the appointment time, date, and place in a calm manner, and added that I would pay for the first visit. I told her it was my hope we would continue to go for as long as necessary to get to the root causes of the issues.

She asked if there were "someone else" around who could see us versus this particular hospital, and I simply relayed that a doctor I spoke with at General had recommended Jefferson in light of the specific issues at hand. "Listen to me, why did it have to come to this?" She huffed. "Why can't we all sit down like civilized human beings?"

I wasn't in the mood to engage with her, and explained that I felt family therapy was necessary because unmoderated conversation among us had proven impossible; there was no civility in their predisposition to gang up on me when they were all together.

"Who said that? *You* said that!" she said.

I simply added, "Please make sure Patrick knows," at which time I told her I had to go and ended the call.

My sister called a few hours later and left a voice message. Quick with her words, she was annoyed and disdainful. "You know, I appreciate that you're taking Dad's suggestion, which actually was *my* suggestion, to see a therapist together, but I think it just should have been discussed with all of us first. I'll let Patrick know, and hopefully there can be a more convenient time for all of us and a more convenient place hopefully, because we all have to work and we all have our responsibilities. And I know you're there and ignoring me, which is fine; we'll deal with that later." Then she hung up.

She failed miserably to hide her contempt but softened her tone toward the end of her message. Whether there was fear in her from this appointment, plain anger combined with concern for the doctor and location, I do not know, but she no doubt held a firm position of extreme displeasure and perhaps with good reason.

The mask would no doubt come off with this doctor—a human lie detector.

One day at the end of August, my sister called and left a voice mail. Her tone was soft and respectful, but I had already learned I needed to be most on guard when it came to alluring deliveries. She wanted to discuss the appointment and asked me to call her.

While her voice was calm and she was not upset or angry, my sense again from the content was that Jefferson Hospital was not agreeable to her. I was prepared to discuss that selection and was not comfortable with another place or doctor, knowing well that my family's behavior made the location more than appropriate.

I had a keen sense of how a discussion with her would play out. A return to the status quo would mean placing myself in a compromising, no-win position, and that was what they wanted.

This was a year of increasingly intense attacks by my brother and sister—continually stabbing me in the back, placing blame on me for everything, and relieving themselves of all responsibility. It just never ended. It was also the year my niece aligned herself with her father's lies and staking her claim in the betrayal. My father and I were aligned; the rest of the family had aligned themselves against us.

There was a reason for the intensifying hostility this year. I came to find out my mother did in fact have a will developed or revised, and there was no doubt my brother and sister knew about it and most certainly helped to author it. I would not know my mother had a will developed in 2004 and revised in 2006, 2007, 2008, 2009, and 2015—and would not know for another fourteen years, until after she died in 2018.

I was never permitted to read the versions of the will or to know they existed.

Clearly, it was planned that way.

Two Conversations from Hell

"It is not goodness to be better than the worst."

— SENECA

A CONVERSATION FROM HELL, PART I

At two thirty in the afternoon on September 20, 2004, I called my parents to ask how they were. My sister answered and explained she was home sick from work. I asked to speak with my father, and she handed the phone to him without incident. He opened by asking how things were with my brother and sister. I always dreaded this question since there was no change but for an increase in their hostility. I mentioned I would call my sister that night and talk to her then, but at the moment I was calling to inquire about him and my mother. It was a very brief call that ended shortly after I responded to his question.

I was not inclined to engage in a long discussion with my sister present. I was also uncertain if anyone was listening in on one of the several phones throughout the house. Preparation was never possible when I knew I was going to engage with my sister.

I had learned long ago that any and all discussions would be one-way and never prove fruitful. The one that night, when I called back to talk to Kayleigh, would be different only with respect to the true definition of a term psychologists call *gaslighting*. Kayleigh and I would talk for more than two hours, leaving me mentally exhausted and physically drained.

In the 1944 mystery-thriller film, *Gaslight*, nominated for seven Academy Awards, Ingrid Bergman plays a woman whose husband, played by Charles Boyer, slowly manipulates her into believing she is going insane. He does everything in his power to isolate his wife from other people, and attempts to convince her she is imagining things (that he actually initiates)—including, notably, that the height of the gaslights' flames lighting the home are going up and down—and that her hallucinations are not real. His efforts are to convince her she is going mad in the hope of having her certified insane and institutionalized. This would free him to search for the jewels of her dead aunt, whom he murdered and which are in his wife's possession.

Psychologists adopted the term gaslighting from this movie to describe psychological abuse in which the victim is gradually manipulated into doubting their own sanity. There are different variations of similar verbiage from my own experiences with my family that were key in my awareness of their gaslighting: "That didn't happen!"; "Are you crazy?"; "You imagined it!"; "That was nothing!"; and "You did your share."

Gaslighting is considered one of the most insidious and manipulative abuse tactics because it is designed to distort and erode one's sense of reality. You will know your abuser is gaslighting you when you question reality and your own sanity with respect to that which you know to be true.

To effectively resist, you must ground yourself in reality. Writing things down, for me, as well as discussing the behavior with my therapist and researching related topics was exceptionally helpful in maintaining my sense of stability.

THE DISCUSSION

At seven o'clock I called the house again, and my sister answered. Following an initial greeting, I asked her what she wanted to talk about. She said she had called Jefferson Hospital to find out more about our forthcoming appointment.

I explained that she and my brother did not need to arrive until just before the appointment time. She opened up at this point, with her voice changing from calm to firm and progressively dissatisfied. She did not see why we were going to see a psychiatrist who specialized in borderline personality disorder and that he was not what she had in mind for therapy.

She said it was also not what she suggested to our father about therapy because "all we do is finger-point." It made little sense to me why it mattered what she suggested to our father when it was more important to attend a therapeutic session. Nevertheless, her position that "all we do is finger-point" was significant in a family in which blame-shifting has always been prevalent. I thought this was precisely one of the reasons this doctor was appropriate for our case.

Kayleigh added with a negative connotation that I had taken it upon myself to make an appointment with this guy without first consulting her, and said again that she had called the hospital to learn more about him. I could understand her annoyance that I took it upon myself to make the appointment without consulting her or our brother. It was reasonable for her to feel that way, but I knew they would have refused to do it themselves. I needed to take the initiative to get to the bottom of the underlying issues they refused to acknowledge. It was another "damned if I do, damned if I don't" situation they were so adept at creating.

As expected, she was resistant throughout the conversation and particularly dissatisfied with the hospital and the doctor. My position was that not all family therapists are qualified in behavioral science and he was, so he was appropriate. Her position was that a therapist she referred to was good for issues within a range of life circumstances such as divorce, grief counseling, and communication skills. I felt the destructive, abusive, and cruel behavior in the family, going back decades, warranted the uncovering of deeper, underlying issues that needed microscopic exploration. She also took issue with the term narcissism, and the next two hours would find me mentally and physically exhausted from a roller-coaster ride of a phone call.

It was far from over.

CONVERSATION FROM HELL, PART II

The closer we came to the appointment, the more my sister's resistance intensified. Upon my return from my trip to Virginia, I called my sister as I said I would. Our conversation lasted an hour and was in the same manner and style as our previous conversation, with no meaningful communication.

She opened the discussion by asking firmly if she had to go to the appointment with the specialized doctor and said it would require her to take time from work and drive a long distance.

I saw no point in mentioning that she had taken time off for other personal reasons. I knew my bringing this up would set her off into a rage. It was apparent she did not want to go, and it had nothing to do with work or distance. I was too tired from my business trip to engage her, and I offered the opportunity for her to back out by stating as I had in our last discussion that the appointment was voluntary and that she did not have to go.

As much as I tried to avoid confrontation, I made a subtle gesture to her that, following our last discussion, I suspected she would try to avoid the appointment. I mentioned that while I was away on business, I had given great thought to our last discussion and had concluded there were many things she was not aware of regarding Patrick's behavior, which she should know.

I mentioned that before my upcoming trip to Idaho I would call and we would talk again if she was interested in learning more. She asked me what things I meant, and I said simply that our brother had left numerous hostile and harassing voice messages that detracted from his having any sincere position of wanting to resolve our issues. She asked if these messages regarded things that had happened thirty years ago, which indicated she either did not comprehend what I had just said or was not listening. I said that I had had no other contact with Patrick all year.

Her response was, "You point the finger at him, and you point the finger at me, and there have been things going on with all of us."

Son-of-a-bitch. Here we go again, I thought to myself.

I firmly stated that never in my life had I ever had any such issues with anyone until I came home from the military, and that I could substantiate with proof everything I said. I informed her that I had not been in contact with Patrick, and yet he continued to leave the most aberrant voice messages imaginable which continued to fuel the fire.

Again, she turned the tables: "You've left messages too."

I had told her so many times that I had not engaged with Patrick whatsoever on my part and that I was becoming tired of repeating myself, but again I did, and said, "I have not."

Her position was that she was not saying I did it "yesterday" but that it had been going on since "we've all been fighting the last couple of years." She blasted, "Since the wedding!" She was referring to Erin's wedding and the conflict over my request to fund Colleen's attendance.

I told her the wedding issue was benign, and she asked why it was made such a big deal if that was the case. I emphasized that I was really becoming sick and tired of repeating myself, and that she should pay more attention to what was being said and make an effort to comprehend and remember it.

At this point she brought up my twelve-page letter from the summer and said that she could pick out some things in that letter that I was now denying. I corrected her and said nothing in that letter was a lie, and that I therefore denied nothing.

As she often did when confronted with honesty or truth, or with my maintaining a rational position, she became silent.

"I would never put anything in writing that I could not substantiate or prove, and I signed the letter," I said.

She commented that this was the kind of stuff that she was talking about, and she asked what kind of proof I had. She added, "You need proof, not just saying, 'Oh, Kayleigh did and said this, or Patrick said or did this.'"

I asked sarcastically, "Right, it's a 'he said, she said' thing, isn't it? If the general public doesn't see it, none of it really happened, did it?"

She asked again, "What kind of proof do you have?"

My sense from her tone was she felt a certain level of comfort in that she could refute the behavior since visible proof didn't exist outside the family. If no one saw it, it could be denied.

She continued, "You can't prove *anything* we've done."

That comment, to me, was in fact an acknowledgment of all they'd done. I explained that I had all of their voice messages and their letters.

She then confused me by asking what a person had to do, in my opinion, to have a worthwhile life.

I failed to see how this related to the conversation we were having, but I responded that one need only be honest and good instead of portraying an image of goodness. I added that truth was freeing. "I told you this before," I said, "it's just as easy to be honest and good than to be evil. People who are treacherously dishonest have a sense of evil yet project an image of goodness."

I was dumbfounded by her response: "That's what *you* say."

Did she believe it was good to be dishonest and that people needed lies? What did she mean by this outrageous comment? I could not allow her to confuse me.

Then she asked with clear contempt and disdain if I taped things, wrote things down, and insisted on knowing what kind of proof I had. I felt this was an attempt to discover whether there was a possibility of their exposure. Regaining my thoughts, I expressed that I did not record discussions because the law prohibited it, but I openly made her aware that I not only took notes from our discussions, but that I kept all voice messages and had had them transcribed.

She sarcastically and arrogantly replied, "Good!" and added that she wished they had taped the times I called. In the same breath, she admitted she knew I only called once and she did not save the message. "I guess it's your word against ours then, isn't it?" she asked.

"No," I answered. "It's your word against the truth which I have. You can make it to be anything that satisfies your need to be resistant, but it will not change for you simply because you deny it or believe your own bullshit."

She was extremely argumentative, saying, "That's why you keep saying you can't come down here—because you are afraid for your life."

"I will not be set up again, do you understand?" I asked.

I reminded her again and, with frustration over having repeated this so many times before, that Patrick said in his letter that he was in fear of his life and his family *from me*. I reiterated again that I told this to our mother by reading excerpts from his letter verbatim. I emphasized that I was not going to put myself in a position now to go anywhere near the house "because none of you can be trusted and I am the target."

I emphasized that this was the discussion I had had with our mother, and I had to repeat parts of Patrick's letter three or more times because each time Mother regurgitated a different version of what I read from his letter in his own words. My mother twisted it, too, and that was what they all did: twisted things that were true to mean what they wanted them to mean, and then forced that version of events onto other people. "That does not work on me," I said.

Kayleigh said she was going to read the letter again. I asked her why she thought I would say something contrary to what was plainly visible in writing, and how that could possibly be beneficial to anyone. I added that Mother obviously fueled the fire even further, and had told Patrick that she and I had spoken. I knew this because he called me and left a voice message reiterating my mother's version of the letter. "You feed off each other's lies," I said.

I explained that when someone tells you they are afraid for their family because of you, the sensible thing to do is to keep your distance. I reiterated that any of them could make up lies about me, and because of their blind obedience to the culture of deception in the family, and to the alliance they shared, all of them believed each other's lies and acted upon them as though they were true.

"Because you hate us so much," she said.

I was dumbfounded and lapsed momentarily in silence. That made no sense.

I told her I did not hate them, but that I hated what they did, what they knew they did and did not care about, and what they took pleasure in doing. I hated their lies, their betrayal to themselves and to the family, and their hostility. I added, "I hate the tears that have been shed by good people because of the behavior by you and the others toward those in my life who are good, and I hate the hatred these good people were made to feel. That's what I hate."

I was angry and found myself bringing up the issue over the "jeans" topic with Michaela and how it affected Colleen. Kayleigh said she remembered.

I was compelled to tell her about Brianna coming out of nowhere to rage at me that "Colleen owes Michaela an apology," and that Colleen had hurt Michaela's feelings. I also explained that I mentioned to Patrick that if Michaela was upset about it, she could have mentioned it to Colleen, who was easy to talk to and a good person.

I went through that entire issue with my sister, including when I had Patrick in the car and he told me his daughter didn't have to know the truth. I emphasized this was both my brother and a father saying his own daughter didn't have to know the truth. In essence, he was saying it was acceptable to him and to his wife that their daughter was allowed to believe she had been insulted by a statement that was purely innocent. I added, "Good parents do not lie to or victimize their children, nor do they initiate actions that destroy relationships and good feelings in others."

Kayleigh said that I had no idea how *she* had to deal with stuff like this from them, and added, "You just have to overlook it."

I was adamant in telling her I did not and could not overlook so many betrayals and lies, and that one could not overlook such consistent behavior for very long.

"What they tell their children is their business," she said.

I took exception to that, and explained clearly that when people lie to the point of victimizing themselves and others, and affect other people's relationships—especially with intent and in the family, and particularly in my life—it became my business. I explained that the street-thug and schoolyard-bully mentality of my brother and his wife would not be overlooked and needed to be scrutinized.

With that, she huffed a clearly sarcastic breath.

I was on a roll, further telling her this was no different than when my brother told me that my then-wife Maureen was "no fucking good" because of Patrick's demand for a personal apology after the baby comment—an apology that was not necessary by the standards of normal people—and that Maureen's phone call was not good enough.

Kayleigh became silent as I explained millions of people apologize by phone every day and that it is socially acceptable—but evidently not to Patrick and Brianna.

As in the past, Kayleigh evaded the entire discussion by saying there had been problems ever since I moved out, alluding to my departure from the house in the mid-1990s after five years at home. She said, "You've been angry with me, angry with Ma, and blaming *us* because you moved out." This had always been her position: insisting that no problems existed before I moved back in, which essentially denied the fact that she had tormented me while I lived at home after my divorce.

I asked again as I had on our previous phone call, but this time in a quip, "So perhaps you would like to kick in the bathroom door a few more times or rage-attack me without reason, or exude some air of superiority over me so Mother can chuckle. Is that what you'd like to do?"

She fell silent momentarily, then said I was fighting with her and would not talk to her for years. "I was not fighting with you," I said; "you were picking fights with *me* and antagonizing *me* with intent while I defended myself, and defending myself isn't fighting, defending myself is just that". I told her in no uncertain terms that I had not started fights with her or with anyone. "Standing up for myself isn't fighting, but that's how you view it," I said, and had to add a sarcastic jab, "Is there something about that you don't understand?"

Then, as always, she changed the topic and said that it was my fighting with Patrick over the "wedding issue" that made me want to have nothing to do with her, and said it was one thing after another.

This was more of the same tactic abusive people use with seeming psychotic thinking; behavior that includes playing the dual-role of both victim and victimizer.

As always, she was draining my energy.

So now, she began to describe how my brother and I were always close no matter what. I countered that it was once the case when we were kids and, in our teens, but not after I returned home from the air force. I explained that he had held a deep-seated malicious jealousy that he hid well, but now manifested through his words and behavior.

I had to work hard to contain myself and to keep my thoughts clear. I told her how it seemed they believed they had the entitlement to do whatever they liked and that they had given themselves the right to total immunity. "Those days are over," I added.

I had to keep myself composed in order to maintain clear thoughts. She had the ability to confuse me profoundly, and I had to work hard to prevent that.

This discussion was turning out to be another futile attempt on my part to get through to her. She asked when the last voice mail came from our brother. "August sixteenth," I said, and added, "Two, in fact, on that day."

"And since then?" she asked.

"Since then, he's been quiet," I said, and punctuated that with a sarcastic remark that he must be taking a break. I mentioned that in total, he left twenty-one messages—and all lies.

At this point she asked, "So, you want to go to a psychiatrist like this doctor to see how fucked up *we* are?"

"There is a consistent pattern of behavior over several decades that still exists today," I said calmly, "and that was the only point I was making." I reiterated again, "There's a pattern over decades I had nothing to do with, and all of you pulled me into it and made *me* the target when I retired from the air force."

She continued to offer contorted attempts at plausible responses while evading the entire point. It was just another fruitless discussion.

I was compelled to tell her there were deeply dysfunctional personalities at play, and reiterated that this behavior was not normal. She wanted to know from me what is it one should do when you can't reason with another.

"You answered your own question," I said, "One cannot reason with the unreasonable, so the only rational thing to do is abandon them and leave them to their own devices, or get the proper professionals involved, and that's what this appointment is about."

Her response left me silent. "There is a hell of a lot worse in other people and in other families, and I do not see our family as being all *that* bad."

I offered the possibility that that could be because she had been living it all her life and it appeared normal to her, and in an attempt to shine the proverbial light, I asked why there would be such great attempts at denial and concealment if there was no conscious forethought or awareness of malice?

She replied, "I'm not making excuses, and I don't want any pity." Then she stunned me into further silence: "Believe me, I don't think there's anything wrong with me."

I entered a mental vacuum.

She said she was going upstairs to read, again, my brother's letter from earlier in the year. I told her to put herself in the position of the reader and the recipient, and she scolded me in her response, "I *know how* to read a letter!" "Good," I responded, and added she should re-read my letter too so she could explain how something good about one parent implies something bad about the other while she was at it."

She became silent for a moment, then changed the subject to the appointment with the doctor again. "Do I have to show up for this appointment? Because if I have to, I need to put in for a day off."

"Again, it is not an all-day session, more like a few hours and is voluntary," I said.

I encouraged her to come and explain every little detail so long as she told the truth. I encouraged her not to lie, and added, "There is verbal abuse, mental abuse, and emotional abuse; there's betrayal, smear campaigns, and lies. Those are the issues that need to be looked at and more. These are not surface issues."

She wanted to know what I believed the purpose of seeing the doctor was, and what I hoped the results would be, adding that our brother "had a very responsible job and he may not be able to go." "*Didn't I just talk about that,*" I thought. Then sarcastically, she asked if someone had to be the president of the United States to be worthy in my eyes.

I responded quietly, "We need to identify the behavior and open a dialogue where continued sessions can be maintained; discover what they are and how to resolve them so we can have some semblance of family that essentially does not and has never existed in the real sense."

She answered with, "I cannot do that," but she did not explain why, and complained that I was being extreme in defining my perception of the issues.

She asked again, "What is it you want by going to this doctor? Confirmation of how you feel and someone to say, 'Yeah, you're right, they are sick assholes'? What is the purpose?" she asked. "How will the remedy take place?," she asked as well. Obviously, at least I thought, that would be up to the doctor.

I had to get off this call, and I attempted to soften the tone to end on as good a note as I could by telling her I had sent Patrick a voice message in May telling him to go on with his life, that I was doing the same, and that if anything happened to Mother or Dad or the kids to let me know. She said I did not include my mother in that discussion, just my father and the kids. "I said it in a voice message, and it was also in my letter," I said. "Read it again before you deny it."

At that point, she asked how long it took to get to the hospital and that she had never been there. "I don't know. You'll find it, and then you will know," I said.

I knew this phone call would have to end soon...like now!

She continued, "We've all done our share, *all* of us."

"I do not accept blame-shifting," I stated vehemently. As defensive as ever, she said again that she did not think they were as bad as I said they were, and I suggested again it was perhaps the environment that had always been her life and, to her, was normal.

At that point, she asked a question that again left me silent and confused.

She asked why it never came out in her own private therapy sessions that there were psychological problems in the family, and then to my astonishment, she laughed and said she must either be "a psycho or a good liar."

I was mentally and emotionally drained, utterly exhausted as I had been from our first discussion. "I have to leave for Idaho for ten days," I said, and reminded her to reread my letter. She agreed, and the call ended.

I again walked to the sofa and collapsed in relief.

Later in the month I called my parents after work one Monday. My conversation with my mother was cordial as it sometimes was without her being cold, and was surprisingly good. While there was no hostility in her tone, she was a bit standoffish. She said my father was doing well, then called him to the phone.

He and I spoke about general things, and then I mentioned the appointment was next week with my brother and sister at the hospital. I told him my sister said she could not take the time from work and that I had not heard from my brother.

I was surprised when he said he thought I misunderstood him. In asking what he meant, he said when he suggested a therapist, he meant a *family* therapist. I explained the doctor with whom I made the appointment *was* a family therapist. At that point, he said the place you are going to is a hospital for people who are "sick in the head, for crazy people."

Clearly, and once again, my sister had weaved a version of events she wanted them to know. I had to explain to my father that the doctor was a specialist, and after meeting with us, if he did not feel he was the right doctor for our case, he could recommend someone else. I hoped this would allay any concerns my father had about the appointment and the hospital to balance the negative connotations my sister had obviously presented to him. "I don't know," he said, meaning he did not like the idea, and then added, "I do not want to be involved."

As best I could, I explained that I made the appointment and was doing my best to fix things. We exchanged caring words, and the call ended.

He just did not understand and was not aware of the extremity of the behavior beyond what he was used to—and what they wanted him to see and to know.

My two discussions with my sister were characterized by consistent denial and resistance to change, and it was obvious she was afraid of both the session and the doctor.

In early November, I checked my mail at the post office and received an envelope similar in appearance to the one I had received in late spring: a plain, typed label with no return address, postmarked at the end of the previous month from now a different zip code. After researching it, I discovered that it came from one of two post offices near my sister's place of work.

Realizing it could be similar in nature to the previous anonymous letter, I did not open it to spare myself the grief.

12

The Appointment

"Anything is better than lies and deceit!"

— LEO TOLSTOY

I took the day off from work and arrived early at the hospital to complete the appropriate administrative documents. I sat outside the doctor's office on a sofa. Ten minutes later both my brother and sister appeared at the door to the stairwell. Since I did not believe they would show, I was surprised to see them.

As my brother turned the corner at the top of the stairs, he was not looking forward down the hall and so did not see me immediately; he was looking at my sister and walking slowly. As soon as he noticed me, his "walk" suddenly changed to a strut, rather a swagger, with his body and head slightly bobbing while his feet turned slightly outward.

He displayed a condescending smirk and immediately stated, "We don't even know where you live!" Following that he asked in what was clearly nervousness, "Did the doctor hear all my voice messages? Did he hear the tapes?"

I remained silent to both the comment and question, and was saved by the proverbial bell when the doctor exited his office and passed my brother with a greeting, which he returned. My sister remained silent the entire time and simply leaned against the wall.

A few moments later the doctor returned and called us into his office. I sat to the left of the doctor, and my brother and sister sat across and facing him.

The doctor requested that I begin.

I remained calm and composed throughout my brief opening, describing my sister's relationship with my mother from observations and my perspective, stating that their alliance was exclusive of all others, and that other family members were designated to fit certain roles. I mentioned that they viewed other people in the household as loyal subjects and held expectations of compliance with their immediate demands and with blind obedience. I mentioned that I believed my mothers and sisters relationship was symbiotic, that my sister behaved with extreme infantilism and sometimes that of a spoiled brat, and that she was severely cruel both emotionally and psychologically and took pleasure in it.

I added that my sister's selfishness toward other members of the family was extreme and had been this way for decades, and notably with my mother's approval and encouragement. I did express a firmer tone over how my brother and his wife treated me and those in my life, and how they always played the role of victim with extreme sensitivity even with respect to things that would not normally be considered offensive.

The doctor asked my sister how she felt about what I had just expressed. She responded, "He says we tormented him for the five years he lived at home," and then explained we were just a small, "stubborn Irish family." She sat still and upright in the chair as an adult would—not sitting back and relaxing. It seemed as though she was in a vigilant state. At the same time, a wide-eyed child was sitting there too—that is, her eyes were wide open similar to flashbulbs. She had always been capable of an innocent, childlike look as she fed her deceptions.

As I watched her, I observed her gazing intensely at him as if in a way was probing to see if he was able to see through what she was saying. I clearly sensed a concern with any discovery on the doctor's part.

I felt sickened as she claimed that she was our parents' caretaker and had always been a good sister. I listened silently as she spoke of her work, and how she took care of my parents at the same time. I did find the caretaker, or caregiver role, as an interesting aspect of her life, and thought perhaps personal research might offer some explanation, at least in part for her behavior.

Turning to my brother, the doctor asked how he felt about my opening statement. Fidgeting in his seat and with vocal pauses and hesitations, he responded by saying, "Well, I'm not the smartest guy in the world." (Actually, he was very smart in the cunning sense.) Simultaneously, and surprising to me, was that both the doctor and I responded in unison to the precise second, "It's not about that," we both said together, while the doctor moved his fingers from clasp hands on his lap slowly upward and pointing to his forehead.

While it was not stated, our point was that *it* was not about being smart, it was about being *good*—much as I relayed to my sister in our telephone conversations and for years.

The doctor clearly mentioned that neither of them wanted to accept responsibility for their actions or behavior and in one instance asked my sister if she could think of one thing she had done to hurt or cause me harm. "Name one thing," he asked her.

I watched as she gazed upward toward the ceiling, rubbing her chin as if in very deep thought, and finally saying she could not think of anything. A moment later the doctor began to speak, and my sister interrupted, "Wait, wait! I *do* remember something!"

The room fell silent with all eyes on her. She continued, "About six months ago, my mother said something bad about my brother's son."

The doctor said sternly, "I wasn't talking about your mother. I was talking about *you*." She had projected her behavior away from herself and onto, this time, our mother.

Then he asked my brother the same question. He responded with an unrelated answer. The doctor was equally firm. "That's not what I asked you. What I asked you was..." and he repeated his question. Again, my brother gave a totally unrelated response, and again, the doctor insisted, "That's *not* what I asked you. What I asked you was..." and he repeated the question a third time. Again, the response was unrelated.

The doctor seemed frustrated and even angry at the constant evasion. This was how I predicted the session would go. I clearly instructed her not to lie or deceive this man. It was the same throughout the fifty minutes.

Admittedly, since Kayleigh and Patrick had actually shown up, I had hopes there would be meaningful purpose behind their visit.

In the final five minutes the doctor asked my brother and sister to wait in the hallway while he spoke to me privately. "Let it roll off your back. There's nothing you can do to change them, nor will they ever admit to their behavior," he said. "I'm afraid I can't help you," he said.

His tone was not displeasing. He called them into the office again.

Neither my brother nor sister conveyed any responsibility for their behavior and saw no reason to believe they had anything to do with the current state of affairs. That was all the doctor needed to hear to cap off fifty minutes of frustration.

The session ended when he simply stood up and shook his head, proclaiming in a firm and strict tone, "I can't help you! I'm sorry!" He repeated these words again as he got up from his chair and was now holding open his office door, thereby indicating he wanted us to leave—now!

We rose from our chairs and departed without a word.

My sister and brother had successfully sabotaged the session, leaving them "victorious" and the status quo remained intact.

We walked to the end of the hallway some forty feet from the doctor's office and stood facing each other. Without any acknowledgment of what had just transpired, my brother asked calmly with a smirk, "Well, where do we go from here?," as if saying, "Well, that was that, so let's all be one big, happy family now."

I removed my cell phone from my belt, and as I dialed my work voice message system, I said simply, "I'm going to work," and walked downstairs, immediately out of the building to my car without looking back.

Based on the two phone calls with my sister, I had suspected they would sabotage the session, and they did. The fifty minutes were frustrating for the doctor and myself.

Of course, he had the luxury of closing his door and never seeing us again.

Five days after the appointment, late in the morning, my sister left a voice message saying she didn't want to argue anymore and that laying blame wasn't the answer, though it had consistently defined their own behavior for years. She punctuated that by saying they were losers and offered a weak apology for "anything I did to you."

Her voice was soft, caring, loving, similar to my mother's alluring voice before the proverbial pounce. She intentionally thwarted any hope for a meaningful session to begin evaluating the core issues with the doctor and had provided every indication that she would do just that in both of our phone calls.

Now, following her success at rendering the doctor's visit void, she wanted to "fix" things and let bygones be bygones?

My brother called the next morning and left a voice message for me too. He followed my sister's path, saying essentially," Now that we have had a few days to digest what happened in the doctor's office, let's just stop beating a dead horse and forget the whole thing." He concluded that the doctor said it was *all of our* responsibility and that was why the doctor became upset.

It was another head-shaking experience. I had no alternative but to disregard any type of seeming sincerity. Sabotaging the session was intentional. Now they were lying about that too.

Over the next few days, my mother called several times asking me to provide her with my son's address so she could send him a birthday card. I did not return any of her calls, and was certainly not giving her access to my son.

With no response from me, she had my father attempt to get it on her behalf, so he called asking for Thomas's address. I saw through the manipulation and triangulation. They believed my silence in not providing my son's address to Mother would mean I would provide it to my father, who would in turn give it to her.

That was not going to happen.

The following day I decided to call my mother to explain that if she wanted to send a card to Thomas, she could send it to me and I would make certain he received it. She repeated what I said back to me in a firm tone that demonstrated her displeasure. She had a history of repeating things I said on the phone so that others in the room would know what was said. This was a common manipulative tactic. Instantly, my worst expectations were realized when in the background my sister angrily screamed out, "HE BETTER MAKE SURE HE GETS IT!"

Withholding a card from him was not something I would do; it was something they would do if they were in a position to do so, much as my card to my niece was returned.

Despite the soothing tone of the many voice messages left over the past week, it only took one sentence from me for everything to return to business as usual. This realization was not unexpected, and yet it was profoundly depressing.

For the following four weeks, there was silence.

I did not have Thanksgiving with my family and was not involved with anyone at the time. I spent Thanksgiving Day quietly at home by myself—saddened, but at peace.

I received a letter from my sister nearing Christmas. By now I was in a state of mind where I had to keep peace within myself at all costs, knowing I had done the best I could to help resolve the issues in a way that was meaningful but to no avail. I knew it would just upset me to read it and decided against opening it, and to this day, years later, I still haven't.

One late morning that same Christmas week my brother left a voice message saying he wanted to try and put things back together and "forget all this stuff," adding that they had been trying to resolve it. He had to spike his sincere efforts at resolution by adding there were no innocent parties here.

It was more of the same. They were not learning despite the obvious results.

Efforts on my part to resolve the issues in the right way were constantly sabotaged with two-faced lies and more backstabbing. Peace with them was rendered impossible since they had proven time and again that they would do anything to keep the drama alive and evade responsibility at all costs.

Christmas and New Year's passed uneventfully, and for me were eerily quiet. I knew the saga wasn't over yet; I just didn't know what else was coming.

But once again, I would find out.

The Depth of Hatred

2005

"Nothing baffles the schemes of evil people so much as the calm composure of great souls."

— GABRIEL MIRABEAU

Two business trips at the turn of the year kept me on the go. While I was away, I spoke with my parents several times with no conflicts; it was always good when we could have a peaceful conversation. To maintain the best chance for pleasant conversation, I continued to call during daytime hours while my sister was working.

Given my extensive business trips, and having been told by my siblings that they would not notify me in the event of either of my parents' passing—Kayleigh in particular was quite clear about that—I asked a friend to check the obituaries daily for me.

It was a morbid favor to ask, but she understood and did so. My days were brutally long and left little time for anything but work.

Between February and April there was silence from my brother and sister. It was peaceful and tranquil to not be burdened with their verbal tirades and projections.

In the latter part of early Spring, I called to check on my parents. During the conversation with my father, he asked if things were any better with my siblings. I reluctantly, and as gently as I could, told him I had not seen any changes in their behavior for the better. We did not speak more about it, focusing instead on his and my mother's health.

That same day a few hours later my brother left a voice message with contempt in his voice telling me every time I called I "ruined that poor man," that I told my father the same bullshit over and over, blamed everyone in the family but me, and that I had started this whole mess. I had not spoken a word about my siblings in some time to either of my parents, nor did I do anything on this occasion but answer my father's one question.

Later that same afternoon, he called again informing me that he had heard the entire discussion I had with my father, and that if I wanted to talk to someone, I should talk to *him*—as though he was an authority over me.

So now he was listening in on my phone calls (of which he reconstructed). It was another example of members of my family having no respect for personal boundaries. I wondered how many of my calls he had actually listened in on.

In his mind I had ruined the family, but if I had asked him *how* I did that, as I had so many times in the past, he would not say. There were several times I asked my sister the same question, and she, like him, could never be specific but always deceptive and evasive.

I did not return his call, otherwise it would have fed into his hostility.

One day in early summer, some weeks later, my brother called again demanding that I end this nonsense and asked what my goal was—what was I trying to accomplish, and saying that I had failed to accept full responsibility for what I'd done.

He continued by saying everything was my fault, that I wouldn't leave him alone, and that he and Kayleigh had tried feverishly to resolve the issues. I had no alternative but to maintain the no-contact rule; I was determined that they were not going to gaslight me.

The fact is I *was* leaving them alone.

My no-contact rule was not initiated because I held some level of guilt or because I had been interfering in their lives, but because it was the only recourse that brought me any semblance of peace. It took years of resilience on my part to reach that point, and it certainly did not appear to me that my siblings were leaving *me* alone.

I could not comprehend what it was he expected me to respond to.

The silence would be broken again on a day in early June when my sister called with a scolding voice message, asking me why I bothered to call our parents or send them cards at all. She accused me of punishing our mother until she died, and labored under false assumptions that my anger and bitterness for them was turning me into a monster.

The more these messages were left, the more I saw no introspection within the family.

The smear campaign was far from over when now it was my niece Michaela who called with a voice message. She proceeded without a greeting to inform me that whenever she came home from school, she had to deal with "this" all the time. She abruptly scolded me for causing the family so many problems, and said she didn't understand what gratification I got from it. She added she'd been quiet long enough, and couldn't do it anymore.

I felt relieved that she at least got something out and didn't bottle it up. The unfortunate part is that she allowed herself to be brainwashed.

I imagine my brother and his wife were proud of achieving such a victory in poisoning the minds of my niece and nephew. Without question, it was obvious they had been brainwashing and badgering Michaela during her time home from school and likely long before then.

Bringing the children into the smear campaign was indicative of their betrayal. Patrick was growing his loyal and devoted fan club.

I felt the day would come when I would be able to speak with my niece and nephew and explain everything, but for the moment I had no choice but to allow their minds to be poisoned by their unscrupulous father and mother, with support, I am certain, from my sister and mother.

As summer approached in 2005, my therapist again urged me to visit my parents only with extreme caution. "The distortions of the truth would prevail at least for the time being, and trust was simply impossible," he said.

Clearly, scenarios will continue to be confabulated, and I will remain the culprit.

They were now being seen for what they really were by my therapist, who was exceptionally helpful in piecing together the parts of a very complex puzzle. He suggested there would be nothing wrong with visiting my parents briefly at this time but only to test the waters. The level of (false) sincerity, however, would continue to reveal itself.

With that, he further suggested not entering the house but rather remaining outside, since my sister-in-law was normally home and I needed to defend myself against the lies they fabricated and exploited on high levels.

"Don't bring up anything or anyone. Enjoy your time with them and keep it brief—thirty minutes or so initially," he said.

I never planned to bring anything up just as I had not on the phone with them. I made a decision to visit for the first time in a year, and I did not go inside the house.

I arranged a visit in late June, and took time off from work. I remained on the front porch while my parents came outside. It was an enjoyable meeting on a warm summer day. We did not talk about any issues in the family or anyone in the family but rather their health, my work, and such things in general. I was a little uncomfortable knowing it was a proverbial battlefield.

Because it was summer, both my parent's front door and my brother's front door had screen doors on them. We stood on my parents' side of the porch.

Some twenty minutes into my visit, the front inside door of my brother's side of the house slammed shut with such a deafening blast that the forty-foot-long wooden porch vibrated, and my father, who was hard of hearing, paused in his talking to look over. I also looked over.

I cut the meeting short at that moment, and departed. I formulated in my mind my brother's wife's behavior and what would spring from that; surely there would be more attacks coming, and I was right. She was a key instigator of problems in the family too.

War drums were beating once again.

There were four voice messages waiting for me upon my return home: two from my brother and two from my sister. Both had run out of time in delivering their initial hostile tirades and had to call again to complete their attacks.

My brother told me one day perhaps I would smarten up and accused me of coming to the house to tell our parents he and Kayleigh had started the problems. We did not discuss any of that. He reminded me that it was my phone call that started the whole mess, on Christmas Eve years earlier—me and my big mouth. He suggested I own up to what I had done and perhaps I would sleep better at night, then ended his call.

He still claimed that the phone call I made in my defense of his allegation that Colleen and I were responsible for the behavior of his stepdaughter toward them was the cause of problems in the family.

Then it was my sister's turn. In her usual contemptuous mode, she told me I had not seen my parents for over a year and then had the nerve to swing by for ten minutes and start accusing her and Patrick of perpetuating the problems, when in fact they had been trying to resolve them. "This is all *you*, buddy. This is all *you*," she blasted, then suggested I get professional help.

This was the first time I was comfortable coming to the house in a year since the abuse and betrayal had intensified to a norm, and not once during my visit, not one time, did either I or my parents talk about or mention anyone in the family or the issues that culminated in the situation.

I thought back to the main inside door slamming shut. Brianna had always proved herself to be a compulsive troublemaker and demonstrated that long before my return home from military service. Based on the results of this visit, my brother's wife was causing more problems in the family, and of course, I remained the target.

The good that came from this, however, for me, was that it was abundantly clear their efforts to patch things up were lies. My distrust of them was even greater after that day.

The remainder of the month and the following month were uneventful. I relished the peace and quiet, although I found myself continuing to check voice messages at home throughout the day at work. I was consciously aware I was doing this but could not seem to refrain from expecting more vicious attacks.

On a Tuesday in early August, I called my mother and mentioned to my father I would take a couple of hours off one day the following week and come by to visit. To my surprise, my father tied my visit directly to my communicating with my siblings and my mother. He said, "If you do not fix this, do not come down."

He was reluctant for me to visit unless I agreed first to talk to my sister and brother, and in response I told him again that my relationship with him and my mother had nothing to do with my relationship with my siblings. I mentioned again that he saw only what they wanted him to see and to know.

I was both saddened and angry when he said that he was in the middle. I knew he was, and they had effectively put him in that position. They were using him as a pawn.

I do not know why, but he said he was ready to go see his lawyer to put an end to all the fighting. I felt the frustration in him. I no longer cared if they blamed me as I was now saving the messages and hate mail that revealed the truth, although I was not sure yet what I would do with them. I was going to fight back but within acceptable norms.

I reasonably concluded that my sister and brother kept me as a topic of discussion in their smear campaign and lies, and that they continued to pretend to be congenial while concealing their anger, seething hatred, and betrayals.

My father said again that I needed to talk to my sister and brother, and that now I had to ask their permission to visit. I remained defiant. Clearly, he was manipulated into giving my brother and sister control over my visits; it was not something he would ever think of or do.

When I spoke to my mother, I mentioned that the following month I had a business trip to Japan. She took on a threatening, controlling, and manipulating stance and said immediately in a harsh, deafening tone, "No one has yet seen my wrath!"

Only God and Satan have wrath, I thought, and I knew she was not the Lord God. I politely told her I had seen her wrath for years and knew it well.

"No one has!" she said again in a seething tone.

This was not helping. As the discussion as usual was fruitless, destructive, and threatening, I simply hung up—and anticipated another barrage of calls from my brother and sister.

It was more than abundantly clear that they had told Dad they tried to talk to me to resolve the issues, but did not tell him what they were doing that kept me at a distance and equally kept the family in a state of destruction.

The unholy alliance among my mother, sister, and brother and his wife generated these phone calls. She immensely enjoyed pitting one adult child against the other, though not in our childhood years.

I traveled on business to Idaho and following conclusion of my work there flew directly to Italy on business. I would be away for two weeks.

October saw no harassing phone calls from my brother or sister as I continued to maintain telephone contact with my parents. All of our calls were pleasant, and there was, surprisingly, no verbal abuse by my mother.

Thanksgiving was approaching too.

It was another time of year that brought feelings of sadness. On a Tuesday in early November, I called my parents and spoke first with my mother and then my father. We talked about her health and how the cold weather had painful effects on her. She had occasional tendencies to exhibit moments of nonhostile interaction with me. I believed that those times would not have come to fruition had I relinquished complete control of myself and given up my personal identity and autonomy to her and my sister's will and that of the others.

I mentioned my trip to Japan the following week and that I had minor surgery scheduled when I returned at the end of the month.

During this call my father said he was using a cane as he was losing his balance since he had had a fall and that he had an appointment for his ear. He said the doctor believed his ear problem was making him lose his balance. He also said he fell down the cellar stairs, and when I asked when that happened, he said it was two months earlier. I did not know about these events.

My first business day in Japan, I checked voice messages on my home phone. Even if part of me knew checking my answering system this often was unhealthy, I also knew the only way to keep my guard up was to be aware of any and all communications from my siblings. My brother left a message for me regarding Thanksgiving, and similar to the countless others, he was harassing, hostile, manipulative, and portraying himself as the victim. His distortions of truth and his projections left him immune from his behavior.

He again, as he had these past two years, focused on that knee-jerk phone call I made as a result of my resentment of his blame-shifting to Colleen and me for the rude behavior of his stepdaughter. He also mentioned all of my "other harassing calls these past two years."

There was no end to this insanity.

That same day I set my alarm to wake up at three thirty in the morning to drive to the air force base and call my mother to wish her a happy birthday. The fourteen-hour time difference was tiring. My sister answered in a sarcastic tone when I asked to speak with my mother. "Certainly! Hold on!" she said.

My mother and I had a good discussion, and she asked me to call again. Upon my return home the following weekend, a call came from my sister with an invitation for Thanksgiving.

As in the previous two years, I did not or, more precisely, could not, share the holidays with my family. This year saw the intensity of their behavior increase.

Little did I realize their behavior served to justify another revision to my parent's will, which I was never permitted to read or know about. While my brother and most certainly my sister knew about the wills, I am convinced one or the other, or both, likely helped author them. You'll see why I come to that conclusion in a later chapter.

I had my surgery and was unwilling to risk driving being on pain medication for ten days, so the holidays passed quietly and remained that way well into 2006 with no hate mail and no hostile voice messages. Even so, I did not dare believe that I was home free.

Bad Seeds

2006

"What is evil? Killing is evil, lying is evil, slandering is evil, abuse is evil, gossip is evil: envy is evil, hatred is evil, to cling to false doctrines is evil; all these things are evil. And what is the root of evil? Desire is the root of evil; illusion is the root of evil."

— BUDDHA

From the experiences with my family, I came to learn more, and gave more thought to what was going on around me in the bigger world. To describe the countless and senseless physical killings of humankind would fill a library. It's the subject of many episodes of many true crime podcasts. But the act of killing does not always relate to the physical sense of murder.

As CEO of Enron Corporation, Kenneth Lay was a multimillionaire and successful businessman. Through greed, he apparently deceived thousands of his employees by telling them Enron was strong, stable, and that they had nothing to fear. Countless lives and families were financially and spiritually decimated.

Martha Stewart vacationed behind bars for four months, having been found guilty of obstructing justice, inside trading, and lying to investigators. She was also wealthy. Significantly, US Attorney James Comey proclaimed in his closing statements at the trial, "This criminal case is about lying—to the FBI, lying to the SEC, lying to investors."

Bernie Madoff was convicted and sentenced to 150 years in prison for various charges. He bilked sixty billion dollars from investors in a Ponzi scheme in which, over a thirty-year period, he apparently deceived thousands of people and stole their money to give himself a lavish lifestyle. His victims included political figures and celebrities alike. He had lying down to a form of art. Pretending to be caring and developing friendships with his investors, he played them with the eloquent grace of a symphony violinist.

There are many who have bilked trusting innocents out of their life savings and hard-earned money. It continues today with identity theft that ruins lives, and can literally take years to resolve the damage to one's finances and credibility.

The television show *American Greed* details these specific evildoers who feel entitled to a comfortable lifestyle at the expense of others. So then, it is clear, in my opinion, that we should appropriately add "money" to Buddha's quote about the root of evil.

As 2006 began, I had had no contact with my brother or sister for some time, with the exception of one occasion the previous December, when my sister asked me out to dinner. I could not due to my surgery and pain medication. Even if I hadn't had the truthful reason, I would have been reluctant regardless, knowing full well she had a hidden agenda.

There always was with her.

I continued to maintain contact with my parents by phone.

On a Friday in mid-April, I spoke to my father, and he explained he had gone from bad to worse in his health. He said something had happened to him ten days ago and that he needed to call his doctor again. I asked what had happened, and he said he did not want to talk about it. I added that my brother and sister and mother were obligated to tell me if something happened to him or my mother regardless of my relationship with them.

He said, as he had on numerous occasions, that my brother and sister told him I did not want to talk to them. I explained to him their lies were too much to deal with, and at that point he wished me a Happy Easter and I wished him one. I mentioned I had business in Texas soon and would be away until the end of April.

I was getting to a point where it was apparent the only place to resolve my family issues was in plain view of the general public. I was becoming increasingly frustrated and angry with the extent of my siblings' success at concealing their behavior and lying to my loving father, who deserved better.

On a Friday soon after this call, I received a letter from my sister informing me that my parents' health was declining. She indicated the numerous times she and Patrick had tried to "speak" with me to resolve the issues, and she let me know how badly I had treated my parents while their health worsened.

While it was true my parents' health was declining as they aged, this was a continued manipulative tactic to invoke guilt and shame in me.

In her view of the world, the solution was my surrender.

The next day I received a letter from my brother written under the pretense of another unproductive attempt to patch things up. He said he was making another "effort" to end the nonsense, and, like my sister, he emphasized the numerous times they had attempted to speak to me with no response. He added that I was no better than anyone else and that how I treated my parents was horrendous. Ironically, he referred to himself as an adult responsible for his actions.

He was trying to baffle me with bullshit, and it wasn't working.

His continued and chronic lying, blame-shifting, and projections were ridiculous, and he wanted me to not only accept his behavior but actually believe things would be better.

They could never be.

The previous June when I had made the effort to "test the waters" during a visit on my parents' porch in which my brother's wife slammed her front door, that was a pretty clear indication things would not be any better.

While Patrick claimed that we as adults are responsible for our actions, I had never seen anything in him to suggest that the rule applied to him (or to his wife for that matter).

Only to me.

Even through his writing I sensed and felt his grandiose arrogance. I also continued to believe the abusive, reactionary impulses from his demonstrated lack of self-control were defeating the purpose of the very thing he, and they, claimed to be seeking. As I had come to see, this letter contained nothing of value nor was it productive in any way.

Because of my recovery period and business travel scheduled in early May, I visited my parents for the first time in several months. My time in my mother's presence was cordial, although I was prepared for an ugly outburst of anger at any time. I called early the morning of my visit and asked my father if he wanted to go out for a cup of coffee. He agreed and asked me to pick him up outside, and to not come inside. I drove to the front of the house, got out of my car, walked him to the car and helped him in.

We went to a coffee shop that was around the corner in a strip mall.

We spoke about his health; he had had a transient ischemic attack (TIA), also called a mini-stroke. We also discussed my work, world events, and other casual aspects of conversation. He finally turned our conversation to issues in the family and reiterated that my brother and sister had told him they had tried to talk to me and that I did not want to talk to them. He just didn't, or couldn't understand the concept of baiting me was intolerable.

Concealing their behavior, demeanor toward me, and hostile phone calls on top of it all continued to allow them to portray themselves in a favorable light in his eyes and to portray me as the black sheep of the family.

I had to be gentle with him—his feelings, he was old, and confused. It was difficult to explain that my brother had been consistently and clearly antagonizing me, taunting me, and provoking me for years as much as my sister and in making me look bad.

I dared not tell him that mother corroborated the behavior; he may have already known that deep within himself, but I did mention what he did know—that Mother did not do much to help, and sometimes participated.

I watched as his lips trembled with sadness, and he looked slightly away and gave a small nod. That was his acknowledgment. I had always suspected he was aware, but perhaps he felt things would eventually be OK. In a way they were always OK between him and I, since my brother and sister both had merged with my mother and thus became extensions of her, and key members of her inner circle. I, on the other hand, had been resistant to give up my identity in order to become part of that sick and pathetic structure.

He would never be able to understand all that. I tried to explain they were, and had been for years, destroying the structural foundation of a functional family through lying and betrayal as best I could in simple English. I also told him that I suspected my sister and brother were doing it for the inheritance.

Kayleigh had always had a huge stroke of greed and was a territorial watchdog when it came to the house, and the driveway "issue" was a prevalent element in that undertaking.

Regarding my brother, I told Dad that I had sufficient proof that Patrick was after material gain and wealth as well—specifically, my share of the will. This had been made apparent many times through his financial-related comments and blaming.

Knowing he could only take so much of hearing what I had hoped he already knew, I was becoming flustered in my attempts to speak truthfully.

To help ease my father's sadness, I asked him to ask Kayleigh to call me that night, and told him when I returned from my forthcoming business trip, I would take her to dinner to talk. He was surprised and happy with my offer, and repeated it back to me as though he could not believe what he had heard. He was smiling and said he would tell her.

I did not know any other way to help him feel better and to show him I wanted the same thing he did. I tried in vain to give him what he wanted, although I knew my sister and brother would sabotage any meaningful attempts on my part.

As I pulled in front of the house, my mother was in the doorway looking out, and I walked my father out of my car and up the stairs. When I turned to the front door, she was no longer there. I had hoped to say hello and talk to her. I opened the door for my father to enter the house, and as we both stood there, we heard my mother in the kitchen uttering some strange sounds of intensely loud unintelligibility.

I do not know what she was uttering, but there were similarities sufficient to remind me of that day in my childhood, the one my therapist had helped me unlock, when I sat eating my sandwich in the kitchen at the age of nine or ten, and slapping herself in the face, uttering incomprehensible sounds.

I went back into my car and departed from the house, deeply saddened.

There were no incidents from my brother's side of the house while I was there.

My sister never called that night, but she left a message the following day saying she was sorry she did not call but was "upset about yesterday." There was no anger or hostility in her tone. She said simply that she had mailed a note and hoped I'd receive it before I traveled again. She wished me a nice day and a good trip. I cringed at the thought of receiving another one of her letters, especially since she was so sincere-sounding in her call.

And once again, she would prove me right.

In the letter I received, she said she'd tried many times to open communication, but my stubbornness was too strong, and I was playing *them* against each other. She added that she had no power to resolve this and that Dad expected too much of her to fix the mess. Of course, she continued with her guilt trip, asserting that I was cruel to my mother.

It was more of the same.

I knew the extremity of her spitefulness to those who refused to comply with her demands. My brother was capable of maintaining a successful image that he was attempting to fix things while secretly demonstrating behavior designed to defeat that purpose. They were adept at playing both sides against the middle and were hurting my father in the process.

To succumb to their bullying and deception would make me a willing partner in the web of hatred and life of lies they made for themselves.

My succumbing would only constitute consent to the abuse.

The Mother's Day card I sent to my mother while on my business trip to Missouri had been returned, unopened, just as my niece's birthday card. I also received the return receipt signed by my mother the previous Thursday—nearly two weeks earlier—so I knew she received the card.

In reflecting on that unlocked memory of my mother slapping herself at the kitchen sink, I came to realize how little I had been aware, as a boy, of what must have gone on behind closed doors in my own house. Through a cycle of abuse and pampering, yelling her into a corner and then putting her on a pedestal, my mother had groomed Kayleigh into their unhealthy, symbiotic relationship. She had made her in her own image, a petty tyrant and the child she'd always wanted, and the rest of us suffered because of it, though we had no idea why.

This continued, as I was realizing, in our adult lives. This was what they did, this cycle of abuse and apology, love and hate, and then they claimed they did not understand why I was not responsive to their requests for reconciliation. I could not understand why she would sign the return receipt for my card and then return the card. This was the victim-victimizer dyad that made up their personalities.

They had to be victims and they were—their own. It was equally incomprehensible to me how my mother could believe this self-victimizing behavior was going to help matters.

It only continued to prove I could trust no one in my family but my father.

I called my parents to ask how my mother made out at the doctor's the previous day, sharing a few moments of cordial conversation with her before speaking with my father. I told him about the incident with the Mother's Day card. He was surprised and said he did not know about it. I wasn't surprised.

This is an example of how members of my family kept their antics away from his view. I told him I would send it to him, and he said he would give it to my mother. He also said my mother was scheduled to have surgery for her heart.

Later that same morning my mother called me. Her tone was calm and relaxed, and she asked that I *not* resend the card. She explained she returned it to me because I mailed it with a return receipt. I sat quietly and listened.

She said she had to get up and walk to the front door to get the card, and it delayed the mailman—"He had to wait for me to get to the door"—adding that there was no need for me to spend money on return receipts and that she knew I did it because I had suggested in the past that she claimed to not always receive my mail. "No one takes your mail," she said.

Of course, in any rational universe she would have simply kept the card and called me about her concern with the return receipt. Sending back the card to make her point was just another indication of the spitefulness and irrational behavior they viewed as normal.

Upon returning home from Missouri, I received a message from a law firm in Center City to a recent inquiry I had made for assistance helping me evaluate any possible actions I could legally take against my brother and sister to cease with their behavior, their bullying, and outright harassment.

While they sympathized with my plight, they indicated they saw nothing they could do and recommended I contact another firm for a different opinion. I did not contact another firm, believing the response would be similar in nature.

On a call to my father in mid-June, he said he could not hear me well and complained that he had told other members of the family for months he could not hear on any of the house phones, and that no one did anything to help him.

I had an idea. "I'll call you back, Dad," I said. "I have to go for a few minutes."

I called the phone company and spoke to a customer service representative, who, after checking my father's home number, told me that while my family's number indicated they were not a customer, there was a program allowing free telephone instruments for those who qualified.

There was also a law that provided special phones to qualified customers, and my father qualified. I called a company in a nearby town that specialized in phone instruments for the hearing impaired and informed the representative I would be there before they closed that day.

The technician said he could install the phone and that he had two appointments the following day but believed he could get to my parents' installation the next day. I advised him, as a matter of conscience, that I had major problems with my brother, who had an unpredictable and hostile personality.

He asked if my brother would give him a hard time and I said that my brother should be working, but I had to inform him for his awareness. I purchased the phone, completed all the forms, and departed the store.

Between June and October 2006, I visited my parents several times. I planned each visit so that I used vacation time, and I always visited during the day. I varied the days and times of my visits so as not to establish a predictable routine and thus to avoid intentional interference or personal conflicts that, from experience, would be instigated.

I also made my visit notifications at most only a couple of hours in advance so my brother and sister could not take time off from work and thus impede my visit. Based on their behavior and malevolent nature, it was clear they would do so if the opportunity presented itself.

On one occasion, after calling to arrange a visit, my mother returned the call to tell me my father had to go grocery shopping and to meet him at the grocery store around the corner from the house. The coffee shop was close by, where we would eventually come to sit for some twenty-six occasions.

While I planned to pick him up and drive him to the grocery store, he said he wanted to drive his own car and did. It was parked in the grocery store parking lot. Knowing how bad his eyes were, I was rather upset that my ninety-three-year-old father was operating a motor vehicle on city streets. My first thought was whether this would be considered abuse and where his "caretaker" was.

In an effort to try and understand her behavior, I also performed extensive research on the long-term effects of a person being in a caregiver role for decades. She was to some extent our parents' caretaker, but she also worked full time. I conducted this research in hopes of offsetting my own personal contempt for my sister and coming to some reasonable, rational, and sympathetic level of understanding.

There is some evidence that long-term caregivers experience stress. The 2003 proposed definition of caregiver stress syndrome (CSS) states, "A syndrome found in caregivers involving pathological, morbid changes in physiological and psychological function. This syndrome can be the result of acute or chronic stress, directly as a result of care giving activities." Chronic caregiver's stress may be similar to post-traumatic stress disorder (PTSD), and the chronic stress of one in such a role can result in physical issues such as diabetes, high blood pressure, and a compromised immune system. There are also psychological results such as helplessness, despair, depression, fear, anger, resentment, anxiety, and grief among others in this 2003 definition.

In my view, the only problem with this valid definition as it applied to Kayleigh was that Kayleigh was not a full-time caregiver. She had a full-time job outside the home, and at no time appeared under physical distress or physical illness. Be that as it may, she had lived at home with my parents all her life, and I remain uncertain as to whether it was by choice, or if she was in some way forced to remain home and not forge a life for herself.

In their 1992 work, *Boundaries: When to Say Yes, How to Say No to Take Control of Your Life*, Dr. Henry Cloud and Dr. John Townsend state that some people were brought up to take care of their parents, and did not sign up for this duty but rather inherited it. This may well be the case for my sister. Was it her destiny to become responsible for our parents? If so, then much can be understood in her behavioral patterns—but only to some extent.

There seemed to be some correlation between my sister's behavior and CSS, but at no time in any of my research did I find greed, territorial adaptation, chronic lying, or other negative traits to be associated with the syndrome. Kayleigh could have sought and maintained a romantic relationship, but I had never known her to be in one, nor did she make any effort to form a close friendship with her brothers, though she must have known our parents would someday die.

Over the next few months, after arranging to pick my father up at the house and go for coffee, my mother would often call me back and say, "Your father wants you to meet him at the grocery store like last time." After several of these messages came while I was en route to the house, it was apparent there was a conscious effort to keep me away.

During one visit with my father, prior to a business trip to Korea, I asked him about it, and he said, "When you get back from Korea, call your mother and tell her, 'My father said he wants me to meet him away from the house,' and ask her why. Blame me. You can blame me." He pointed to himself.

My mother said it had been my father who suggested I meet him there. With this I came to realize it was not he who had the idea, it was her or someone else's idea. She had made another untruthful statement. Following my Korean business trip, I did *not* call to ask her about it as my father suggested, knowing it would have only generated more rage I did not want to deal with.

My birthday was coming up, and having returned from South Korea I had two days off. The fourteen-hour time difference made it extremely difficult to readjust, and I had not yet gone to visit my parents. I received two cards in the mail for my birthday, one from my sister and one from my parents. Since my mother was unable to walk and my father would not be able to see well enough to select a card, it was more than likely my sister who selected and bought both of the cards.

My sister's card wished me a good day and good luck in the year and had a hand-written note: "Sean, I hope you have a nice day on Monday. I have been meaning to write all summer, but it has been very hectic here. I will write soon. Enjoy your day."

My God, I thought. *Another one of her letters coming.* I cringed.

Two weeks later, in early November, I received a three-page letter from my sister.

In stark contrast to the birthday card and her well wishes, Kayleigh's letter was seething with hatred and anger. As with her many other letters, there was nothing meaningful or sincere to respond to. It was amazing she believed a letter such as this would prompt me to join them during the holiday season. In fact, I believed her letter was carefully timed to ensure I would *not* come down for Thanksgiving or Christmas dinner.

Starting with her intent to write for many months without knowing how to begin or end, she stated that for a long time she had believed I was very troubled emotionally and psychologically. In referring to our visit with the psychiatrist, she said she was very sad to see what had become of me.

The next time I spoke to my sister, I informed her that a survival strategy I had to employ to protect myself from their lies and betrayal was asking a friend to videotape my outside visits from a distance, in which my sister-in-law clearly slammed the front door as I enjoyed a nice visit to my parents on the front porch.

I explained it was not intended to be malicious, only to counter their lies if I was set up, which I was, with the visit resulting in several seething phone calls by her and my brother. I hoped to compel them to evaluate their behavior through fear of exposure in some way. I thought if I could distract them with fear of themselves, it would take me out of their crosshairs.

Hiding the truth about their behavior from the general public was always one of their primary strategies, and as I mentioned before, I found myself drawn into spy-counterspy strategies as a key element of self-protection.

The truth is my visit was not videotaped, but I was forced into a position whereby I would try anything, even scare them, into changing their behavior.

This also failed.

On a Monday in mid-November, my sister invited me to join the family at either of the coming holidays if I had no other plans. I was dumbfounded. First, I received a card on my birthday—a nice card with a note saying that she would write a letter, which ultimately came and was full of vitriol. And now, a nice voice message with an alluring tone, inviting me to share the holiday with them.

I had given great thought to plan for my son, Thomas, to come for a visit at the holiday and had been debating taking him to see my parents. While I struggled with the notion, I was now absolutely convinced I could not take him to a place where there was a strong likelihood he could be subjected to devaluation or other maltreatment.

I made the difficult decision to fly my son home, and several days later I informed my father my son was coming to visit. He was surprised and happy to hear it, and I asked if he and my mother would be able to spend an hour over coffee or perhaps get something to eat together. He asked me to call him back later that day, which I did. He said my mother could not go out, and asked if I could bring his grandson to the house for a cup of coffee or tea.

I was not prepared for that question. I sadly let him know that it was not a possibility. With the hostile tendencies of my brother, his wife, and my mother and sister, I did not want to expose my son to the potential for any negative elements. I felt bad for my niece and nephew as much as for my son and my father.

On Thanksgiving Day, I called my parents, and my sister answered the phone. I politely wished her a happy Thanksgiving. In a contemptuous and arrogant tone, she said, "Happy Thanksgiving to *you*!"

I sat silently with the phone to my ear for a moment, refusing to respond to the tone.

She hung up but before doing so I heard her say, "He hung up."

I assumed my silence made her think I had put the phone down, but she should have realized there was no click, nor did she ask if I was still on the line. I called back, and my mother answered and said, "You hung up."

I responded, "No I didn't; that's why I called back. Kayleigh hung up." I explained I had wished my sister a happy Thanksgiving and she returned the greeting sarcastically, then hung up when I had a moment of silence.

I put Thomas on the phone, and he wished a happy Thanksgiving to my mother and then asked for my father and also wished him a happy Thanksgiving.

On the day after Thanksgiving, I met my father and took him to meet Thomas and Thomas's girlfriend at the same coffee shop where my father and I usually met. It was a nice visit, and they enjoyed each other's time and company. We were all happy at that moment and very pleased that my father and my son were able to see each other following so many years of absence. After less than an hour my father said he had to go. I was hoping for more time.

He looked at me and said, "I don't know what to tell you," assuming he meant he knew I was not taking my son to the house to see my mother and that I should.

Knowing the hostility that my sister-in-law, brother, mother, and sister exhibited as part of their personalities, and the impulsivity—especially with my mother disavowing my son not once but at least three times—I could not possibly take Thomas there.

They were unpredictable, and I did not know what would happen.

Thomas was aware of this, and I left it up to him as to whether he was comfortable going to the house. He was willing to see Mom "away from the house," for my father's sake and happiness, but his grandmother could not leave the house.

An hour after taking my father home and departing with my son and his girlfriend for my home in New Jersey, I checked voice messages on my house phone from my cell phone. I instinctively felt a message would be there, and sure enough, there was. While they were unpredictable in some ways, they were equally predictable in others.

My sister said it was cruel that I couldn't take my son to see my mother after all these years, that our parents were old and sick, and I better start using my head. I did not respond.

Nearly a week after Thanksgiving my brother left a message at my home while I was at work. It was similar to my sister's. Clearly, they were coordinating their positions.

Again, I did not respond.

I contacted another attorney in Center City immediately after hearing this message. I had reached the point where I was now contemplating legal action to stop their harassing phone calls. In contacting this law firm, I asked about the possibility of getting a restraining order against my brother and sister.

After relaying all of the voice messages and letters from the past several years, the history in general, and what I believed was a clear tendency of potential violence on my brother's part, I was told that I should seek a restraining order through the courts and that as long as I could prove my case, a restraining order should not be a problem.

To my relief, I was informed I did not require an attorney to do this.

In the early months of 2007, there was no contact and I did not pursue legal action, but soon enough the renewed harassment, abuse, and escalation to threats would make it inevitable.

During my research, I discovered that there's one particular type of person I've mentioned several times that requires a brief yet closer examination. This type comes in many forms, shapes and sizes, and can be found in schools, the workplace, and in any institution, as well as in families.

Essentially, they're everywhere, and society is just now claiming "enough is enough" to the point of enacting legislation to put these people in their proper place by outlawing their behavior.

Unfortunately, laws are slow and the bureaucratic process never seems to work fast enough. I'm certain you've met this type in your life, too, and perhaps may even know one or two; or worse yet, maybe you have to live with one, or have one or two in your own family.

Let's take a look at this insidious creature.

The Bully

"I would rather be a little nobody, than to be an evil somebody."

— ABRAHAM LINCOLN

Bullies are not confined to schoolyards, the internet, or to teenagers. It wasn't until I put pieces together of my family's behavior that made it abundantly clear they were, by any standard or definition...bullies.

My sister was in fact bullying me during our two conversations that she devised in hell: *mind-fucking* is bullying. The one-hour visit in the therapist's office with my siblings, the countless letters and voice messages and in-person discussions during my visits were all based on this technique. Bullying.

It's pretty obvious to me that narcissistic people are bullies. It's what they do.

Bullying comprises elements of conversations in circles, projection, and gaslighting, all designed to disorient you and to keep you off track; to deny what you know is true. These conversations are an effort to discredit, frustrate, sow confusion, inject guilt, and to make you think *you* are the crazy one.

My only regret is that I did not know then, when the conversations were happening, what I know today.

REINTERPRETATION AND MISREPRESENTATION

Any valid emotion, differing opinion, or stated comment from the victim is a character flaw in the eyes of the abuser, who misrepresents, reinterprets, and reinvents their own truth. My sister reinterpreting my statement that Dad had a place reserved for him in heaven to mean my mother had a place for her reserved in hell is a prime example, and feeding that reinterpretation to my father was designed to destroy his love for me. My brother continually stating, "This is not what I've done to you," but "what *you* have done to *me*" is another example. Toxic people are notorious for putting words in your mouth and similarly-related behaviors that build on each other. You can't lie without reinterpreting or denying the truth.

MOVING THE GOAL LINE

The difference between constructive criticism and destructive criticism is when a personal attack is prevalent. Nitpicking and scapegoating are two examples of this difference. When an abuser moves the goal line, that abuser will always be dissatisfied with their victim's performance no matter how hard the victim tries to please them.

Even when I provided evidence to my siblings of their behavior that validated my complaints, there was denial and argument, which compelled me to provide more evidence, which was again denied, projected, and used to create rage. By pointing out one or two irrelevant instances of something I did "wrong" or some flaw in me and maintaining a hyperfocus on it, they attempted to divert or distract my strength of will. This occurred even in those times I bent over backward despite the abuse and gave them the benefit of the doubt.

Doing so did not change or stop the abuse. Stressing irrelevant topics was designed to provoke me into "improving" myself to meet their demands and their expected standards, which, as I've just stated, was impossible because the goal line was constantly moving.

EVADING ACCOUNTABILITY

At times I considered this a "What about me?" syndrome. My sister, brother, and mother did this all the time. My efforts to stick with an actual topic of discussion regarding their behavior were often redirected to *my* (perceived) behavior. They were accountable for nothing; I was accountable for everything. Redirecting discussions benefits a narcissistic person. Talk about their negative behavior, and they will divert attention away from it, primarily on to you. Derailing discussions only maintained the current state of affairs which was to their advantage, as they benefited from the circumstances.

For example, in the doctor's office with my siblings, the doctor asked my sister, as you have read, if she could think of just one thing she had done to cause me grief. Looking up in deep thought and eventually saying she could not think of anything was followed momentarily by stating she *could* think of something, then commented on something my mother said regarding my son six months earlier. This is a good example of evading accountability.

When the doctor asked my brother the same question three times, and when Patrick gave off-the-wall and unrelated responses that prompted the doctor to (three times) proclaim, "That's not what I asked you," is another example.

Should you find yourself in a position of mind-boggling communication going in circles or in any consistent no-win situation, the first thing you should look for is the exit door—as the good doctor showed us—even though this may be painfully unbearable and heartbreaking.

OVERT AND COVERT THREATS

Since the day I returned home, my siblings perceived me as a threat that needed to be dispatched. As such, they used their sense of entitlement, territorial beliefs, false sense of superiority, and grandiosity to challenge my sense of self. For the five years I lived at home and for twenty years after, they attempted to instill fear in me; to disagree with their demands or expectations of their standards was to my own peril. But it was actually to theirs.

NAME-CALLING

Whenever Patrick or Kayleigh called me names or lambasted me for some perceived slight, they did so in a rage. What better way to manipulate your victim's emotional state? It is an easy and quick way to degrade a person and insult their intelligence. This is the lowest of the low, another way an abuser undermines your credibility. Name-callers do not have the intelligence level to implement higher levels of interaction and problem-solving.

SMEAR CAMPAIGNS

You've seen this throughout this book. When any toxic person cannot control the way you see yourself, they start to control how *others* see you.

Smear campaigns satisfy a corrupt ego, and that is all they do. While the Bible does not explicitly state that Cain was untiring in his focused efforts to destroy the standing of his brother, Abel, there must have been a major smear campaign before he committed outright, jealousy-founded murder. It would be ludicrous to not consider an effort by Cain to undermine the character, reputation and credibility of Abel before he inserted the fatal knife.

The real intent of a smear campaign is to sabotage your reputation and your character so that you do not have a support network. Harassment goes hand-in-hand with a smear campaign. Smear campaigns allow the abuser to hide their own abusive behavior and project it onto you while at the same time preventing you from exposing them.

The surprise phone call from my niece, blaming me for all the problems in the family was based on my brother's and his wife's successful smear campaign; brainwashing of a young child.

Victims in an abusive relationship or who have narcissistic family members often are not aware of what is being said about them, but ultimately find out once they have been discarded.

Slandering you to your loved ones and creating stories describing you as an aggressor while portraying themselves as the victim are tactics designed to ensure the roles of abuser and victim are reversed, at least as far as the opinions of third parties are concerned.

The constant baiting to get me to respond with violence was comprised of methodical, covert and overt deliberate abuse and devaluation. Reactions to provocations will be used against you to prove you are the abuser and they are the victim.

Consider what I call the "toothpick test". "Let's say I have a toothpick, and I poke you once on the arm. Annoying yes, but there is no physical damage. You say, "Stop that." A few hours later I do it again without warning; this time I poke you two times. You say, "You know what? I told you to stop that. Don't do it again." I wait a while and do it again; but this time I do it three times.

What if I continued this? What if every day I poked you with the toothpick? Poke, poke, poke. Each poke is insignificant and not damaging, but day after day, poke after poke, eventually you're going to haul off and whack me.

You can back a lamb into a corner, but eventually it's going to come out fighting. That is the process of instigating a psychological principle called *projective identification*: the abuser doesn't want to throw the first punch, but they want their target to so they can say, "See what he's like? I told you. He's abusive. He hit me!"

You have to look deep and maintain your self-control; don't take the bait from a bully. This is why I stayed in therapy throughout my time with my siblings; I was in a constant defensive mode and therapeutic discussions were one of my anchors.

The most effective way I could handle their smear campaign was to stay mindful of my behavior and your reactions—constant self-check. This is especially true when you are baited with intentional provocations. For this reason, as I did, it is crucially important to document any form of harassment, bullying, or any other negative elements of abuse.

When the mask of the abuser comes off, as it always does, your character and integrity will clearly be evident.

If you have a family member or members who are bullies, as mine were, you're going to have to fight for your life in more ways than one.

TRIANGULATION

My family was notorious for this sick method of communicating. Triangulation is the act of bringing another person or group of people into the dynamic of a relationship or interaction to belittle a victim. Manipulation on a grand scale, one person will not communicate directly with another, and instead use a third person to relay communication to the second. This forms a triangle. Used mostly by narcissistic people or those with narcissistic tendencies, it is employed when ganging up on a target. All of my family did this, including my father but only because he was brought into it.

Triangulation validates the abuse while at the same time invalidates a victim's reactions. My sister's alliance with my mother, brother and sister-in-law was the prevalent triangulation vehicle. It was impossible for me to "reverse triangulate" because there was no one to align with.

BOUNDARY LINES (OR THE LACK THEREOF)

The more violations an abuser, who is a bully, can commit with immunity, the more they will occur. I can't count the number of sweet promises, fake remorse and empty words used to bait me back in. If you give in and believe the promise, you will pay the price.

But then again, when has a bully ever respected personal boundaries?

A Time of Reckoning

2007–2008

"The truth is incontrovertible. Malice may attack it, ignorance may deride it, but in the end; there it is."

— SIR WINSTON CHURCHILL

The first few months of 2007 passed with quiet solitude. From mid-April to mid-May I took a business trip to Missouri, out in the middle of nowhere.

With Mother's Day approaching, one day I drove to a nearby town at lunchtime to mail a Mother's Day card. Before I headed home, I made arrangements for flowers to be delivered in time for Mother's Day as well. It was coincidental that this was the second year in a row I was away on Mother's Day and at the same location as the previous year.

A few days after my return home in late May, I called my parents and initially spoke to my mother. She said my father was in the bathroom and was not really inclined to talk to me. I told her I would call back the next day. It was one of those harsh workdays, as this business often is, and I was still settling back in from another nearly three-week trip.

So, I called my parents the next afternoon. My mother answered and I was surprised that she seemed in good spirits. We spoke briefly, and then I spoke to my father. This call lasted only for a few moments; I had a lot to do to resettle while at the same time preparing to return to Missouri in a couple of weeks. I had little time off, but mentioned I had some time that week and the next day for us to have coffee. My father had recently celebrated a birthday, and I wanted to see him. Earlier that morning I bought his birthday card and ordered a fruit basket from a local nutrient-oriented supermarket.

On the phone, my father asked me to hold on as soon as I mentioned I would visit the next day. When he came back to the phone a few moments later, he said tomorrow was not a good day for me to come. He whispered the words "not tomorrow" after I questioned him about it. He had obviously mentioned it to someone there—with whom I do not know.

He suggested that Friday was a better day. I agreed so as not to upset him. He asked me to hold on again and then came back to say Friday would work for a visit. Obviously, he had to get someone's approval or permission. I asked him directly if it was my mother who made the decision that I could not come tomorrow. He whispered, "No, not your mother." He was trying not to be heard.

Then he whispered again, "Everyone is home tomorrow."

As we had agreed, I visited that Friday and the visit went well. The remainder of 2007 was relatively quiet and peaceful. The holidays passed, and for the third consecutive year I did not spend any holidays with my family.

The new year also came in with peace and quiet, and I hoped that 2008 would be better.

It would prove to be the worst year for my family thus far.

It was now a cold day in mid-February 2008, and I was about to depart for a business trip to Japan the next day. I took the morning off from work to visit my parents. It was a good visit, and there were no incidents from either my brother or his wife. I was standing by the kitchen counter when my nephew walked into my parents' house from the back door. I was surprised!

"Hi, uncle!" he said with a smile.

I smiled in return and extended my hand in greeting; we shook. "It's good to see you. You look good—it's been too long," I said. He returned the greeting. We spoke briefly about his school, and I mentioned I was happy that he was doing well in college.

After a few minutes, he departed. It was the first time I had seen him in more than three years, and it was a nice, brief visit, but I was saddened by his sudden departure. I had been in the house for just fifteen minutes when he walked in, and I could not stay much longer since I had a meeting and had to return to work. The drive back to New Jersey was not the best at midday.

I mentioned to my parents I would call them from Japan and then see them when I returned before heading out on another scheduled business trip back to Japan.

I had a ninety-minute return drive home, a haircut appointment, and had to turn in early with a wake-up call at three o'clock in the morning to make my early flight.

Shortly after arriving home my sister called my cell from her place of work, and we spoke briefly. I told her I was unable to talk, and she stated she would call me later.

When I returned home, two messages from my brother waited for me. His tone was more vicious than I had heard from him in the past. Both messages were left late in the morning.

The first was brief: "I'm gonna tell you *one* time—don't you *ever* talk to my kids!!" The second was left twelve minutes later. "You've caused enough damage to this family with your *big fucking mouth*! Stay away from my kids. Leave them out of your poison."

With the exception of my father, a hubris-nemesis complex ran rampant in the adult members of my family. This is a pathology that puts great energy into hatred and revenge. The complex gets its name from the word "hubris," which is the pretention to be godlike and untouchable, and "nemesis," which not only means one's enemy, but is the name of the Greek goddess of divine vengeance.

In this rare pathology, two forces that normally contradict one another become one, a fusion that generates awesome energy and ambition. To play the role of Nemesis, one must possess total power. The two forces, now compatible, feed on one another.

Because this complex revolves around a combination of hubris and vengeance, the dynamics may lead to destructive, high-risk behavior. Any effort to deter, compel, or negotiate with anyone who has a hubris-nemesis complex can be dangerous.

Am I qualified to discuss this pathology? No. But the behavior is consistent with the research, so if the shoe fits, the shoe fits. These messages from my brother implied, at least in his mind, that I had purposefully sought out my nephew, which I did not.

My caller ID showed he had made these calls from my parents' home phone versus his own. It was evident that he was concealing his behavior from his children, who were home for a visit from school. As was his normal pattern of behavior, concealing himself was designed to maintain a good image in front of his children. He would not dare reveal his behavior or intentions to them.

It had been evident to me for a long time that Patrick was the one poisoning their minds, and clearly it was he who had the big mouth. He continued to pursue a thinking pattern of disowning his behavior and actions and projecting them onto me. This was the behavior that caused me greater concern than the sheer stupidity he demonstrated; it revealed him to be out of control and dangerous for a very long time.

As loud as he was in leaving these messages from my parents' home phone, it was also evident he must have had my mother's consent to do so.

This false sense of superiority he believes he has over me is going to get him in serious trouble, I thought.

He was a ticking time bomb.

My sister called a short time later, again from her place of work, and we spoke briefly. She was distracted once again, and I asked her to call me later, but not too late since I had to sleep before my three o'clock wake-up.

During our conversation later that day, she expressed her disappointment that I did not "sit and relax" during my brief visit with our parents. Apparently, my mother, as she often did, made this complaint and my sister had willingly relayed her discontent and specific complaints to me. Triangulation in the family continued to be alive and well.

I told Kayleigh that I had things to do that day, and had no idea before that day whether I would have any time to come down to visit. I also mentioned the hostile environment at the house had not changed, and I told her about Patrick's calls, which were apparently triggered by my nephew's innocent exchange with me. I told her that I had received two messages from our brother and that each had a tone of seething hatred, which indicated a tendency to come close to violent behavior.

Before I could explain further, she was distracted again and had to go. The next morning, I departed for Asia, and our discussion was not completed—nor would it be.

The following several months were quiet with no aberrant or hostile messages by any family members in what I had come to call "The Alliance." In between my continued travel requirements in 2008, I visited my parents several times without incident.

On one visit in June, I enjoyed an hour-long visit with my parents. It was a beautiful summer day with the windows open and screen doors filtering in a warm breeze. On this particular day, the driveway was vacant which allowed me to park my car where it had once caused so much consternation and disruption to my life from my mother and sister. As I left the house with a happy heart, I pulled out of the driveway and turned left toward the main street.

Out of the corner of my left eye, I noticed my brother standing inside the screen door on his side of the multifamily home. I did not make it obvious that I noticed him. By this time, following extensive research, I knew he wanted and needed attention—any kind. Even through the screen door his body language was noticeable in its silhouette: erect and straight, both hands on his hips with his chest puffed out.

I continued on without him realizing I noticed. The position reminded me of the arrogance and superiority in this type of body language I had read about so many times.

My thirst for knowledge and truth related to my family members never abated. I intended to take two extensive online courses in body language to enhance my awareness of the culprit we call the liar, but my workload and travel schedule between Korea and Japan prevented me from doing so. Nevertheless, I was motivated to educate myself, and I studied more than a dozen books from reputable professionals and experts in the field of lie detection. Thanks to long flights to Asia, which gave me ample time to read, I was armed with an extensive arsenal of unspoken communication skills and indicators to maintain a more defensive advantage.

On a side note, I quickly learned that body language alone cannot and must not be the sole determining factor in evaluating if someone is lying or otherwise being deceptive, even though the body rarely lies (if you know what to look for).

Other factors must be considered, such as instincts (our God-given internal radar), the subject's past behavior, previous observations of questionable or defective thinking and behavior, and judgments that create distress, problems, or chaos. Other strategies include evasive maneuvers such as physical finger-pointing with anger or rage when confronted with the truth, and a noticeable value system inconsistent with virtue, and normal societal views. In that vein, I used this vast knowledge with great caution and with an eye out for a key factor: *consistency*.

If one *consistently* brings out uneasiness in you from your past and present interactions, your internal radar is working as designed and presents a warning indicator to pay close attention —and possibly keep a safe (or safer) emotional, psychological, and physical distance.

I am not, on any level, an expert such as a psychiatrist, interrogator, or investigator who can rightfully make the claim to, and be classified as, a human lie detector. They can spot liars from a hundred miles away. I can only spot one from forty, and that is sufficient for me.

An instinctive feeling of gut-wrenching revulsion is normal in healthy-minded people who are in the presence of liars, deceivers and people that are self-righteous in the false belief of superiority. I discuss liars and hypocrites further in Chapter 20, based on my own experiences.

I had a break from travel in August, and on a Sunday in the middle of the month, my sister called and said my father had been rushed to the hospital after suffering another mini-stroke.

On Monday, I took a few hours off early in the morning and drove to visit my father at the hospital. Our time alone was good for us both. He was happy to see me and I to see him. He looked very tired in his hospital bed, and I was saddened knowing he and I never had a real opportunity to spend the time together that we deserved.

The following day, Tuesday in the early afternoon, I called my father's room from my cell phone and my sister answered. We spoke briefly, and she handed the phone to my father. Despite my talking loudly he could not understand me. He handed the phone back to my sister. In the background, I heard my brother talking and until that time did not know he was there. He was clearly within a couple of feet of my father.

While I was on the phone with my sister, our quiet talking regarding my father was broken by my brother loudly commanding her to "Hang up! Hang up!" I was agitated by this outburst, yet I remained silent thinking that my loving, kind father who could have possibly been on his death bed, frail and in the twilight of his life, heard my brother—his own son—yelling to my sister to hang up on me. Patrick gave no thought to the fact that my father loved me. Nor did he care what or how my father felt at the moment of his hateful command.

There was a complete lack of conscience, utterly no remorse for this level of cruelty, and certainly no respect shown for my father.

I asked my sister who it was that said that, knowing full well it was my brother. She was silent, which confirmed it was my brother. I asked, "Was that Patrick?" She let out an audible sigh. I told her to pass on to him that he better keep his behavior in check.

As I ended the call, I told her I had mailed emergency contact numbers to her that same day for my next three-week business trip to Korea. Just before I ended the call, I asked her to try to talk some sense into my brother before he got himself in serious trouble.

Knowing his hatred was more powerful than his ability to stop the demons in his mind, I added that this had been going on for four years, ever since the day he succeeded in conspiring with our mother to betray me regarding the will.

I ended the call before she could respond; now it was my turn to get in the last word.

Although it would make no difference, the one good thing was that my sister heard my brother's pointless and vicious outburst for herself. There was no denying that. I was more concerned for what my father had heard and felt. He was an old, dying man who had given my brother everything. Regardless of his jealousy or other negative feelings toward me, Patrick should have shown my father respect.

For several hours after this incident, I continued to play over in my mind what had transpired. I could not stop thinking about it and channeled my anger into positive thoughts of what could be done within the realm of societal acceptance.

After all, I knew what my brother was doing. He was in fact continuing to provoke me to initiate behavior that would have resulted in my being viewed as the culprit and he, of course, as the innocent victim.

My thoughts focused on initiating some form of action to stop Patrick. *Who could I call to file a complaint or grievance against him for his behavior?* I thought. *The police or hospital staff?* My father was clearly in danger of psychological and emotional abuse, and I felt the need to do something.

The more I saw my brother's deep disrespect for my father, coupled with demonstrated and mindless disregard for his emotional state, the more determined I became.

I decided to call the patient advocacy office at the hospital.

Ms. Karen Sawyer took my call. I told her what had happened and briefly summarized the present family environment. Specifically, I mentioned my brother's behavior over the past several years and his proclivity toward verbal and other forms of abuse, although no physical violence had been demonstrated—at least not yet.

In identifying myself and responding to certain questions, I explained that I was the second child of three and that I had lived away from home since the age of seventeen.

In response to her question, I relayed that I felt my father was in no immediate physical danger. I did state, however, that my brother's behavior on that day was not good for my father's emotional well-being, and that I was concerned that my brother's outburst and specifically his chosen words were cruel to my father's ears.

I informed her my sister had been present in the hospital room at the time, that she did not correct him, and that my brother had a history of demonstrating narcissistic and antisocial personality traits, in my opinion. I elaborated specifically that Patrick was motivated by extreme greed, malicious envy, and jealousy that made him hateful and unpredictable, and that he had demonstrated a tendency toward uncontrolled rage.

She asked specific questions about my brother and myself, I assume to ascertain further who I was and who he was. I summarized my life from when I left home as a teenager for military service to date, and relayed that my brother's chosen path in life left him entirely dependent on my parents while I forged my own way.

Ms. Sawyer was receptive to the potential outcomes of jealousy-fueled anger. She understood precisely what I meant, and indicated she would visit my father to talk with him. She also said she would talk to the head nurse on my father's floor to inform her of my brother's behavior.

My father would remain hospitalized for several more days and I felt relief after notifying a hospital official of my brother's cruelty in the presence of my father. Whether my brother liked it or not, my father loved me and was proud of me.

I should add that over the many visits with my father over coffee, I had played him the taped voice messages from my brother. All of them. My father knew who his betrayers were.

I was preparing to fly again to Korea on business the following Thursday. I was not looking forward to another sixteen hours in the air. I took a few days off, and the morning before I departed, I visited my parents. My father had been released from the hospital and was home by this time.

It was a good visit, as they had been during the past two years although it was brief since I had much left to do to prepare for my return trip to Asia. In my line of work there are not enough hours in the day, it seems—or weeks in a month, or months in the year.

As I headed down the front steps to my car which was parked directly in front of the house, I felt the sense of relief that I had come to expect when no conflicts erupted, especially when neither my brother nor his wife initiated a confrontation while I visited.

However, on this day, I was taken by surprise by the depth of a loud and vicious tone that came out of nowhere. Just as I reached the sidewalk to my car, my brother, standing inside his front door against the screened door, yelled with such forceful rage that I jumped even standing on the street: *"I'm not done with you yet!"*

I turned and found myself yelling back to him, "Come out here, you fucking coward!" I surprised even myself, since I had maintained self-control all these years and was never the kind of man to look for a fight. I'm not a man to run should one find me either.

It was instinctive. It was totally out of character for me, but my pent-up frustration got the best of me. I stood there and watched as he retreated inside the house. Based on his tone, I was absolutely certain he was either coming out with a weapon or that there was going to be a physical confrontation on some level.

It was all in his tone; in the air was impending violence. Feeling the potential, I dialed 911.

I explained to the dispatcher what had happened and that my brother had retreated and was not standing in his doorway or outside at the moment, but that I did not know if he had retreated to get a weapon and was coming back out.

I continued to stand outside my car for a few moments and then entered my car to talk more quietly, all the while looking back to the house to see if he came out as the dispatcher suggested to me. He remained in retreat within the house.

I provided the address and verified the correct spelling of my brother's name and let the dispatcher know I did not want to upset my parents with this, and provided details on their medical condition and overall health. After a few moments of explanation to the 911 dispatcher, I was asked if there were issues going on "this very moment" and whether Patrick was inside or outside the home.

On the basis that nothing was going on and Patrick was inside, there was no sense of urgency for the police to respond. Indeed, the dispatcher informed me that if no activity was in progress, the police *could* not respond.

My frustration after these many years of bullying by my brother had reached a point of intolerance. I had given no thought to calling 911—it was instantaneous—and I went to the police station without hesitation after to discuss specific issues and to document a history.

The officer asked if my brother had threatened me, and I responded honestly that he had not done so directly. I repeated what was, in fact, to me a threat on the basis of the tone and his words: *"I'm not done with you yet!"*

The police officer shook his head slightly and said I could go to the courthouse and file a complaint, but it was not a direct threat from the perspective of the law, and that since I was leaving for so long, I would not be here to work out a complaint even within the court system.

Essentially, with my pending departure the next day, the process could not be implemented. I left the police station for home. There was nothing I could do.

While driving home I replayed in my mind what had just happened. While there was no actual confrontation from Patrick, I felt a degree of satisfaction that there was now, finally, something on public record—a recorded 911 call.

Nevertheless, thinking about my self-disciplined silence and complete avoidance over the past four years, I felt a degree of disappointment that I was unable to prevent myself from lashing out verbally. I thought to myself that I must guard myself against his provocations and try to prevent further such reactions.

It was what he wanted, after all. A reaction.

I went on my three-week business trip, but my return home was short—just eleven days before I was scheduled to leave again on a second trip to Korea. This next time, I would be away for five consecutive weeks.

I returned from Korea on a Friday in mid-September. After a few days of resettling, I visited my parents on the following Wednesday morning. There were no incidents or confrontations from my brother while I was there or as I departed.

When I returned home from work though, there was a new message from Patrick. He left the message in the late morning at just about the time I departed my parents' home, and he must have been watching out the window waiting for me to leave. It occurred to me he had also known when I left my parents' house that day in late August. I recall feeling then he had been stalking me, watching out his window to see when I left the house.

As with the January calls after the visit in which I saw and spoke to my nephew, Patrick also made this call from my parents' house rather than his own. The effort I felt, again, was to keep his behavior concealed from his children, designed to maintain his image as a good son, a good father, and good brother in their eyes while spewing his hateful venom toward me secretly.

The term "plausible deniability" also came to mind again, but then, if he pushed the buttons that landed us both in court, there would be no denying the dozens of voice messages and more of the "evidence" I had accumulated and had in my collection.

In this call he reiterated his late-August threat, but he raised the bar: "Hey Fredo, you two-faced bastard. How do you feel coming down here knowing what you did to your parents? Who do you think you are—fucking balls you think you got! Why don't you take that phony cane"—referring to one I had used since my foot surgery—"and stick it up your ass. And don't forget what I said!"

What he had said a month earlier was, as a reminder, "*I'm not done with you yet!*"

These were more than just related statements; nor were they mere idle insults. As far as I was concerned, they were connected and were a direct threat.

The reference to "Fredo" was to the fictional character in Mario Puzo's novel *The Godfather*, the second oldest of four children. In one scene in the Frances Ford Coppola film adaptation, Fredo is with his father, Vito Corleone, when men working for a drug kingpin attempt to assassinate Vito. Fredo struggles to get his gun out and fails to return fire to the would-be assassins. He sits on the street curb near his wounded father and cries. To help in his recovery and to protect him from reprisals, his oldest brother, Sonny, sends him to Las Vegas under the protection of an ex-hitman.

After Sonny's assassination, Vito, the godfather, chooses the youngest son, Michael, to succeed him as head of the family.

In the film, Fredo's personal inadequacy and inability to act decisively on his own behalf become character flaws of great consequence. He is shown as far less cunning and adroit than his younger brother.

By the beginning of *The Godfather Part II*, Fredo becomes an underboss to Michael but has little to no real power. Fredo later betrays Michael when he is approached by a representative of a rival gangster during negotiations between the gangster and Fredo's family. Fredo quietly agrees to help the rival gangster in exchange for compensation. With the information gleaned from Fredo, the rival gangster makes an attempt on Michael's life.

At the end of *The Godfather Part II*, Fredo befriends his nephew, Michael's son Anthony, and plans to take him to Lake Tahoe on a fishing trip. As things turn out, Anthony is called away. Fredo is thus alone in the fishing boat with the assassin, who steers the boat far out onto Lake Tahoe. As Fredo prays he is shot in the back of the head.

Whether or not there was intent to commit the ultimate act of violence, it was a major revelation of what was in his mind. His attempts to instill fear in me were to no avail.

The cane I carried in my vehicle was not phony, as he suggested. He was aware that I had had surgery and struggled at times with mobility.

The signs of his hostile nature were present and had been for many years, and while at that time they were repressed by signs I did not recognize, I saw them all clearly now. In realizing my brother's extreme hostility and abusive tendencies, when I visited my parents, I used the cane while walking in the house for the sole purpose of having it readily available as a defensive weapon in the event he initiated violence—whether I actually needed it or not.

I called my parents several times a week while I was in Korea, and I also remained in touch with my attorney via email. Based on a thorough review of the recent phone call from Patrick along with what she knew of our history, my attorney determined it was now time to pursue a restraining order.

I returned from Korea on a Friday in early November. My attorney and I agreed to meet a week later at the district court, where I would stand before a judge and make my request for a restraining order.

I took the morning off from work with plans to visit my parents. It would be the first time I had visited them in six weeks. As had been the case on recent visits, I had some level of anxiety over the uncertainty of what to expect if my brother was home.

My sister mentioned several times that he had a good job working from home. Whether or not there was truth to his home employment, it was my general belief she was either protecting him or making an attempt to create a positive image of him by simply lying. I did not know.

His recent behavior and threats had to be dealt with—that I did know. He made any enjoyment of peaceful visits with my parents uncertain and unpredictable, and had no respect or regard for their age or condition in spewing his venom or for the fact that I had a right to visit them in peace regardless of how he felt about me.

As I turned the corner to my parents' street, I intended to pull my car in front of the house as this visit would be very brief. An SUV was parked in front of the home. While there seemed sufficient space to park behind it, I felt my visit would be brief enough so that I parked directly in front of the SUV so that I didn't have to back out later. This placed my car in front of the driveway slightly and not with ill intent, but it did block the exit route of a car I believed belonged to my niece.

My father was at the front door waiting to open it for me as I walked up the stairs. He waited for me since I had called in advance and he knew when I would arrive. Together we walked into the kitchen.

As I always do, I kissed my father and my mother, and then my father sat down. I stood in the doorway between the kitchen and their bedroom; I was now always in a defensive position when in the house and could no longer relax while visiting. I had to constantly be aware of my surroundings with visual range both to the front and rear doors.

I handed my mother a card for her birthday, which was coming up in two days, and she thanked me.

The sound of power tools came from upstairs, and my father said my brother and another man were putting a new floor in the bathroom. With the knowledge my brother was in their house, I became even more alert because I believed his lack of impulse control, seething hatred, and omnipotent mindset could lead to a violent eruption at any time.

About fifteen minutes into my visit the house phone rang. My mother picked up the portable telephone from the basket attached to her walker, and she answered the call. Despite being approximately six feet from her, there was distinct clarity and seething hatred in my brother's tone in commanding my mother, "Tell that *asshole* to move his car!"

My mother responded to him with a feeble "OK," and turning to me, she requested I move my car. "You have to move your car. Michaela has to go to work," she said. Without thinking it through I departed from the kitchen and out the front door to move my car across the street. Then I returned to the house.

Later, as I drove north, I wondered if my niece was truly home and needed to go out or if my brother was simply exerting his self-perception of absolute power and control over me—with my mother as his chief enforcer.

This was an interesting visit for three reasons. First, it again confirmed the decades-long dynamics of "triangulation" in the family structure, passing messages to one member of the family through another. Secondly, it was déjà vu all over again with my car and reminded me of the psychological torment I endured from my mother and my sister when I lived in the house for five long and miserable years. Third and lastly, it was utterly ridiculous for Patrick to be upstairs and calling my mother in the kitchen downstairs when he could have come down and asked politely to move my car.

Nothing in the abusive and hateful family structure had changed in all these years except that now my brother was also a designated chief tormentor, chief antagonist, and chief provoker.

On days following a visit to my parents, the routine of checking voice messages continued. I was relieved that my brother did not leave any threats or antagonizing voice messages and assumed he was much too occupied installing the new bathroom floor and had sufficiently satisfied his ego.

Two weeks before Thanksgiving, I met my attorney at the courthouse. We went into the county clerk's office where she assisted me in completing four required documents; then we proceeded directly to the session where we sat for forty-five minutes. Summoned before the judge, we walked to the bench, where I raised my hand and swore to the truth of my testimony. My attorney started the discussion with the judge, who requested a few moments to review my affidavit. He was perplexed and uncertain as to whether an actual criminal restraining order was necessary versus what he felt was more appropriate in a civil protection order, or "injunction."

The problem he faced was that there was no indication of actual physical violence and my brother had no criminal history on record. The difference between a criminal and civil restraining order is that a violation of the civil order would not result in criminal liability, a criminal record, or arrest for a violation.

The judge also stated that in the absence of an actual criminal record or history, or physical violence, and being receptive to the situation based on the "recent evidence of behavior," he did not see the possibility of imminent physical harm despite the context of my brother's voice messages that were written out in the affidavit and despite clear and convincing severely hostile tendencies.

I listened intently as he spoke.

At one point, my attorney and I both attempted to convince the judge of my brother's proclivity for violence with the recent context of his messages and the history of his behavior as clear indicators. The judge admitted there was likely something he might have been missing, and I believed he was, but the full history to present would have taken an entire week of testimony.

I explained to the judge that all of the abuse was concealed within the confines of the family and away from the external world where denial can be argued with relative ease, and that I had sufficient evidence to make that claim as well, reminding him of the voice messages and hate mail. Nevertheless, unless physical violence was actually demonstrated, his decision, based on the criteria of the statute, was that my complaint did not meet the requirement for issuance of a criminal restraining order. He suggested I pursue relief in Superior Court through a civil protection order that essentially provided similar benefits of protection from harassment and imminent danger, but without criminal liability for a violation.

To my dismay, the civil protection order would hold no criminal penalties for a direct violation. I needed my brother to have a wake-up call, and knowing his lack of self-control, a few days in the slammer would certainly get his attention.

In essence, the judge's position was that he felt sympathy for me in view of my brother's "rudeness," which was a gross underestimation of the real matter. He at one point asked if I would have a relationship with my brother after my parents passed away, and I responded with "no." In that vein, since my brother's threatening and aggressive behavior was only prevalent when I visited my parents (notwithstanding the multitude of his phone call threats and aggression) it was his judgment that my brother's "nonphysical aggression" was then not a physical threat and that my visits were based solely on the fact that my parents were alive.

At one point in our discussion following my explanation of the interaction of my family with the established structure, the judge asked me directly whether there was a history of mental disease or disorder in the family. I explained while no formal, clinical diagnosis had ever been performed on any of my family members, this was based solely on the aggressive concealment of the family's hostile tendencies from the external world.

I explained that through both therapeutic sessions with a professional to understand the behavior, and from extensive research, I had learned and came to believe in my view there existed behavioral traits consistent with narcissistic personality organization in four family members that contained some elements of antisocial personality functioning.

In the end, since my brother had not actually been physically violent and the conflict was dependent upon my visiting my parents' house, the threat, in his view, would be removed when my parents died. While there was some reasonableness in his view, his decision to not grant the criminal restraining order against my brother achieved two things. First, his decision had the potential to perpetuate my brother's threats and harassment, which I could not afford to underestimate, and secondly, in so doing, he placed me in a position of "damned if I visit my parents and damned if I do not."

Under these conditions, at least for the present, evil was granted a victory.

My attorney told me that she would initiate the appropriate documentation on the following Monday in Superior Court, and we would proceed to seek relief.

MOTHER'S BIRTHDAY, 2008

A few days before the court date I had made flower delivery arrangements for my mother's birthday and spoke briefly with her that afternoon. I also spoke with my son the previous day, and during our discussion he requested I extend his best birthday wishes to her "even if she doesn't love me." I was silent momentarily as I processed the tone of his voice and his feelings. He was saddened. I told him I would pass it on to her, which I did.

"Thomas said 'happy birthday,'" I said to my mother when I called. I hoped for a reciprocal greeting since his birthday was within the coming week.

She replied simply, "OK."

I waited a moment in hopes she would return the greeting as either a sign of reconciliation, conscious, or remorse, but it was not to be. I politely ended the call.

THE RESTRAINING ORDER

The court agreed to issue a ten-day temporary restraining order against Patrick. Before the end of the ten-day period, both Patrick and I would be required to appear together in court.

There was no doubt I had to be well-prepared for the next phase following submission of an injunction order. It was my awareness that whether an injunction or criminal restraining order was initiated, my brother, in all his omnipotence and self-righteousness, would rage; and I was uncertain how other members of the family would react, though I had a pretty good idea.

I possessed a multitude of evidence, but would prefer to call it "truth".

I contacted the patient advocacy office at the hospital where my father had been a patient and spoke with Karen Sawyer again. She remembered my call.

This was the event in which Patrick demanded my sister hang up on me as my father lay in his hospital bed. I attempted to relay to her as much documentation as possible of the newly escalated and continued behavior.

My thoughts were that any violation of a court order would bring the event in August to light as part of my defense and would be a relevant part of Patrick's behavioral pattern of demonstrated aggression. It is well publicized by a highly respected and well-known professional scholar that hatred, envy, sadistic aggression, and violence go hand in hand as core effects of aggression, which my brother clearly demonstrated on a progressive and consistent level.

I asked Ms. Sawyer if she would be willing to prepare a statement on my behalf based on her recollection of my call to her in August, as it appeared it would be a relevant, documented matter to bring forth in a court proceeding.

I explained to her that my brother's behavior had escalated to the point where court action was necessitated, although he had not actually been physically violent. She said she would contact the hospital attorney and ask their opinion and permission, and would leave a message on my cell or home phone.

Later that morning, while I was at work, she called my home and left a message, letting me know that on the advice of the hospital legal department, she would be unable to submit a statement, but she wished me well going forward with my concerns.

While she was unable to send a written statement, I felt satisfied she had validated the event by recalling our discussion regarding my brother's outburst the day my father lay in a hospital bed, during which my sister had been present.

On a Sunday in late November, I called my parents to see how they were feeling. It was the first time I had called since my brother had been served with the restraining order. My mother answered the phone in a fit of rage and accused me of causing more problems in the family and telling me I had no idea what I did to the family.

I anticipated this. While the guilt trip tactic was not new, it was unexpected. I thought they would back down by realizing the behavior had been exposed.

It was naïve of me to believe my brother would be man enough to *not* tell my sick and aging parents about the restraining order, and that he would accept responsibility for his behavior. Instead, he had to run to Mommy and Daddy, and tell everyone what Sean did to him. While my mother's rage and guilt trip were a common theme, they were always unnerving.

My father, who had always been close to me in spite of the separation, was of a similar mindset as my mother, and it was hurtful to hear him tell me my brother was not capable of doing the things I claimed. He sadly requested I not send a card for the holidays and not come down to visit and then hung up on me.

I was both livid and saddened.

I thought my father must not remember the messages my brother left, which I had played for him when we had coffee together. I'm certain he was not thinking about it at that moment, and nevertheless, even if he had, there was nothing he could do about it. He was essentially alone in the home.

Still, his sadness in those days of our coffee meetings remains fixed indelibly in my memory. It was conceivable my father was simply supporting the rage of my mother, for certainly he, like the others, would not dare defy her.

My mother continued her infantile, ridiculous, and destructive accusations that I had caused all the problems in the family.

I wrote an email to my attorney and explained what transpired. Her response was detailed and informative, indicating what I needed to think about and tell the judge following the ten-day period of the temporary restraining order, when my brother and I would both stand in open court before the judge. I should focus on the issue of immediate danger.

Clearly there was an immediate danger she agreed, based on the gradual progression of his behavior, his letters, and all the voice messages over the years. She emphasized in her view there was a definite threat regardless of his protection by other members of the family and went on to say that if my parents attended the hearing—and it was already made known by my brother's attorney they would be attending on his behalf—should they state they did not want to see me and my brother did not know where I lived—which he did not, as far as I knew, but in the age of the Internet, he might have—the judge may deny the continuance of the order.

My attorney went on to say that I could not force someone to talk to me, and if I believed my parents were being abused or manipulated by my brother, I could involve the state elder services to investigate. However, I was in a very difficult situation, and unfortunately the law cannot make people think differently.

One of the most prevalent aspects of my family functioning, to me and to each other, was lying. My attorney said what I needed to concentrate on was, "Why now?" Why, after all these years, did I now make a decision to request court intervention? The answer was simple I told her: Patrick had not crossed the line before now, nor had his behavior become a cause for concern until now, and his demonstrated potential for being unpredictable had intensified only within the past few months.

She then agreed and understood, saying I should be prepared for what my brother (and other members of the family) would say about me and my behavior. I had previously informed her to be prepared for lies, mudslinging, and false accusations, but we had corroborating evidence. We held a meeting in her office the following day to discuss the issues. I brought all of their letters, the anonymous letters, and voice messages with me.

The following day at six thirty in the morning, my attorney called to inform me my brother, through his attorney, was requesting a "truce" and wanted to come to an "agreement" instead of attending a formal court session for continuance of the protection order.

"Of course, he would. He can't explain his behavior without lying to the judge," I responded to my attorney.

He would be utterly unarmed and without defense of the behavior, and God help him if he lied to the judge. This was another strategy to conceal his behavior and sidestep putting himself in a position to have to explain himself. She also relayed my brother said, through his attorney, that he heard my message "loud and clear."

I had great doubts.

I received an email from my attorney who forwarded to me a draft agreement she received from my brother's attorney, and asked me to review it and comment on it.

It was totally unacceptable. It essentially rendered the purpose of the terms and conditions of the summons and restraining order meaningless, minimized the severity of his behavior, and thereby not only forced me to accept the behavior but left the door open for him to continue with the behavior. It was utterly ridiculous.

I prepared a return response to my attorney that morning with a revised agreement that was more appropriate to identifying the specific behavior, and thus might help him think about his tendencies and lack of self-control.

My attorney worked up my inputs in a revision that was acceptable to me. It was more stringent and included protection of my new car. I had always had some level of fear while inside my parents' home that I would come out to find it "keyed" or otherwise damaged, and it was not beyond Patrick's capacity, or his wife's, as demonstrated by their primitive behavior and street-thug mentality.

One thing that became a major concern was that there were no provisions in this agreement for violations of any kind. I asked my attorney about this and she responded by reminding me there could not be provisions for violations in a civil protection order.

She explained, "The only remedy you will have is to go back to court and file a new request for a restraining order."

Later in the day, after sending the revised agreement to Patrick's attorney, she called me and said, "Your brother agreed to the revised version. I will have the agreement for your signature on Friday morning. I am giving his attorney my word that this is acceptable to you as he is giving me his word that it is acceptable to his client. Please let me know if this is acceptable to you." I provided my concurrence, reluctantly.

Now we'll see what he and they do to demonstrate good intentions, I thought, but I was expecting vindictive and spiteful behavior.

As was always the case, I would be proven right.

I called my parents to wish them a happy Thanksgiving Day. For the past several years I had slowly, despite the extreme betrayal and "setups," attempted to make my way back to some level of normalcy for my father's sake. My brother's behavior in the past year had made that all but impossible, and I had reached the point where I had enough.

It was a good phone call although it was another year gone by where they made it impossible to invoke any humanistic resolution to the behavior. While there was no anger on my mother's part, I heard anguish and felt the broken heart in my father's voice. He was again deprived of the one thing he wanted by those who surrounded him—his family.

The day the agreement would be signed in court had come and I had a nagging feeling my family members would find a way to circumvent the agreement. They were exceptionally cunning. I arrived thirty minutes early and took the elevator up to the courtroom floor. As I turned the corner there sat my brother and his wife. I did an immediate turn around and took the elevator back downstairs.

There was no possibility, without witnesses, that I could remain in that small area, and I certainly was not going to put myself in a precarious position. I decided to wait for my attorney outside so that we could go up together.

When my attorney arrived, we sat in the courtroom during a session already in progress. My brother and his wife sat on the opposite side of the courtroom with his attorney. My attorney announced to the court official there would be an agreement, which was to the official's apparent delight. Both my attorney and my brother's attorney signed the agreement, passed it along for my brother's signature, and finally walked it over to me for my signature.

My attorney and I departed the courtroom and the courthouse.

The following two days were quiet as I prepared to depart for another business trip, this time to South Dakota.

After checking into my hotel, I called my parents. It was the Christmas season, and was reflected by the snow and cold of the northern frontier and the beauty of decorations around the city. The call was cordial. I had hoped that the volatile situation and hostility would cease from some personal acceptance of responsibility, and indeed the emotional upset appeared to have subsided. I felt a great deal more peacefulness.

I returned home the end of the first week of December. With bitter cold in South Dakota and subzero temperatures, I was happy to be home. While winter in New Jersey is also cold, the temperatures had not reached the unbearable lows as the Midwest.

I called my parents and speaking to my mother was fine. I was surprised she did not vent any anger, and I felt some level of relief that her hatefulness appeared to cease—at least for the time being. A few minutes later speaking to my father, I mentioned I would come to visit before my next trip which was coming up the following week.

My father was angry and said, "No," and added that I should not send a card or gift to him or my mother for Christmas. I could hear and feel great pain and anguish in his voice. I tried to comfort him by explaining things were fine and not to worry. I also told him I would speak with my sister and would call her that night, which I did after dinner.

Kayleigh was extremely angry when I called her. I asked if she wanted to go out to dinner, and she responded sarcastically, "Why? So you can tape me?" I responded calmly and explained I did not tape our conversations. I relayed that I had needed to save the hostile voice messages because they were so bad and had to protect myself from the provocations, threats, and lies.

As with many other conversations with her, her anger clouded any hope for a meaningful discussion of the facts, and she said she did not want to be involved. "I want peace," she said. Most people want to know what happened when issues escalate between others.

But she maintained the same position she had for several years. "I don't want to know," and added, "I know what goes on in this house," alluding to her interactions with my brother and his wife. But let him tell her some lie about *me*, and she would have been on the phone leaving another venomous voice message.

I continued to have no allies in the family but for my helpless father, who now seemed to be, through force applied by other family members, aligning himself with my mother and sister.

I explained I understood her position of wanting peace and was not surprised at issues she had with my brother and his wife. I emphasized it was nearly impossible to communicate since all discussions from their end were designed to fend off, evade facts, distort the truth, and were punctuated with hostility.

Kayleigh defended Patrick and said, "He would never do what you claim he was doing," yet when I attempted to explain the specific details and offered to play back some of his voice messages, she again said she did not want to hear them.

She remained defensive of my brother on the one hand and on the other hand would say she did not want to take sides. Her contradictory position was enough to drive one to insanity.

Clearly, I remained the target.

On not one occasion over the years was she willing to understand or become aware of the full situation by asking me what had transpired. She just did not care, and the internal dynamics of my family continued to deteriorate. Since it was a fruitless endeavor to get her to change her view of the family, I offered to have a drink with her to welcome in the new year under the concept that "the new year would be better." I did it for my father's sake.

She agreed, and I asked her to select a place close to where she worked and I would meet her there. I then said simply that I had to go and would call her again the following week.

The second week of December, I planned in advance that I would visit my parents on the coming Thursday. My sister explained the hairdresser would be at the house for my mother. I did not view this as an issue.

While driving on the highway between ten thirty and eleven o'clock that morning I received a call from work regarding major issues that came up at one of my assigned work locations. I had to return immediately to the office. Fortunately, I just departed and was not that far from work. I felt I could make the trip to the house later in the day, or reschedule my visit for another day. Such a change of plans had happened before with no consequences.

I called to let my parents know I was delayed and my mother answered the phone. I explained that I had a problem at work and had to go to my office and would reschedule my visit. She became extremely angry. The hairdresser was there. I was disturbed that my mother would demonstrate anger in front of someone from outside the family when there was no need.

On this particular occasion, my mother was simply not accepting of the fact that I had responsibilities to my work that needed my immediate attention. She was aggressively adamant that she wanted me to come to the house right then.

I did not want to engage my mother in this ridiculous discussion. She said she would call me and asked what would be a good time. I indicated four o'clock would seem to be a good time to call me, at which point she commanded, "Make sure you're there!"

The only condition that made this day different from other occurrences was the presence of the hairdresser. Obviously, she wanted me to be there with the hairdresser so she could chastise me in front of the perfect audience. *"She needs an audience,"* I chuckled to myself." *"What better way to highlight me as a no-good son in front of a stranger, and what better audience to believe than an aging, sick woman?*

The failure of her attack plan was upsetting to her, not that I could not visit at that time.

It was another setup, and it failed.

At four o'clock I called and my mother answered. Exceptionally hostile as she had been in the morning, she accused me of intentionally not coming to the house because the hairdresser was there. She unwittingly validated the conclusion I had come to earlier in the day.

It's not the first time I thought if the behavior wasn't so ridiculously infantile, it would almost be entertaining.

I explained matter-of-factly the hairdresser being there had nothing to do with my decision and that my work required my attention at that time as it had on many previous occasions.

She simply repeated her accusation that I had elected not to visit because the hairdresser was there. Without being direct, she was letting me know she *needed* me to be there at the time the hairdresser was at the house. I politely told her I had to go and would plan another visit.

It was a week before Christmas, and I was again on business in South Dakota. Later in the morning, on a break, I called my parents to see how they were. The previous times of cordiality were all but gone now, and hostility again prevailed in my mother. She answered the phone, and when I asked how she was, she responded with a contemptuous "Fine!!" I was becoming increasingly frustrated, yet I asked politely as I could to not talk to me in that tone.

I asked if she knew I had dismissed the restraining order against my brother, and she acknowledged she was aware. I fell silent in my thoughts to ascertain why she would remain angry. "We have an agreement, he admitted to his behavior and phone calls by signing it, and said he would not continue to do what he was doing," I said.

I attempted to emphasize that this resolved more problems than it created and said that her anger served only to perpetuate problems.

She became angrier, and told me she raised us all well and that the restraining order had hurt her as a mother. I fell silent as she rambled on about how she raised us to be "good." "After all I did for you that you would do such a thing as take out a restraining order against your brother…You broke my heart!" Her attempt to manipulate me into guilt and to minimize my brother's behavior failed. Out of nowhere came words from her that I had never heard from anyone and that took me by such surprise to the point where again I fell silent: "I don't care if He sends me to the deepest corners of hell. I—don't—care!" she said with a slight pause between these specific words.

After the restraining order, Patrick interfered with my visits in another way. Knowing when I visited, he would rev up his motorcycle in the rear yard just below the kitchen window, effectively ensuring conversations could not occur by drowning out any opportunity to speak.

I cannot count the number of times discussions were driven to silence while we waited for the blaring of his motorcycle revving to stop.

His behavior would persist in other passive ways in the future to impede my visits, and would take on a form that psychologists call passive-aggression.

The Unredeemable Family

January to May 2009

"Battle not with monsters, lest ye become a monster, and if you gaze for long into an abyss, the abyss gazes also into you."

– FRIEDRICH NIETZSCHE

The turn of the new year found me on a plane to the United Kingdom for two weeks on business. After my first week I contracted a sinus infection, yet I managed to complete my work requirements even as the infection was becoming progressively worse. The plane ride home was extremely painful—especially on approach into the city because of my inability to "pop" my ears to decompress the pressure.

For the following two weeks, I worked on and off from home while recovering.

In February I called my sister to arrange an after-work cocktail. On at least two occasions previously our arrangements were canceled due to snowstorms that struck the city.

We agreed to meet at the Harp and Crown near her place of work in central Philadelphia. It was my intent to refrain from any discussion about the family. I hoped that my physical separation these past four years would have fostered some level of introspection within her that would create a positive change in behavior.

You think I would have learned my lesson by now.

I hoped that, if the present environment was unacceptable to her, there would be some self-evaluation that would lead to reconciliation, but I doubted it.

Our initial conversation at the Harp and Crown was good, but after fifteen minutes she brought up my brother and the restraining order. "He does not have it in him to do what you claim," she said quietly. I emphasized that he did, and said I had more than sufficient proof which my lawyer and the judge had agreed with. I added that because she stuck her head in the sand, that doesn't mean truth is nonexistent. I emphasized that restraining orders are not given out like candy.

"Well, we didn't tape phone calls, but I wish we had and that we had saved them," she said, implying that I had.

"An attack against one is an attack against *all*," she added without hesitating.

So now the restraining order was an attack against the whole family. I figured she might attempt a diversionary response to take focus off of my brother. While her thinking was truly defective, there was some semblance of truth to it: except for my father and the children, in a real sense they were all responsible for the restraining order.

She stated in a low voice, "The family is ruined."

"The family was ruined long before I came home," I responded.

I further thought it would help her to understand by reasonably explaining that there was more here than met the eye. Our brother had crossed the line with his threatening behavior, which had been escalating since early 2008; and again, I offered to present facts to her that had been accepted by my attorney and the courts as proof.

Again, she repeated she did not need to see or hear anything and said, "I live there."

I did not care what they thought. I had the truth in hand.

Realizing we were in public, I placed myself closer to her ear and said softly, "I can resurrect the restraining order any time based on his behavior or his *agents'* behavior—meaning you or anyone who picks up the behavior or acts on his behalf."

She looked directly and calmly at me while in succession tapping her index finger on the bar several times, just as my sister-in-law had that one day to tell me I was responsible for all the problems in their family. She said, "But he did not do anything to you *today*."

"You've done your share," she added abruptly.

I found myself again becoming frustrated with her as I always did when I gave any attempt to reason with her.

"Tell me what I did," I asked. "Be specific."

She merely repeated, "You've done your share."

Then what came from her put me in a state of momentary silence while I processed and analyzed it. "There is such a thing as middle child syndrome you know," she said in a low voice.

"That has nothing to do with me," I said. "If you knew what middle child syndrome was, you would never relate it to me." I felt my frustration rise as she used this complex as an excuse to justify years of abuse.

It was another attempt to insinuate that I had the problem. It was a ridiculous assertion that brought our discussion, as had all the others over the years, to a never-ending circle of meaningless babble. Nothing had changed in her strategy of evasiveness.

MIDDLE CHILD SYNDROME

The characteristics of middle child syndrome include having a sense of not belonging and fighting to receive attention from parents and others. These were never representative of my character. Those suffering from this syndrome tend to possess a general feeling of being ignored and have a general lack of drive, and these were neither part of my character.

One of the most significant traits of those with middle child syndrome, which surprised me when I researched it, was that they seek direction from the firstborn child, often feel out of place due to being underachievers, and tend to go with the flow. These qualities were obviously not who I was and I could never see myself seeking direction from her.

God forbid!, I thought.

Other characteristics include being a loner and taking no pleasure or interest in bonding with another person in a meaningful relationship. This was also not who I am and in fact was more representative of Kayleigh and Patrick.

Reflecting their lack of achievement, which was ridiculously far from my having become professionally and personally successful, those with this syndrome work only enough to get by.

My sister, as was always the case, had failed to do her homework. It was not surprising, however, as I evaluated this assertion from her days later, that she would attribute the family's cruelty, abuse, and betrayal toward me for so many years was because I was the middle-born and "struggled" for attention.

In addition, those with middle child syndrome tend to not work well under pressure and often start several projects, completing none due to lack of focus, which was far from any aspect of my personality. They further require flexible working hours—which I never had, and from what I came to understand, since relationships are not of major importance to them, the best possible match for a middle child is the last-born, which would be my brother, who appeared to fit the definition more than I. My brother and I have absolutely nothing in common, and based on his behavior, I certainly would never look up to him for guidance either.

My sister's attempt to label or identify me with some form of personality or character disorder was utterly preposterous, but not surprising.

The time was approaching when our meeting would have to end. I saw no effort on her part to communicate with meaningful effort.

My family had apparently learned nothing from their behavior. The defensive strategies, excuses, and projections were stronger than ever.

Yet I offered to meet with her again. While walking to my car I questioned why I would continue to make efforts when it was abundantly clear these meetings were a waste of time.

Maybe I am going insane, I thought. "*How many times are you going to keep trying before you realize it's not going to work?*"

Several studies by birth order theorists claimed that birth order influenced personality, but that was largely negated in a July 2017 article in *Psychology Today*.

One area that did gain my attention involved the oldest child. In any family, the oldest child is for a period of time at the center of attention. When the second child arrives—as in my case, two years later—attaining this center of attention for the first child may become a neurotic need and may persist well into adulthood, producing a personality that craves power and influence. Another proverbial dot seemed to connect, and secretly I was pleased Kayleigh had pointed out middle child syndrome to me, or I would never have known this.

She was unwittingly arming me.

It was certainly true my sister's mindset was one of power and total control. It was an aspect of her personality all her life due to my mother alternatively abusing her and placing her on a throne and conditioning the family—by force if necessary, and as was often the case—to accept my sister's anointed superiority.

This grooming and the resulting sense of entitlement by my mother allowed my sister to control every aspect of the family environment in our mother's own image. My mother's severe parental mishandling of my sister was always the key to the demise of the family.

On a Thursday in mid-February, I took half a day off and planned to visit my parents before my return trip to South Dakota the following week. It was the first time I would see them since the agreement was worked out with attorneys—almost three months. To arrange the visit, I called and spoke to both my father and mother. The call was cordial.

During the call, my father said I should park my car across the street. I asked if I could park in front of the house because it was easier. He said he had to speak with my mother. After a few moments, he came back to the phone and said I could park in front of the house as I always did.

Along the property in front of the house was an old sidewalk whereby you had to carefully position your car to get it off the busy street. When I pulled up to the house later that morning, Patrick's car was parked in front of the house, positioned directly in the middle of the sidewalk. It was impossible to park in front of or behind his vehicle.

For the years preceding the restraining order, during all my visits, the front of the house had been consistently vacant of any vehicles and I had often parked there.

In this case, had I parked in front of his car, I would have once again blocked the driveway. Meanwhile, the driveway on the opposite side of the house, which was his, had sufficient space to park three cars. I would never park on that side of the home, though, since my car would be out of my visual range.

I parked across the street where I was forced to park for the years I lived there.

From that day forward, during all of my visits for the coming years, Patrick's car and at least one other vehicle were parked in front of the house, making it necessary for me to park away from the house.

Resigned to this foolishness, I went in. After some fifteen minutes in the kitchen, and following cordial conversation to ease any tension resulting from it, I felt the need to ask my mother about the parking situation.

Her answer was, "Well, the agreement said you have to be one-hundred feet away from his car," and she looked directly at me with a smirk, revealing a level of joy that she only feebly tried to hide. They were now twisting the provisions of the agreement, which my brother had wanted and signed.

Everything was distorted to their benefit, and more importantly, my mother continued to demonstrate her alliance with my brother's aggressive behavior.

She was continuing to feed the beast.

I decided that I would monitor what was clearly harassment and an attempt to impede my visits, although it was my mother now who was doing the bullying on my brother's behalf, thereby acting as his agent, whether she realized it or not. This was another condition of the agreement; there would be no further acts to impede my visits, including by my brother's *agents*.

I took an hour to relax and think things over, and decided to call her and ask for a favor.

I asked politely if she could leave the front of the house open for me to park during my visits, just as had been done in the past, prior to the issuance of the restraining order against my brother. I did not ask her to relay any specific message to my brother since I did not want to be part of the triangulation or dysfunction. I also mentioned that cold temperatures have an effect on me since my surgery, and my right foot was acting up on me.

I purposely avoided mentioning that the driveway on the opposite side of the house normally had sufficient space to park several cars. In this way, I hoped to keep tensions low.

That didn't work.

"I raised you kids right and good!" she blasted with fury and contempt. "You broke my heart when you took out the restraining order against your brother."

I sat and listened quietly before attempting to diffuse her anger by stating I did not know why she was upset and that I was merely asking a favor.

She calmed down momentarily but her anger prevailed. "Are you planning to cause more problems in the family?" she blasted with blind fury.

I wished her well and said I have to go, then hung up.

As I recall the many photos of my brother blocking the front of the house with his cars (and in one case a video recording him doing so after I called my mother to tell her I was coming down), I confirmed that this passive-aggressive behavior was designed to impede my visits.

I flew to South Dakota on business the following Monday for the week. I called my parents on two occasions while there to see how they were feeling and were cordial and friendly.

My father was lying down during both of my calls and said he did not feel well. I was anxious to get home and wanted to see him, but I would only be home the following weekend before driving to Delaware on business.

By mid-March I returned and was settling into my office. It was my first day back in two weeks. In the late morning my cell phone rang and I noticed it was my parents. I answered, and my mother said, "Hang on." The next moment my father spoke and said I should not plan to visit the next day as my mother had a doctor's appointment in Center City and he and my mother would not be home. She did not tell me herself, and had him pass on the message.

This triangulation business was very annoying.

I waited a day following their appointment and called my parents. It was a cordial discussion with my mother, and then she said she would pass the phone to my father, but wanted to ask me a question when I had time. I told her I was driving, but I could talk.

I knew trouble was brewing when she began manipulating the outcome of any conversation by using her health, saying she did not want to get upset and did not want a heart attack. This method of manipulation was getting really old as well.

She said she had been living, walking, and sleeping with the agony of my telling her the other day that she was "not a good mother."

"Are we back to that?" I asked. I told you whoever said that lied to you. I had never said that and never used those words, and did not know where they came from. She was adamant that her memory was perfect and that she did not forget.

I said again she was mistaken and denied the ugly accusation. I reiterated that what I *did* say was that she clearly favored my brother and sister over me to the point of conspiring, scheming, and lying about me, which was destroying the family.

Now she was more angry and flatly denied ever initiating that kind of behavior—*ever*—and always treated us equally. I found myself being pulled back onto a battlefield of psychological confrontation.

"Do you know how all this started?" she asked.

I knew I would never forgive myself for asking this, but I asked her anyway—how.

"Your phone call to your brother on Christmas Eve a few years ago."

Then out of the blue she changed the subject. "You left home in 1969 and didn't come home except on vacation! I sacrificed my life for you, and you left me!" she said angrily.

This was a new development.

During my research, I learned that narcissistic mothers believe their children are extensions of themselves, and that many actually force their children, through guilt and other forms of abuse, to give up the autonomy of their personal identities to live their lives serving the needs of the mother. But that means never leaving home to forge a life.

Every time my mother went on a hateful tirade, I saw more of what I believed was narcissism in her; things that came out of her mouth revealed what was in her mind.

I said, "I left home because I was coming of age when the Defense Department was going to likely issue me a Selective Service number and send me to the army. I decided to go in the air force instead, remember?"

Her tone softened. "No, I don't remember that," she said.

"Yes," I said, and explained the draft had been in effect and the oldest male children in families who were eighteen years old were being drafted into the army and sent to Vietnam. "You don't remember Vietnam and how many boys were being drafted out of high school?" I asked. She remained silent.

I explained the draft ended in 1973 and the requirement to register for the draft ended several years later in 1975. "I was leaving home whether I liked it or not. The Defense Department was taking me," I said.

I was a bit disturbed with her for making me feel as though I had done something bad by joining the air force and leaving home.

She suddenly ended the conversation by saying, "Here's your father," and handed the phone to him. We enjoyed a few kind moments before the call ended.

I was debating whether it was even worth having another afterwork cocktail with my sister, but ultimately, I felt that despite the many failed attempts to describe my brother's behavior, another attempt to try and get through to her may be worthwhile. After an hour, I decided to call back and ask my mother what time my sister would be home, but deep inside I was increasingly frustrated.

My sister answered and was flustered. I asked if she had had a bad day at work. She immediately went into my call earlier and relayed how I had blamed our mother for issues that developed in 1969.

Here we go again, I thought, *another reconstructed version of the truth.*

I told her that Mother was chastising me for leaving home in my teens, and my discussion was merely how the draft was in effect and that I was likely going to receive a draft number like thousands of others.

She fell silent as I explained I had no idea what our mother was talking about and that my discussion had nothing to do with blaming anyone for anything. My mother was creating more havoc in the family by placing her own twist on the truth and by recreating the discussion.

I was always angry that members of my family knew how dishonest my mother was yet *still* joined her in this macabre dance of psychological fusion.

My sister then asked if I recalled the special hearing telephone, the one I had bought for my father a few years earlier, and I acknowledged it. She proceeded to tell me the volume was up on it, and when I spoke there had been others in the kitchen with my mother who could hear all I was saying—and they agreed with my mother's version of our discussion.

"Of course they would," I said. "Every one of you reconstruct the truth and support each other in your lies."

"Everyone agrees with Mother because you always have." "No one has a mind of their own, and each of you fear her," I added.

I had not sensed that my mother was once again setting me up and creating more problems in the family, and that once again her alluring voice was meant to bait me into falling into another of her language traps. I told my sister I could care less who was there and especially did not care if it was one of the two from next door. I knew the truth.

Then I hung up.

I took time off in the late morning one day at the end of March to visit my parents again. In making the forty-mile trek from my home in Wrightstown, New Jersey to Philadelphia, I had, as I often did, that nagging pang in the pit of my stomach from not knowing what unpredictable event might take place. Upon arriving at my parents' home, my brother's car was parked directly in front of the house, positioned dead center between the driveway and the telephone pole.

I was beginning to believe that when I called my parents for a pre-planned visit, my mother was informing my brother, who then would move his car in front of the house to impede me.

I was going to find out, and knew I had to plan it.

As ridiculous as it sounds, this issue over parking my car in front of the house was clearly to soothe my brother's ego. Her intervention on his behalf provided Patrick with some release for his rage, now that he could no longer contact me with threats and explosive anger. She was providing him an outlet through herself.

While this may have buttressed the rage that stirred within him, her unredeemable intrusiveness made my brother a "winner," at least in their minds.

"Someone had to soothe his itty-bitty feelings!" I thought.

I expected my mother to chastise me or make derogatory comments, but she was well-behaved other than a few cold comments to my father about his eye and where the best doctors were. He was clearly in distress, and I felt bad for him having to listen to my mother scold him in his discomfort.

I watched this interaction with disgust. "Call your doctor at General Hospital and have him refer you to another doctor, Dad," I suggested. He said he would wait one more week to see if the medication was working but could not wait six months, which was how long they had told him to wait before returning for another visit.

I provided my father with a list of my planned business trips for the year and a few into the following year, and asked him to provide the list to my sister so she would know where I would be and when. I departed about thirty minutes later—told them both I would call while I was away. Then my father made a comment: "I don't know, Sean. I don't know."

I knew what he was referring to. It was an opportunity for me to say to him, "Dad, Ma said this was over one phone call I made in my own defense four years ago—one phone call and all this destruction." I felt the need to repeat myself: "All this destruction for one phone call in my own defense of a lie against Colleen and myself." He remained quiet, and so did my mother.

His broken heart and anguish were on the surface as much as his frailty. It was in his eyes and upon his face while my mother showed a blank look, totally oblivious to her husband's pain and heartbreak. My disgust mounted. He got up from his chair and walked me to the door. I kissed him on the cheek and told him I loved him and would call him.

On one afternoon in early April, I called my parents several times with no answer. My calls were spaced out over a couple of hours, so following my second call I was concerned. I was not certain if they had doctor appointments and waited until early evening and called again. There continued to be no answer.

I decided to call the hospital, believing my father may have been admitted since he had been fairly recently. He was not, and the representative transferred me to the emergency room.

In making my query to the emergency room representative, I mentioned and spelled my name and provided my father's first name. "No, he's not here," she said, followed by, "What's your mother's first name?"

"Sinead," I responded.

"She's here." She asked if I wanted her to call my sister to the phone—Kayleigh was with my mother—and I said simply I would call my sister's cell phone. I hung up and then realized I did not have her number programmed into my cell phone. No matter; I thought she would call me. I waited that night, but no calls came.

The next afternoon I called my parents' home, and my father answered. I asked how he was, and he said, "Not good. Your mother is in the hospital. She was admitted last night." I told him no one had called me. I told him I would call him back, and then I called the hospital.

They connected me to my mother's room, and a man answered the phone—it was my brother. I said hello, which was met with silence; a moment later my mother came on. I asked how she was, and she said she was not feeling well. Voices in the background made it difficult to hear, and then my sister came on and said the nurse was there and that she would call me later.

I waited several hours for her to call, and then in the early evening I decided to call the house. My sister answered, and following my greeting she said she had intended to call me. She explained there was no news other than that they had found fluid in our mother's lungs and around her heart, which was a sign of congestive heart failure.

When I asked Kayleigh to call me after she received word on the tests, she said the hospital was contacting Patrick, not her, and that Patrick and Brianna had a planned engagement that night that they had to keep. I thought it strange that if a major issue were discovered or, indeed, if my mother passed away, the hospital would call my brother who was out and not my sister who was home—and who lived several minutes from the hospital.

It was very mysterious.

I asked her to call me when she received word on the results and if I was sleeping to just leave a voice message. She also said the hospital was contemplating transferring my mother to another hospital if additional testing was required.

Before our call ended, I asked if she had a cell phone, and explained I thought I had the number but realized I did not. She explained she did have a cell phone but did not turn it on often. It was one of those "go phones," she explained, and she only turned it on if she had to. She did not offer the number or mention she would make an exception to keep it on during this time, and I did not suggest it.

In view that I could not contact my brother per the agreement, nor would I regardless, and in view of the fact that Kayleigh would not offer her number and keep the communication lines open, I was effectively in the dark, at least temporarily, when it came to our mother's condition.

I realized that, from this scenario, the conditions were designed, orchestrated, and in place to effectively remove me from notification channels. By all appearances, it seemed I had to find out what I could about my mother on my own volition.

The first weekend in April arrived, and there were no calls on Saturday night. Early Sunday morning I contacted the hospital to check on my mother. I explained it was my understanding she had had tests performed the night before and I was wondering what those results were. The representative acknowledged that tests were conducted and my mother was fine, but the doctor would provide additional, in-depth information later that morning. She also mentioned that my mother had had a comfortable night; the representative herself had been on duty all night and monitored her. She indicated a catheter was inserted to monitor fluid output.

When I asked if my mother could go home that day, she said it was a possibility.

There was no communication from Kayleigh.

Later on, Sunday, I was up and prepared for my forty-mile drive to the hospital in Philadelphia. I was under some level of anxiety on the drive given that I hadn't heard from my sister. I had asked her to coordinate with Patrick the time I would be at my mother's bedside. I planned to be there between eight and nine in the morning as I told her, but because I hadn't heard from Kayleigh, I was uncertain who else would be there.

I arrived at the hospital just before eight o'clock, and I found myself cruising the hospital parking lot looking for Patrick's car to ascertain whether he was in the area. Not seeing it, I parked and made my way into the hospital and up to my mother's ward and to her room. She was alone and awake when I walked in and was resting comfortably. I kissed her on her forehead and handed her a get-well card.

She did not appear overly pleased to see me. We spoke briefly about how she was feeling. I offered to get a newspaper or something she may have wanted or needed. Twenty-five minutes into my visit she blurted out, "What I want to know is why you said I'm not a good mother!"

I had hoped to avoid this. There was a woman in the other bed in this shared room, and I was not about to engage in this discussion.

"We talked about this," I said. She snapped back in an angry tone and had that all too-familiar look. "He did not lie and does not lie!," she said in anger.

Her election to draw lines of battle between her and me since the restraining order seemed like it was meant to distract my attention from my brother, but if this was the case, she would not be successful. Internal alarms sounded, and this discussion was my cue to cut the visit short. The last thing I wanted was for her to suffer a heart attack. My family would no doubt accuse me of upsetting her enough to kill her, which would unquestionably be my fault.

The other woman in the parallel bed would no doubt corroborate that I upset her, and thus my role in the discussion upset her enough to kill her.

I had to always think ahead to stay ahead; anticipate, evaluate, and initiate the best option at any given moment.

I paused for a moment and told her I had to head back; that I had a lot to do. I calmly wished her a great day and hoped she would be able to go home soon. I kissed her on her forehead and departed her room.

So, the prevalent victim-victimizer dyad was in full force even on what could have been my mother's deathbed. I was grateful I did have some thirty minutes with her without disruption and in a somewhat peaceful interaction until near the end of my visit.

I thought it was appropriate to call Kayleigh and thank her for coordinating my visit with my brother and giving that time to our mother and me.

I called her just after eight thirty. After a friendly, mutual greeting, she became flustered. Not angry, but very flustered. "Well, I mentioned it to him," she said abruptly.

Still flustered, she continued, "You know there's going to come a time when we're all going to be at the same place at the same time." She did not directly mention the funeral parlor, the church, or the cemetery, but it was clear what she was referring to. I acknowledged that I was aware of that, but privately I did not feel it was beneficial, at least not at that moment, to state that the provisions of the agreement would remain in effect.

The following morning, I did not hear from Kayleigh on how our mother was, how the tests went, or if her condition had changed. I called from work early that morning and spoke with the nurse who said my mother was fine and that they needed to perform another test. The nurse was in the room with my mother and told her I called to check on her. I thanked her for the update.

The next day I called Kayleigh at home to see how our mother made out with her tests. It was determined that she could go home as early as the following day. She added that Dad appeared to be happy, as though our mother had returned from the dead. I was certain he was happy, and so was I that my mother was in good enough condition to go home. With Easter coming in a few days, I ordered flowers be sent to her and my father.

EASTER SUNDAY

Following Mass, I called the house from my car and wished them a happy Easter—my sister as well. Neither of my parents sounded very good, sounding old and tired. I wanted to visit them and have dinner with them, but with the increased hostility and tension it was not a good idea.

After Easter I was in North Carolina on business for the week. While at Raleigh-Durham Airport waiting for my departure flight to return home, my cell phone rang. It was late morning—almost noon. The number was not one I recognized but I answered the call. It was my brother. He said they were taking my mother back to the hospital as she was not responding to verbal conversations, instructions, and was unresponsive to her surroundings.

I told him I was in North Carolina and on my way home. He added, "We should put our differences aside at this time and work through the present circumstances." I told him I would talk with him at a later time, and I ended the call.

I called my attorney to let her know my mother was going back in and relayed what my brother had told me. She mentioned it was an emergency and not to place too much credence on a perceived violation of the agreement. She mentioned his willingness to "put our differences aside" was a good sign and that I should allow things to proceed as they appeared. In responding that I knew him and what appeared to be good may not be what it seemed, she acknowledged that as a reality, yet encouraged me to let things proceed to "see what happens."

I spoke with my sister that night and was deciding whether it would be beneficial for me to come to the hospital, and she indicated my mother was not yet in a room and she may not be admitted formally until later that night. I was uncertain if it was best for me to make the journey that night or if I should wait until the morning. She mentioned that if our mother were dying, she would call, and obviously I should come down. We agreed it was best for me to just wait and come early in the morning.

I arrived at the hospital at seven o'clock the next morning. In checking in with the ward desk nurse, I asked first how my mother was and if she was still sleeping. The nurse said she was in the room by herself and she seemed to be comfortable, then pointed in the direction of her room. Mother was half asleep and did not look very good. With tubes in her arms and breathing tubes in her nose, she looked worn out. I kissed her on the forehead and asked how she felt.

She was alert, yet her eyes seemed to look into space—aware but not aware, closing for several minutes before opening again. I could see her moving in and out of sleep as though forcing herself to remain awake.

I attempted to make conversation in those moments her eyes were open, letting her know that Patrick had called me while I was in North Carolina and he had let me know she was coming back into the hospital. She made no response and remained quiet with her eyes closed. My sense was she was just not up to any real conversation, so I simply stood by her bed quietly.

Not more than five minutes passed when she asked if I had any plans for the day.

I casually mentioned I had no plans but to return to work later in the morning.

"You should go then," she said softly.

I thought about staying longer, but that was overridden by other thoughts, specifically that the last thing I wanted was for her to become upset and have nurses rush into the room while I was alone with her. As I mentioned, I would be seen as a perpetrator if something happened. Witnesses were unquestionably essential at all times to protect myself.

I acknowledged her wish, kissed her on the forehead, and told her I loved her. Instead of returning to work I decided to take the whole day off. I needed time for me.

During my drive north, I played over in my mind the brief twenty minutes I had spent with her. It was clear to me that she was going to continue denying herself our love through her abusive behaviors as she had for the past sixteen years, right up to her last breath.

Even on the possibility of her deathbed she was unwilling to be at peace with me, much less give to my father, the man who had given her more than sixty years of his life, the one thing that meant the most to him and that I was struggling to achieve.

I found some level of peace and solace within myself knowing we have absolutely no control over one who simply refuses to be part of our lives and in fact does everything possible to be abandoned. While long ago I had tried to accept it and still continued to make efforts, my mother's inherent nature to be self-rejecting was and will continue to be one of the most bewildering and disappointing aspects of my life.

In the afternoon, I called the hospital and requested to be connected to my mother's room. The phone in her room rang with no response. This had happened earlier in the day as well. I thought perhaps the doctor was with her or some tests were being performed. I called the hospital again and requested this time to be connected to the floor nurse. In speaking with the nurse, she said, "Patrick's been here all day with her." I mentioned that I called and was not sure why, but there was no response from the phone in her room.

"Hang on a minute," she said.

Following a couple of moments, I heard her say, "Your son Sean is on the phone, and he wants to know how you are. Can I tell him—is it OK to tell him how you're doing?"

It appeared she had walked in the room with the phone as I heard loud voices in the background that I assume were family members. "Yes?" she said, then I heard, "OK."

A moment later it was quieter with voices no longer in the background, but I knew that didn't mean she was alone. The floor nurse explained how things went with my mother that day and some tests that were performed and that she may be released the next day or Sunday.

I was quite pleased to hear the nurse check in with my mother to ask permission to give me status on her condition. The Health Insurance Portability and Accountability Act (HIPAA) is a protective measure of patient privacy and rights, and I was glad it was being practiced.

Later that day, upon my return home, I resettled from my business trip and caught up on essential errands. I discovered a voice message left on my phone around eight thirty a few days earlier—the day after I had arrived in North Carolina.

With my caller ID revealing both the calling party and number as "Unavailable," I was a bit suspicious. In listening to the message, I heard four pops, then distinctly heard the caller hang up. Whoever it was, they waited for my voice greeting to play entirely, which is approximately twenty seconds. It was a bit harrowing since the sound was either of gunshots or simulated gunshots. I had never received a message of that type before.

I contacted the phone company, explained the matter and asked for help to trace the number, but the kind woman said she did not have the capability to perform that level of detail on a call from her system and suggested if it was a major concern, that I contact my attorney. In turn, my attorney could make contact with the telephone company's legal department and request a subpoena of my phone bill.

That was the only way. The information could be provided by the phone company's legal department to my attorney, but could not be made available directly to me.

She also advised me that *57 will initiate a trace and that when three instances of the same number are tracked, the phone company initiates a procedure to notify me. I decided to not pursue it further but saved the message to a microcassette tape—another one for my collection as my brother would say—and mailed a copy of it to my attorney.

While at home on Sunday my home phone rang at lunchtime. I answered with a greeting and heard the caller hang up. In checking my caller ID, I noticed both the number and calling party again revealed "Unavailable."

I immediately dialed *57 to initiate a trace and received a recorded message from the phone company stating, "Unsuccessful trace. Your call cannot be traced by this method." The recording further instructed me to dial a number that was provided and if there was an emergency to contact my local law enforcement agency.

My mother was released from the hospital early the following week. I coordinated with Kayleigh to drive down and visit, but decided instead to take some time off from work later that week to visit. I called in the early afternoon to let her know I had a change of plans and would take some time off later in the week. It was a relatively short conversation.

Toward the end of this call, though, Kayleigh said, "Can I ask you something? I held off asking but feel now that I need to ask you."

"Oh my God, not now!" I thought.

Sure, go ahead," I said.

She asked, "Did you call here last week?"

I explained that I had, possibly twice and reminded her that I often call our parents when I'm away on business to see how they are.

She asked, "Did you use a special phone?"

"No. I have my personal cell phone with me, and I use it exclusively. I have a federal government cell phone, but I never use it to make personal calls." I also reminded her that my caller ID is programmed in my personal cell phone to identify me and that my name and number should always appear on her caller ID.

I asked her if there were a specific reason for her questions, and she said, "Something is going on with calls coming in."

I purposely did not inform her that I was also experiencing odd calls, including the bizarre message of several pops that compelled me to contact the phone company, and that I also had had a hang-up or two. While I was not certain Patrick was behind these calls, it was not beyond the realm of possibility—stir the proverbial pot with both parties, let them question each other, then sit back and enjoy the chaos!

Several weeks passed since I had returned from my last business trip, and my hectic work schedule did not allow for time off to visit my parents.

My next business trip would be the longest of six weeks with a break mid-way to go home briefly before flying back again. I was scheduled to leave on Mother's Day, return at the end of the month for one week, return to the site for the last three weeks in June, and return home prior to the July Fourth holiday.

It was going to be a very long and exhausting forty-five days.

Knowing the last week before I departed would be utterly hectic, I took a few hours off to visit my parents. On the drive to Philadelphia, traffic was not as bad as it usually was. NJ-68 and US-206 were surprisingly light, and I-95 and I-276 were wide open.

I arrived at my parents' sooner than normal. When I arrived at the house, a large truck was parked in such a way that it took up the entire parking area where I normally parked across the street. Another one of my brother's cars was parked directly in front of the house.

As usual it was centered precisely so that only one vehicle could fit. I pulled slowly past the house to see my niece or nephew's car in the driveway and felt that, since I was only staying a short time, I would park there. I knew I was blocking the driveway, but I believed there would be little chance that my car would be in the way just because I was there.

What was I *thinking*!

My visit to my parents was going well. They were both in the kitchen, and we spoke of my mother's visits by two nurses that morning, my father's eye issue, and in general how they were. We also spoke briefly about my upcoming trip to California. I handed my mother a Mother's Day card and kissed her, explaining I was flying out on Mother's Day.

About twenty minutes into my visit the house phone rang. My mother answered, and I could hear my brother's voice: "Tell him to move his car. Michaela has to go to work."

"Oh, OK," my mother responded. She turned to me. "You have to move your car. Michaela has to go to work," she said to me even though I was able to hear Patrick clearly.

I simply shook my head and uttered with a chuckle, "It never ends, does it?"

My mother sounded offish. "It never ends because *you* always have to have *your* way. Then she asked with an arrogant tone, "What, are you calling me a liar now because Michaela has to go to work?"

The fact is it would not have been a lie from her; it would have been a lie from my brother —she was just the conduit. He had initiated it, but as always, she was inclined to defend it.

I said simply, "Well, it's time for me to go. Take care, and I'll call you while I'm away." I made my way to the front door with my father, kissed him on the cheek, and told him I would call him while in California.

In the car driving north I thought I could have moved my car for my niece to pull out and then pulled back in, but I was not certain she even had to go to work or if my car was really in the way. Besides, there was nowhere else to park in proximity to the house.

On the other hand, I did not want to be pulled into the sickness again. Nevertheless, my brother, once again, had plenty of room to park on the opposite side of the house and could have left the front open for me to visit my parents peacefully, as he agreed.

So much for putting our differences aside, I thought to myself, referring to his call to me while I was waiting for my flight in North Carolina the previous month.

It would have been best had he shown our mother that he was no longer willing to do what they were doing, but that would defeat his real intent, the intent he had had in mind since the day I retired from military service. Namely, to create the conditions to ostracize me so he was the family hero and the "good" son, regardless of what lies and betrayals were required to do so—and what he could take from me.

While it was his alliance with our mother that made me seek out legal protection in the first place, it was his astonishing stupidity that prevented him from seeing it was she who helped me succeed in obtaining the restraining order. I could never have obtained the restraining order against him without our mother enabling and protecting him as she had done again that day.

They were not learning their lessons, and it still did not seem to penetrate their minds that anyone who aligned themselves with our mother was setting themselves up to come under the searing light of scrutiny.

The enabler, regardless of how sick the enabled person is, is always sicker.

Forms of passive revenge rather than behavioral change was more soothing to Patrick's injured ego, and it felt better to get even than to undergo self-evaluation and make changes.

In late May, I walked through the door of my home around two o'clock in the morning, having returned from my first three-week business trip to California. I would only be home for nine days, and knowing I was returning to California, a colleague had agreed to hold my suitcase in his hotel room so my return trip would be easier.

After a long day of errands, I was finally able to settle down that evening. Glancing at my machine sitting on my desk, I saw the red message light was flashing.

There were two messages waiting.

The first message was harmless from some unknown company. The second was sent in the early afternoon on Friday—a week earlier. It was similar to the one I received during my business trip to North Carolina that featured what sounded like a hammer driving a nail or gunshots. As with the previous message, the caller played the full extent of my voice greeting and then clearly a hammering sound or something similar was heard, followed by the click of the hang-up. There was no mistake this message was intended for me.

It was too late to initiate a trace action by pressing *57, even though I suspected it would not have worked much as the last time.

I hadn't heard from my attorney following my previous request to contact the phone company to investigate based on the message from mid-April, so I sent her an email on the first day of June relaying this recent message, and to let her know I returned briefly from California.

As with the other odd messages I received, I added this one to my collection.

July to December

2009

"It's better to be hated for who you are, than to be loved for someone you're not. It's a sign of your worth sometimes, if you're hated by the right people."

— BETTE DAVIS

A few months passed with continued business trips and the occasional yet uneventful visit to my parents. My sister called at the beginning of August and said my mother was in the hospital yet again and may go home the following day. I asked her what had happened since she seemed fine when I had spoken to her the previous day.

She said it was not possible that I had spoken to our mother the day before because she was in the hospital all day that one day from early morning. I was perplexed and fell silent. I had to think about what day it was. I was certain that I had spoken to our mother the day before, but I conceded. "OK, then maybe it was earlier in the week that I spoke to her," I said.

I wondered if the multitude of consistent and lengthy business trips was taking its toll on my perception of time. I had not had a decent break in several years. We spoke briefly, and I asked her to let me know when our mother was released to go home. The call ended.

I need a real vacation, I thought.

When my mother was released from the hospital, I took a few hours off from work to visit and called in advance. As had always been the case since the restraining order had been issued, my brother's car was again centered perfectly in front of the house, impeding my ability to park without blocking the driveway.

They're certainly keeping with the spirit of the agreement for him to stay away from my car, I thought to myself.

Then I recalled what my therapist had said about it on a recent visit: "It's a perceived victory, one merely symbolic in nature to soothe his injured ego from the restraining order."

I recall adding, "It is also a sign of aggression," to which he agreed.

My visit to my parents went well. My mother looked old and tired, though, and she sat in the living room in a La-Z-Boy chair with the footrest fully extended to elevate her legs.

It was a day of fairly high humidity, and the ceiling fan was on. I asked about the air conditioner, but my mother said she did not want it on. I assumed it was because my father was often cold. I knew their eyesight was not the best, so while I was away, I had purchased a magnifying sheet. I thought it would help them read. I showed my father how to use it and said he could read the paper with it. I told my mother she could use it, too, for reading.

I also took from my pocket a postcard my father had sent me when he visited Ireland in the seventies. While I was in air force boot camp, my father went to Ireland because an old friend of his passed away. I explained to him and my mother that I had been going through some old papers and found it. He smiled when he saw it, and I knew he could not read it, so I read it aloud. The smile on his face was heartwarming.

Following a general discussion for about thirty minutes, there was silence. I was beginning to feel uncomfortable. I had a meeting to attend and felt maybe it was time for me to leave, and my mother had said a nurse was coming by within the hour.

I told her and my father I hoped they felt better, kissed them both and mentioned I would call them.

I knew they could pass on while I was away. I missed my father already. My mother I would also miss, and I thought fondly of the certain acts of kindness and love she showed while I was in uniform. Despite her bad health and arthritis back then, even if she had to bring a cane, she would always come to the airport to see me off after a visit home, and she would cry as I went through the gate. This was short-lived, though; on my next visit things would pick up just as they had before.

It was these intrusive, unredeemable qualities of hers that I had learned to dismiss.

Just before Thanksgiving my sister called to ask about my travel schedule for the next year, specifically if the contact numbers I had provided for South Korea were still valid. I said they were and informed her I had a new personal cell that was a global phone and could be reached anywhere in Asia. I provided her the number.

Following small talk, primarily about my schedule, I asked if the family was planning dinner the next day, Thanksgiving Day. She said they were. I informed her I had sent flowers to our mother and father and that they should be delivered that day and mentioned I bought them a card but did not mail it. I was thinking about making a visit to the house tomorrow. I did not have plans to have dinner, though.

Kayleigh said, "Well, you can come down, but you know who will be here," meaning my brother and his wife. This also translated into meaning the restraining order and agreement, which he had agreed to, might not be respected.

The agreement had been and still was that he did not have to avoid me, but he was required to be respectful of my time with my parents.

It would have been better, but it was wishful thinking on my part, had she said, "You can come down, and I'll make certain your time is not interfered with," or, "I can let you know when Ma and Dad have free time so you have can your time with them."

Following our call, I sat quietly thinking about the conversation. I could not help but ask myself if my brother, stuffing himself at the table of my always generous and loving father, after conspiring with my mother to betray me (and thus, my father) for so many years, felt like a good and honorable son, and if his wife felt like a loving daughter-in-law.

On Thanksgiving Day, I arrived at my parents in the early evening. It was the first time I visited on Thanksgiving Day in five years. My sister opened the door. Walking up the front stairs I noted my brother's car was parked in front of the house, as was either my niece's or nephew's car. There was only one car in the driveway—my sister's—and it was positioned in the back so that my niece or nephew could have easily parked there and kept open the front for my car. By overlapping the front end of one car across the driveway entrance, my niece's or nephew's car blocked any entrance into the driveway itself.

On the opposite side of the house, my brother's side, as always, were available spaces for three cars.

When I arrived, my mother sat at the kitchen table and my father was pouring a glass of water at the sink. I put my hand on his shoulder, and turning around to notice me, he put on a great, big smile. I kissed him and then kissed my mother. We talked in general terms about my work and how they were feeling, doctor appointments and things of that nature, and about thirty minutes later I departed.

I had hoped to see the children, but thought that day would come another time.

As I looked at the photos of my niece on the wall of the entryway, Kayleigh informed me that Michaela had graduated from college and was now in graduate school. I was not aware of this until now. I was proud of her for that. I knew she planned to become involved in a benevolent field of helping others, and from what I was told, she was well on her way.

I had continued to hope she had a humane value system that was unlike the value system of the family she grew up in, or she could conceivably cause more harm than good to her patients— those who were in pain.

It was Christmas Day 2009. I had planned days in advance to visit my parents on Christmas and had coordinated it with my sister. I did not have a specific timeline when I would arrive due to other engagements but mentioned I would let her know. I was driving late on Christmas morning when my sister called my cell phone and asked what time I felt I would be there. "In an hour or so, around noon," I said.

"OK, that's good—see you then," she responded.

I arrived a few moments before noon and parked my car across the street as I had come to do. My visit was quiet and relaxing. In fact, the entire year had been relatively comfortable, without my brother overtly badgering or threatening me. I even contemplated the possibility of staying for dinner.

It would be the first time in five tormenting years that I felt comfortable doing so.

The restraining order and subsequent agreement allowed me time to breathe and relax on my visits to some degree, and I wanted to try and get things back to some level of civility—even if slowly—despite the years of betrayal. I especially wanted this for my father. I wanted so badly to give him the one thing he wanted, and I knew he would have been very happy if I had sat with him for dinner.

I did not discuss the possibility of staying for Christmas dinner with my sister in advance of my visit, and decided instead to just wait until I was at the house and could feel things out, then decide if I would, or should, remain for dinner.

It was a nice visit. I brought cookies of various Italian kinds in a large Christmas bag for the whole family to enjoy, and brought each of my parents a bathrobe as gifts. I kissed them both and presented my father, mother, and sister with a Christmas card each.

Throughout the visit my mother was coughing consistently, which concerned me. When I asked about this, she said phlegm would catch in her throat, and she had a difficult time dispelling it. General discussion about their health, doctors' appointments, my travel the following year, and other topics were discussed, but we said nothing about the family.

While again this year I bought my niece and nephew cards, I kept them home in a box with other cards I accumulated for them over the years. I did not know if they would be at the house and felt I would play it by ear.

I thought I could ask Kayleigh about the kids and, depending on her willingness, ask her to bring them over so I could say Merry Christmas to them. If that were possible, I felt I would explain to them, seeing them as I was for the first time since Christmas 2004, that I did not forget them and had held their cards these past five years. I was not likely to go to the point of explaining there was no possibility of mailing them since they would be refused and returned. I would not have opened up that discussion.

During a general discussion, I commented on how pretty the Christmas tree was. My sister agreed and said she believed it was the best tree she ever found. I did not disagree; it was the perfect tree. Its shape and decorative style were out of a storybook.

I mentioned that I had not noticed whether there was a nativity set under the tree, and recalled the nativity sets under our Christmas trees as children.

My mother and sister recalled those as well. With that, my mother began speaking of a nativity set that was old—very old, she said, referring to when she was small. I asked if it was under our tree when we were small children, and she said it was not.

She suddenly spat, "My fucking stepbrother stole it!"

"Stepbrother?" I asked, as my sister prompted my mother that she did not have to swear.

There was no response to my question, and I did not pursue it, but it was the first time I was ever aware my mother had a stepbrother growing up. You may recall, though, that Patrick had informed me that my mother was beaten up when her "brother" locked all the doors throughout the house to ensure she did not escape and her aunt broke down the door to save her.

I can only surmise, based on how she described him stealing the nativity set and her choice of words and her tone, that it was this non-biological brother who physically abused her, although to this day I still do not know if my mother had any biological siblings. Following my return from the military, the opportunity to know about her biological family and how she grew up never presented itself.

With my mother upset about her stepbrother, I changed the tone and topic. "Are the children here?" I asked Kayleigh.

"Yes," she said. "They're next door."

I waited in hopes she would ask if I wanted her to get them, but she did not. I had wanted to wish them both a Merry Christmas, and felt it was not something that would be denied at Christmas, although I was somewhat reluctant to suggest it not knowing whether it would ignite a fuse. Another part of me felt she might have offered in an effort to bring the family together, but that was not to be. Instead, I thought I would call her on my way home and ask if she would pass a Christmas greeting on to them for me.

I felt a pang deep in my chest. Despite the traitorous behavior of their parents, I had wanted for years to connect with my niece and nephew, more so now that they were much older.

Nor would I have the opportunity to sit and have dinner with my parents on this day that may very well have been their last Christmas. I continued to see no genuine effort to reconnect the family, and all of my past efforts to resolve the issues and gain some level of togetherness felt intentionally thwarted.

Approximately thirty minutes into my visit my father said he was tired and wanted to lie down. Several minutes later, I suggested it was time I should be going.

I felt bad about it, but did not feel it was a good idea to stay any longer. Neither my mother nor sister offered or otherwise suggested I could remain for dinner if I wanted to.

As I was about to leave, I noticed my father looking at my sister with sad eyes. She gazed back at him. He was clearly communicating to her without saying a word.

It was also clear my sister was listening, but she did not acknowledge what he was saying verbally or nonverbally. The eye contact was maintained between them. I turned back to look at my father again. His sadness was written upon his face and was in his eyes. I heard his silence loud and clear, and I knew she knew exactly what he was saying in his silence.

My sister walked me to the front door. I was compelled to ask nonchalantly, and in a somewhat joking manner so as not to ignite her fuse, how many cars were in the family. She said she bought my father's car from him since he no longer drove, and she sold it, and that everyone else in the family had a car. I left the question at that, knowing full well she was aware of the purpose of my query. She never answered my question.

Driving away I wondered again about my niece and nephew, how they felt, and what they were thinking. They had remained silent but for my niece's phone call years ago, clearly initiated by the badgering of my brother, his wife, and their smear campaign. Nevertheless, I missed them and wanted to reconnect with them, and to connect my son to them.

The future generation of the family depended on it.

I was struggling with the thought of calling my sister to ask if she would pass on my Christmas greetings to them, not knowing if it would set a fire, which was not beyond the scope of possibility. I spoke to my girlfriend at the time and asked her. I could not think clearly in making a decision.

She encouraged me to call, and I did. Kayleigh became agitated but said she could and she would and that I needed to know something: "The children have an extreme dislike for you."

"They do?" I asked. I let her know I did not do anything to them and that I always loved them despite the situation in the family.

Increasingly firmer, in a tone of contempt, she said, "You have *no* idea the hell this house went through for a week over the restraining order!"

I explained, as I did in the past to her, that a restraining order is not an attack against anyone, but is intended to stop attacks. I further relayed our brother had requested a lesser form of the restraining order—an agreement—requiring him to abide by respectable standards when I visited, and he had agreed to do so, which by the way, he and mother circumvented.

I mentioned the agreement I concurred with was a sign of leniency and compassion on my part versus pursuing the restraining order process, and that he admitted to what he was doing. "I don't know why it's a problem now, when he admitted to and accepted responsibility for his behavior," I said. I added that even though I gave him what he asked for, there were still clear signs of aggression in the form of vindictive and spiteful behavior. "I still don't see any changes in his behavior."

"Don't *even* go there," she said. "I *don't* want to *hear* it."

"If the children dislike me, it's because their minds have been poisoned with lies and a continued smear campaign," I said.

She blasted in a tone that caused me to move the phone away from my ear, "*No* one talks about you! Patrick doesn't even *mention* you!"

She could not possibly know this unless she lived with him, which she did not. She did not know what was spoken in his house or what they did or said. But it was clear to me that, based on the continued behavior, I was clearly on their minds and in their discussions.

As always though, despite my brother and sister's hatred for each other, she defended him.

"He's their father!" she said firmly, and added, "It's Christmas. I don't want to talk about this now, and I don't want to be involved!"

Unfortunately, she was already involved.

At that moment, I heard her say in a sweet, alluring voice, "Oh hi, aren't *you* pretty today." My niece had entered my parents' house. Even over the telephone I could hear the fakeness in Kayleigh's tone. I felt sickened.

I pressed the End Call button on my cell phone. I could only surmise that what my sister said was truthful, that the children extremely disliked me over the restraining order. But I had problems with that.

My niece's phone call from years ago had happened long before the restraining order.

I suppose the restraining order was too shameful and embarrassing, and detracted from Patrick's image as a good son, brother, and father. A major aspect of the personality structure and behavior of my family members, as you have seen, was to design concealing tactics to maintain an *image* of goodness instead of *being* good, and came at the expense of the family.

Keeping a separation between the children and myself while stepping up a major smear campaign through the lies would effectively separate us, and in this way the restraining order against their father would be effectively used as a basis for the children's dislike of me.

But why would the children not question their father's behavior that precipitated the restraining order, rather than disliking me for its initiation? An even more important question: Why would the children not demand to speak with me about it to learn my side of the situation in order to come to a more truthful conclusion for themselves?

Was it beyond the realm of possibility my brother or his wife had intimidated the children and demanded they not contact me, lest the truth be told?

No.

The children were both approaching their midtwenties and were old enough to be aware that restraining orders are an element of the law designed to curb potentially violent behavior. So then, why would they not want to speak to me about it?

NEW YEAR'S DAY 2010

Within the first forty-eight hours of the new year, I would board another plane to begin another long year of business trips, and started by spending the entire month of January and most of February in Europe. I felt the need to see my parents before departing and still had much to do in preparation. I called my mother late in the day on December 31 and told her I would have limited time before my departure and wanted to see her and my father that night.

It would be my first New Year's Eve with them since 2003. Mother said she was not going anywhere and I could come down, asking me what time I would be there. I mentioned I was uncertain but it would be in a little while.

I do not believe she mentioned this to my father or sister. I arrived around five thirty and rang the doorbell. Kayleigh answered with a not-so-subtle mix of contempt and surprise on her face. It was clear she was not happy to see me, and likely was not aware I had arranged to visit.

I walked into the kitchen to see they were eating dinner from take-out containers. My father was surprised to see me and mentioned he never expected I would come down that night.

I tried to offset any discomfort, encouraging them all to keep eating and enjoy their dinner. My father offered me some of his dinner, but I declined and encouraged him to eat and not to worry. I would never take food from him, even if he offered. In his old age and frailty, it was more important for him to finish his dinner. I kissed my mother and father and stood at my usual place in clear view of the front and rear doors.

We spoke about various topics and it was overall a comfortable time. I was unsure whether anyone in my brother's family would come over, but I heard movement and my guard was up.

My visit was a brief forty-five minutes. At one point, my mother brought up, primarily to my father, the recent news event of a mother fighting the political process to be interred at Arlington National Cemetery next to her recently killed son, a casualty of war in Afghanistan. I mentioned I felt her pain and understood, and offered a recent experience the past summer while I was managing a defensive system installation in Delaware.

Dover Air Force Base is where the Department of Defense Mortuary is located. Regardless of service branch all deceased soldiers re-enter the country at Dover. I described the aircraft—a large, cargo type that would offload flag-draped caskets—and the ceremoniously respectful soldiers and airmen who would carry each casket to a large, waiting white van. I described my heartache as I watched a priest and the parents walk off a parked bus in proximity to the aircraft and mothers turning to bury their faces in their husbands' chests.

I was not close enough to see their faces, and I almost felt I was invading the privacy of their moment of grief, but it was something I could not pull away from in all its sadness. I would see this same event several times in the six weeks I remained there.

It was a very sad thing to watch, one that prompts a myriad of feelings. I merely stated, "I feel the pain of this woman who wants to be buried near her son."

In hindsight, I suppose in some way I hoped that, by saying this, my family would see something human and heartfelt in me that would prompt them to realize that I, in fact, was not the enemy. On the contrary, I have a large capacity for empathy and compassion, and held anguish for the families who, during this holiday season, and others past, grieved family members and relatives and friends they had lost to war and in other ways.

If my mother or siblings felt anything of that nature while I was on active duty, they never showed it or said it.

It was only from my father that I ever heard similar words in the years since I returned.

I helped with cleanup by taking my mother's empty takeout container from her to make the table more comfortable. Shortly after, I mentioned I needed to be going. I was happy it had been a nice visit with no anger and no upset, and to see my parents for the last time that year.

My sister walked me to the door. She said she had wanted to call me last week to talk about our phone call on Christmas Day, when I had asked her to pass on my greetings to my niece and nephew. She said she had "things" she needed to talk about that related to resolving the issues. I turned and listened.

She began with the restraining order, saying it had ruined everything in the family. It had always been a point of contention for her even though it was my only recourse. She simply refused to accept that. For years prior to that, they consistently told me I did this and I did that that ruined the family or someone in my life said this or did that that caused problems for them.

It was always something *I* did or said, or something someone in my life did or said, that ruined the family.

Not one of them, except for my father, had any concept of humanistic values or the real meaning of family outside of the environment they called "home"—and that was permanently engraved in their defective personas and defective thinking.

As I had several times in the past, I explained that for several years, specifically since the meeting regarding the will, the behavior from our brother toward me had been relentless and ultimately, I felt, could lead to violent tendencies. I explained I could not possibly come down to visit until the behavior stopped, or it would have only exacerbated the situation.

To my astonishment, she changed the subject to our visit to the psychiatrist's office and said they were all still angry that we went to see him through "force" on my part, and they felt the only reason I selected him was to show him, or try to convince him, of how crazy they were.

"Nothing is further from the truth," I said.

I reiterated our two painful telephone discussions before the appointment five long years ago (Chapter 11) and reemphasized they did not have to go—it was purely voluntary—and reminded her I told her that several times. "No one made you go. You did not have to go," I said.

I mentioned again a family therapist was not the right person to see the core issues of the behavior and that my intent and hope was that we would continue to see this specialist regularly to get to the bottom of the behavior. "It was never my intent to show anyone whether anyone was 'crazy,'" I added.

What was interesting is that more than once she castigated me for bringing things up from years past (which continued into the present), while this one and only visit to the doctor was five years earlier.

I was shocked that she brought this up and that they would, after five years, continue to harbor anger over this. Even after I expressed this to her, she said she felt I had demanded they go to see him, which was totally untrue. I did not know how she could conclude that anything of meaning could be discovered in one fifty-minute session—other than sabotaging the session and making the doctor angry with their lies and evasion, which they both did, until he ended up literally throwing us out.

Then she spoke of a lack of trust in the family and a refusal to accept responsibility on *my* part. This was surprising but perhaps should not have been. I again told her I accepted responsibility all my life, both personally and professionally, but would not accept responsibility for others or for those events that had nothing to do with me. I added she had always projected everything on to me and that I was not responsible for their betrayals and abuse from the very first day I came home.

"Oh, that's rich. That's really *rich*," she said in a condescending tone.

She was degrading me—or rather, my integrity—and the truth again was evaded, but only in her mind. It was another meaningless interaction, and the no-win situation for me prevailed.

In the span of five minutes, she negated everything I said, denied my voice and my views, distorted the truth, refused to accept the reality of the situation, defended my brother, continued to blame me, and, as she always did, left me utterly frustrated and confused.

She was so toxic that she was a direct threat to my mental and emotional health.

"I don't want to be involved. I feel I'm in the middle and ready to tell both of you to go fuck yourselves," she said firmly with a small chuckle and a badly hidden smirk.

I was almost compelled to say, "Thank you," but knew that would only fuel her rage and upset my parents.

Clearly, she had sided entirely with my brother all these years. I imagine it was easier to live in the same house with him in peace if she simply did not know the truth. Otherwise, she would have to acknowledge it and deal with it.

"People keep bringing up shit that happened years ago," she said.

I could not help but respond as I often did: "We had that discussion before, did we not?" I explained the behavior from them for decades was the same behavior that existed today. "It's no different," I said. "My only mistake was coming home from the air force."

I didn't know how she would take it, but in retrospect, I felt she would consider that I meant there were never any problems in the family until I came home, and she would feel it was an admission on my part that I was responsible for all the problems in the family. The truth is, there were problems in the family all her life, including my twenty-three absent years.

That ludicrous thought was replaced with one that I just did not care what she felt about my homecoming. I knew what the truth was, and it was evident my role was to be the designated family scapegoat as well as their dumping ground for shame, guilt, and every other negative emotion one can feel.

My conversation with Kayleigh was five solid minutes of mind-boggling confusion.

Finally, as I opened the front door to exit, she said, "They want to resolve this."

"I want to resolve this too." I responded without hesitation, but I knew it would only be on the family's terms and by maintaining the status quo, which would never be acceptable to me. "I will call you when I return at the end of January, and we can plan a drink at the Harp and Crown," I said.

"OK," she responded as I closed the door behind me.

I did not know what good it would do to sit and have a drink with her again, but it would make my father happy. I could not relate to her thinking in which she completely disregarded any aspect of truth and reality.

Red flags continued to fly with underlying hostility, and I knew it would be that way until I gave in and saw things from their perspective.

That was not going to happen.

One of the most frustrating thoughts I had over the years were those occasional times I wondered how Kayleigh was able to function in the real world. In her work, surrounded by real people, did she perform normally? Did she think and act with rationality? Did she not have a need to gather all information available in her line of business before making a decision and acting on it with full awareness of the facts and truth? Did she become another person when she walked through the door of her home?

These questions often plagued me.

As the year came to an end, as much as I knew they would be physically draining, the seven planned months away from home on business trips—three to Asia, two to Europe (one of which would begin in less than forty-eight hours), and five trips scheduled in the US—I would welcome the peacefulness of distance they brought.

In early February, with Valentine's Day approaching, I took time off from work to visit my parents. I bought a nice Valentine's Day card for each of them, some chocolates, and a helium-filled balloon.

I decided to test the waters to see if, after the passage of some months, my brother had ceased his aggression and ridiculous behavior of parking one or two cars in front of the house to impede my visit.

I would test my theory by capturing the act of his moving the cars in front of the house after I notified my mother of my visit, or conclude that the many times his family cars were parked in front of the house were merely coincidental.

I continued to my parents' house as I normally did, but this time I drove past the house to see if any cars were parked out front. There were none.

When out of range but within view of the house, I called and informed my mother that I had some time off to visit her and my father that day, and explained I was preparing to go back to Europe in a few days. She was agreeable to my visit and said she would see me soon.

"I'll be there in about thirty minutes," I said.

After fifteen minutes had passed, I drove by again. This time two of my brother's cars were parked in front of the house in their usual position: one centered perfectly so that it did not allow space for two vehicles, another in front of it with its front end overlapping the entrance to the driveway, which had sufficient space for another vehicle though now its entrance was blocked.

I was convinced these actions were meant to impede my visit.

My visit was cordial except for a momentary defensive position I had to take when I walked into the house. "You're here already? You just called me!" my mother exclaimed.

"No, I didn't just call; I was on my way when I called you, which was a half hour ago. Traffic is light at this hour on the highway, so I sailed down quickly."

"Oh," she said, and nothing more was said about it.

In making my drive north following my visit, I recalled what my sister had piously said regarding Patrick on New Year's Eve: "He wants to resolve this." I could only, once again, shake my head in bewilderment.

I saw no change in their behavior, so I did not know how they thought a resolution could be attained. It saddened me greatly to know our father would undeservedly die a heartbroken man from the actions of his traitorous younger son and the others, who would have nothing if not for him. They were so engrossed in themselves, with their vengeful, vindictive behavior and tell-tale signs of greed, that they didn't care for the loving man my father was, much less that he deserved better than what they were giving to him.

It was obvious by now nothing would ever change that.

The Next Generation

"There is a generation that are pure in their own eyes, and yet is not washed from their filthiness."

— PROVERBS 30:12 (KJV)

There was no doubt that my mother took something terrible within her, from her childhood, into her relationship with my father. I understand this. On top of that, there is no question that, from what I was told, she was abused as a child or teenager. I also realize that as she was developing into adulthood, there was no help for her even if she had wanted it. Narcissistic personality disorder was not categorized in the *Diagnostic and Statistical Manual of Mental Disorders* (DSM), published by the American Psychiatric Association, until 1980. That is not to say I have come to the conclusion she was or is a narcissist, or that any member of my family is—just that the behavioral traits appear similar.

I tried in vain to have compassion for my mother, for her physical pain and for her to be all alone with this struggle in her mind, but it was often difficult when the knife was inserted deeply and intentionally in my back.

I believe that my sister held the key and could have been the solution. Granted, as a child she was powerless, but there came a point in her life when she was old enough to say "no more" to my mother. Instead, she relished the false sense of superiority and power over the entire family my mother bestowed her. Rather than merge with my brother and join forces to preserve the family and overcome my mother, she became the abuser, feeding off my mother while my mother relived her anger, and perhaps her life, through my sister.

This appeared to be the key destructive element to the family.

My brother was not equipped to deal with the extremity of our mother and sister's unshakable alliance, and my homecoming made me a casualty of their psychopathology. I know now I was not viewed as a brother and a son, but as an object of ridicule to be devalued, reformed, and reshaped to the culture of their whims, needs, and desires.

Moreover, their betrayal of me to the demise of the family was, as I would learn at the final reading of our mother's will, for their financial and material gain. My resistance to their abuse and lies made me worthy only of being ostracized, betrayed, and destroyed by any and all means necessary, and the more I defended myself, the more they increased the abuse.

In a famous quote from Socrates, he says, *"When the debate is lost, slander becomes the tool of the loser".*

My brother's jealousy and greed were so clearly evident it would have been foolish of me to deny them. Had he accepted any measure of responsibility for his life, none of what transpired would have ever materialized. He can claim all he wants that what started the problems was my phone call on that day in my and Colleen's defense, but that just signifies the depth of his hatred and intent. If it was not the phone call, it would have been something else—and often was. It depended on what was most convenient and expedient at the time.

They would dispute this with ferocious adamancy.

Nevertheless, despite my attempts to secure for him a professional position that paid a substantial salary, his inner demons compelled him to "get even." Nothing I did for them would ever have been good enough. He needed to be "better than me." That was his motivation as much as his wife's—to assassinate my character in order to take from me and secure the illusion of a better position for himself within the family, regardless of the effect.

In essence, my mother had sufficiently conditioned my sister to represent her anger and hatred, which she then passed on to my brother. I have greater insight today as to why, as a child, my sister remained in her room with the door closed more often than not.

While I never heard anything specific from my mother to my sister (it was no doubt designed to be concealed from the rest of the family), there is no question my sister grew up injected with shame by, and fear of, our mother. I can only conclude from the behavior and interactions at home I witnessed over the past twenty-six years that my mother's perception of her children was that she had brought us into the world for one purpose: to serve her needs. Those who did not kowtow with blind obedience would face her wrath.

The children—my niece, my nephew, and my son—were always a concern for me. They represented the next generation. The seeds of ruination of this generation of my family had been planted decades earlier, from my mother through my sister in their unhealthy relationship; and my brother's ruination of the family had been founded on his failure to accept responsibility for his life and the undesirable choices he made that were so intolerable for him to face that he had to psychologically give them to me.

In their eyes, I was responsible for all the problems in the family. Me and only me.

The next generation of my family, on my brother's side, was born surrounded by hatred. Nevertheless, it remained important to me that my niece, my nephew, and my son connect and establish their relationship if that were possible. It would depend on the extent to which my brother and his wife had poisoned the minds of their children and whether the children were mature enough to realize something was amiss in their parents' behavior.

Still, my niece, nephew, and son would one day be the only blood family remaining and would need each other. Just because my siblings and I had failed in this regard did not mean that my son and his cousins' relationship should have to suffer.

Someone had to accept the great responsibility to attempt to bring my son, my niece, and my nephew together if that were possible. That could never be a possibility, though, until the ruined family structure was leveled like an old, decaying building; until a foundation was developed from scratch through disclosure of the truth, and the proverbial house was rebuilt. This would also mean acceptance of responsibility on my family's part.

Does that mean the truth could—and more than likely *would*—have devastating consequences to the relationship between my niece and nephew and their father and mother, as well as my sister? Possibly. It is not an objective, nor am I concerned with that distinct likelihood. There were many factors that would or would not result that depended primarily on the system of values developed in my niece and nephew.

Several times I had informed my sister that sweeping the behavior under the psychological rug and not addressing the core issues was a major error in their thinking. But I had experienced only false attempts that had served to maintain the status quo, which worsened the situation over time. It was for this very same reason that their "clear the air" sessions amounted to no less than demonic dialogues, or psychopath conventions, that achieved nothing and left the core issues utterly ignored. As adults, they not only did not know how to communicate, but their open hatred and contempt for each other was a barrier to any meaningful effort to do so.

It is not my intent to expose the false relationship between my niece, nephew, and other members of the family. That is between them and is of no consequence to me. The severity of consequences to evil people exposed for what they are is neither a concern for me nor a concern to good people in general. I have already heard once from my brother that his daughter does not need to know the truth, and have since seen efforts related to that intention initiated with great energy. That, in and of itself, speaks volumes.

What mattered to me most, as my parents got older, was saving the next generation of my family and, if possible, my own sabotaged relationship with my niece and nephew.

To this day, now in 2021, my niece, my nephew, and my son do not know each other. There was one time when my niece and nephew were toddlers and my son was perhaps ten years old that they met. It was so long ago that I do not recall the precise year.

During the years since my return not one member of my family had indicated a desire to initiate contact with my son or as much as query about him for genuinely sincere purposes.

They were too busy playing God, and devising ways to disrupt my life in some way.

I initiated those calls in hopes of creating a comfort level that would eventually allow my father and mother to see my son before they passed on, but my mother made certain that a meeting with him would never take place.

Through the many years of what I tolerated from my family, I had to protect my son and shield him. He was not aware of any of the abuse and betrayals that took place until recently.

By contrast, my niece and nephew were, unfortunately, surrounded by hostility all their lives. I could not stop their exposure to what they were born into, nor could I amend the hostile environment they were raised in.

The only thing I could do was to love them as best I could from a distance.

I never told my son of the events that transpired within the family; I felt it was best Thomas not know, and saw no reason to detail the abuse to him. I vowed he would not find out about it until another time in his life. I also vowed he would not become infected by the contagious cycle of abuse that I had to fight against within myself.

Today Thomas is well into his forties, and I have since explained it all to him.

After the revelation of the will, I had two choices. First, I could accept my family's behavior and live in denial of the years of betrayal and mischief. Alternatively, I could get away from it, having no choice but to save myself. I knew there was no end to their behavior and my limits had been reached years ago. I simply could not do it any longer.

As a consequence of severing the relationship, my brother was placed in a position where he was forced to explain to his children the reasons why "Uncle" did not come around anymore. To do so truthfully, however, would potentially destroy his relationship with his children because he certainly could not openly admit to his greed, jealousy, envy, and treacherous sins.

Thus, the smear campaign was his only option, and had to be constantly maintained and intensified. Someone had to be the bad guy in the eyes of the children, and it was certainly not going to be him, his wife, or any one of the other guilty parties. Of critical importance at this point was his goal to protect the false self and images he and his wife displayed and maintained.

The bad guy would have to be me.

Evil is bred in families. There is no question my mother was abused by someone. In turn, my mother clearly became emotionally and psychologically abusive to my sister when she was a child, and in turn, my sister merged with my mother, becoming abusive to my brother while I was away for twenty-three years of military service. My brother and his wife, in turn, became infected. Then my niece and nephew were born into an abusive and hostile family environment, and they became infected, and the cycle recommences with the next generation when my niece and nephew have children.

The draft and my departure for the armed services were my escape.

If it were true my niece or nephew had parked their car with their father's to intentionally impede my visits or to express their extreme dislike of me, as childish as this may appear to you, it was not a good indication of their development and what they would take with them into adulthood. They were old enough to know better and choose to not be part of that behavior.

If my brother demanded it of them, they not only had the right and obligation to say no, they should have done so.

2010

Following nearly a year of relative peace without drama or anger during my visits, the calm was broken without warning.

On a Friday in May, I had returned from a three-week business trip to Asia and was still undergoing the transition from jet lag. I decided to take a few days off and visit my parents. Remembering the quiet, nice visits of the past year, I anticipated a joyful time seeing them again.

I kissed my mother and father, and after a few moments of conversation, my father said, "Your mother wants to tell you something."

Puzzled, I asked, "Ma—you want to tell me something?"

She responded calmly, "Yes, I want to tell you something." As she often did, she held out her hands, palms outward as if holding me at bay, as she said, "I don't want to get upset. Your brother told me the last time you were here [just before my trip to Asia in early April], as you were leaving you spit on his car, and then you walked by the driveway and spit again."

I went from my quiet and calm to a controlled anger. I looked her directly in the eye and told her that was a goddamn lie.

She said, "They watched you leaving and were looking out the window."

I entered another defensive position and said again I never did such a thing nor would I. It was not who I was. I reminded her that it was something *he* would do, and that I always walked down the front stairs directly, straight across the street to my car and did not pass the driveway.

She had a way of changing topics when she was unable to pull out a victory on one subject. This time was no different. She brought up why I left home and described the night I waited up for my father to ask if I could join the service (more than thirty-five years earlier), forgetting that I, in high school, was facing potential conscription into the army and joined the air force instead.

She even accused me of voluntarily reenlisting following my first four years, angry that I did not ask her permission first, and then coming home on leave to blame *her* for my position that I did not have a family when I was a small boy.

I was stunned into utter silence. This was so off the wall I couldn't process it fast enough.

"What the fuck are you talking about?" I asked. I told her it made no sense that I would say I had no family as a small boy when in fact I did; I did not understand where that came from.

Essentially, she was finding a way to ridicule me for my decision to remain in the air force, and she had concocted a partially true story to do so. Yes, I had voluntarily reenlisted, and I did not ask her permission to do so, but I had never said I had no family as a child. It was a massive guilt trip based on some imagined scenario, and I was totally unprepared for it.

I was in a whirlwind. In my defense, I told her if she wanted to continue to believe the dishonesty of her own lies, I could care less.

She went silent.

My father interjected at that moment how proud of me he was, as he had several times. He added that he was happy he signed me up to join the air force. I told him I was happy with that, instead of letting the army draft me with the Selective Service number that I would likely have been issued.

My mother intervened again. "Your brother does not lie."

I stood my ground and told her I did not care if she believed his lies, and reminded her that I worked hard and traveled extensively and had no time for such foolishness, nor was it my character to concoct drama or deception.

With that topic exhausted, she turned her crosshairs again onto my son Thomas, complaining that he never sent her a card for her birthday. She knew he had, and that I had made many attempts to connect them by phone and eventually had planned to bring him to the house to see her, but that effort had been destroyed by her disavowing him three times over several months some years earlier, which she was clearly maintaining to this very day in 2010.

I explained, first, that given how I had been treated upon my return home, I did not want him to be treated the same way; nevertheless, I had made the effort to make the connection. Secondly, I explained that she had returned so many cards to me that I had sent—and I was her son!—that I did not want *my* son to feel the anguish from her rejection of his love. "If you did it to me," I said, "you would do it to him, and I have never seen so much hatred in one person as I have seen in you."

She again became silent, looking downward on the table.

I knew I would have to cut this unpleasant visit short, and I finally told my father I would have to make my way home. He asked me to call my sister.

Then my mother turned her crosshairs onto my father. She immediately blasted to him, "What does *she* have to do with this?" while giving him a long, hard stare of utter contempt.

He looked at her in bewilderment, as I had often seen before, a silent confusion, as if asking, "What did I say?"

I sensed his fear of confronting her, but I could not refrain from confronting her myself. "There has to be drama, chaos, and havoc in the family, doesn't there, Mother? Otherwise, you're not happy, are you? There can't be any peace, can there?"

She did not respond. I immediately came to my father's defense and said, "You didn't say anything bad or wrong, Dad." I completely invalidated my mother's cold, harsh words to him as I touched his shoulder softly. It gave him comfort from the cruel glare she was giving him.

It was that look of evil I had seen so many times before.

I again turned to my mother and stated I could not accept or understand where the degree of hatefulness had come from in her. She adamantly proclaimed she was not hateful and became exceptionally upset by my assertion.

Sitting in her chair at the kitchen table, she forcefully pushed her walker away and into the center of the kitchen in a childish way.

I walked over and gently repositioned it by her side where it was, at which time she again pushed it away from her in the center of the kitchen. I walked over calmly for the third time and wheeled it gently back to her, and again she pushed it into the center of the room.

At that point my father said, "It's OK, Sean"—meaning to just leave it there—and then said he was in the middle and did not want to be. I was saddened for him. This was one more time my mother had waited for me to come to the house and had a plan, aligned with my brother and based on a lie, to unleash her venom.

And she was acting like a spoiled, rotten child.

My father told me not to worry about it. I found myself again fighting to feed her the truth. If she was interested in the truth, the family would not be where it was and she would not be creating such conflicts. Every time I defended the truth to any member of the family, it seemed to feed their tirades and exacerbate their hostility.

So much negative energy could not be diffused.

Then my father looked up to me from his chair and again said he was proud of me, as he had said several times in front of my mother.

At that point I knew I had to leave. The sickness in my mother's mind was alive and well, and my planned, peaceful visit was again disrupted by my brother's bizarre lie and my mother's continued interference.

I kissed my parents and made my way out the front door, straight down the front stairs, and across the street to my car while thinking to myself that I was going to have to mount a camera in my car to monitor my comings and goings to legally protect myself.

My next thoughts were about what Patrick would do when the chain was broken—that is, when my mother left the stage. Who would he run to with his deceptions, to perform his dirty work and instigate more problems in the family?

Driving home I thought with bewilderment about a previous discussion with my sister in which she relayed that mothers get involved directly between their children and that's simply what they do, and my thoughts took me to the reality that they do this only when their children are small, but not as adults.

The childhood structure had never been broken. I can only reiterate that when one does not leave home, one does not grow up.

A week later I called to wish my mother a happy Mother's Day. My niece, I believe, answered the phone. I did not speak to her but merely asked for my mother. She said a few words that I did not hear with any clarity, and she handed my mother the phone.

I delivered my message, and she thanked me for the call. I asked who had answered the phone. "Was that Michaela?"

"No," she said calmly, "it was me. It must have been my voice." She was not angry in her tone but calm and simply matter-of-fact. I felt momentarily confused and then realized the ridiculousness of her lie. I did not think to ask if she had received the flowers I had sent, nor did she offer to acknowledge she received them or thank me.

Several days before my father's ninety-seventh birthday, I had time to visit my parents and I took half a day off from work. In calling my mother I mentioned I was visiting and she acknowledged it, and added that the hairdresser was coming to do her hair.

While it brought back memories of the time in which she was exceptionally upset that I couldn't come while the hairdresser was there, I continued on my way.

I wanted to see my father.

After parking my car across the street, I positioned a video camera I had bought on the dashboard facing the house. For several months, I had been doing this to capture any aberrant behaviors and to protect myself from any lies about my behavior regarding my visit. It would be something to add to my "collection," as my brother would tell me and, of course, would be of interest to my lawyer.

I rang the bell and then entered the house. My mother sat in a chair in front of the kitchen sink with the hairdresser working on her hair. The hairdresser was a nice woman who exchanged greetings with me. My father and I went into the next room and sat quietly talking. I spent most of my time with him on this visit. When I sat down beside him, almost immediately he whispered, "Is there something you can do to fix the phone?" I told him I would fix it and not to worry about it. We discussed his hearing, and I casually mentioned his hearing aid might be the problem. At that point he said he had just paid eleven hundred dollars for a new hearing aid.

We spoke about different topics, and I mentioned to him his birthday was coming up in a few days. He had a surprised look on his face and a huge smile as though he wasn't aware—and he wasn't. "It's my birthday?" he asked with surprise.

"Yes, Dad, very soon," I said, smiling back to him.

The joy I saw in him was warming, but it was replaced with sadness when he whispered to me, "I think it's going to be my last one."

I had to show no signs of sadness from his statement, which put me in a serious mood. I shuffled it off by stating, "Oh no, Dad, you're going to have many, many more birthdays—many more," waving my hand as I said it matter-of-factly. I hoped it gave him some comfort. I couldn't let him know my sadness from his awareness that he was in the twilight of his life.

He started talking about the phone again and asked me if I could fix it, but this time he said it loud enough to where my mother heard—and the gates of hell opened.

"What did *he* just tell you?" she exclaimed.

"What do you mean, Ma?" I asked, professing ignorance for my father's sake.

"What did he just ask you?" she said again in a demanding tone.

"He didn't ask me anything," I answered, knowing that she would berate him.

Nothing more was said about it—we escaped!

During a brief break while my mother's hair was setting, I enjoyed a few moments of casual conversation with the hairdresser. Simply responding to her questions about my work and my life, I was humbled by her compliments and the gratitude she showed toward my profession.

I offered comfort by letting her know the general population wasn't fully aware of the devoted work of so many to help keep people safe.

After a few more minutes, my visit was coming to an end. I kissed my father and told him I would see him over the coming weekend; this year I planned to come to see him for his birthday and bring him a cake, although I did not reveal that.

"You're coming Sunday? Why?" my mother asked firmly.

"Because his birthday is coming soon and I have to travel again," I said. Then I wished her a nice day and extended my goodbye and best wishes to the hairdresser.

Before I left, I took a picture of my father with my cell phone. I needed it for me—to remember him in the moment for giving me all of his love.

My visit to my father had been an opportunity for a one-on-one visit with him. It occurred to me that each time I had visited over these last years, even through my mother's coldness, her alliance with my brother and sister in their lies and other such negative behavior, I felt and followed a positive energy with and from my father.

From my mother, there was nothing but coldness, emptiness, and unpredictability. From my father, I received what I needed for my heart from him, and he received what he needed in his heart from me. Despite the negativity, my visits were a win-win for both of us in that respect. I realized the negativity from the others was not in my power to change.

Letting it fall away was all I could do.

On a Friday at the end of July, I returned from two and a half weeks on business in Oklahoma, and for the next several days I resettled while preparing for my next flight out a week later for a weeklong business trip to New Mexico.

The following Tuesday I arranged to visit my parents. While driving to the house, my cell phone vibrated. I missed the call, but when I played the message, I heard my mother deliver a brief message in which she told me not to bring any cameras. She ended with, "I'm *warning* you!" I pulled over in a rest stop some miles ahead to replay it.

She was firm, demanding, hateful, and scolding. She said simply, "... and Sean, *no cameras. Don't* take any cameras over—I'm *warning* you!"

I was livid, but resolved that it could not stop me from seeing my father, and she sure as hell had no power to stop me from mounting a camera in my car. It was ridiculous.

I called back, and Mother started to yell but then took a softer tone, telling me that I could come down. As part of her typical behavioral pattern to keep one at bay, she said that she was sick and did not want to be upset. It was the same old trick of using her health to get in her last word and ensure you complied lest you be the cause of anything that happened to her. "If you want to come down, then you come down," she said. "I don't want any problems."

I told her she had to stop being the middle person and stop believing the lies. I said it even though this particular accusation had a basis in fact: I did take photos on occasion to record Patrick's attempts to impede my visits, but I would never admit to it to keep peace for my father.

"Why would you say I took pictures of their cars in front of the house?" I asked.

"Because they saw you," she replied. "They were looking out the window. They saw you taking pictures of the cars blocking the front of the house." I did not admit to it and in fact denied it, but I had to; I needed evidence he was violating the agreement not to impede my visit.

Then she hesitated and backtracked, saying, "No, *they* didn't see you take pictures—*I* did." Now she had changed her position.

"You didn't see me either," I said. "You can't walk from the kitchen to the front door in less than fifteen minutes, and it only takes a minute to walk to my car. So, tell me, how did you see me?" She fell silent.

I was angry and she knew it. "I'm calling my lawyer. I've had enough of you and your betrayals and those liars next door!" "Oh my God—oh my *God!*" she whispered.

Clearly, she was thinking about the possible outcome. This would reveal a consistent pattern of behavior that they effectively concealed from the external world—and in this case, that could again involve the law. She was clearly worried.

She left a message on behalf of my brother, doing as she had since the restraining order had been served and acting as my brother's "agent." I was silent as I listened. She asked if I was still there, and for a moment, I remained silent. "You hung up," she said, and then she hung up.

I called back a few moments later and told her that today was not a good day for me to visit and that I would look at my schedule for Thursday. She was very soft-spoken and said OK.

I was also thinking this might be the opportunity I had waited for. By accident I had deleted the voice message, but she did not know that. If I played my cards right, I could put the fear of the law in her to help her stop the demons, stop making me the family scapegoat, and stop everything she was doing. Although I did not have a recording of the voice message, I did take a photo of the "Received" call from her on my cell phone. It was all I had.

Whether or not they had been discussing the potential outcome of me having said I was contacting my attorney, I could not be certain.

But it was my hope they were afraid—very afraid.

A Dichotomy of Evil

"Love all, trust a few, do wrong to no one."

– WILLIAM SHAKESPEARE

I have used the word "evil" in this book so many times I have lost count. I have reason to believe I have seen its face expressed in human form in that unmistakable, chilling look of venom.

While I read dozens of informative books, one in particular was so profoundly influential and eye-opening that it forms much of the basis for this chapter: *People of the Lie: The Hope for Healing Human Evil* by Dr. M. Scott Peck.

Dr. Peck states, "Evil has nothing to do with *natural* death; it is concerned only with *unnatural* death, with murder of the body or spirit."

The courts, the law, and the general population view murder only in the physical sense in the taking of a life. Can a consistent pattern of abuse designed with the intent to cause non-physical harm that leaves no outward scars, yet designed to destroy the spirit of another person (or persons) be considered evil?

The answer, to me, is obviously yes.

My mother, sister, brother, and sister-in-law strove to break my spirit which included those in my life. To delve at any length into my views on moral or cultural relativism, or to emphasize my research and personal studies on the psychology of evil isn't really necessary.

We're gifted as humans. If during our daily interactions with another person, the instinctive nature of our internal radar locks on to feelings, even in passing, as revulsion, confusion, a momentary loss of mental balance, a sudden emotion of risk and trust, and similarly negative feelings that are not and have not been part of our lives, or a normal aspect of our character, we are likely in the presence of a person worthy of great caution.

The conscious act of disguising or attempting to conceal acts of one's abusiveness, one's severely narcissistic behavior, and any intentional action of harmful behavior to others reflects an awareness these acts are in fact harmful, and concealment is in and of itself an act of evil, to me.

The family image of respectability to the outside world was guarded like Fort Knox, but this is equally a weak link in that the act of concealment, by itself, is an admission.

BLAME THE VICTIM

We've seen blaming-the-victim in our own system of justice—it's a strategy of concealment to ascribe abusive behavior directed *toward* an abused person, to *that* person.

A woman who dresses in a revealing manner, confident in the beauty of her femininity, was not asking to be raped or worse. A person who won a million-dollar lottery was not asking to be scammed out of their winnings.

One of the most prevalent character traits I experienced was a ferocious refusal to accept responsibility on any level; "It's all *you* buddy—it's *all* you!" as my sister once said.

My father was the only one who offered to listen, but only out of plain view of the others as he did so many times. Once he heard the voice messages and we spoke over coffee, his sadness seemed to be grounded only in the acceptance of his inability to resolve the problems.

It was apparent that he was effectively silenced decades ago.

Having read several books on parenting from experts in the field, there is a consistent determination that a parent should only defend one child against the other while they are small and innocent, such as when one child shoves the other.

There is equally a determination that, as adults, a parent should never, *ever* take sides with one sibling against another, and should *never* become involved in disputes. My brother and my sister consistently ran to her for revenge and to have her inflict her punishment. I was utterly confounded in realizing we did this when we were tots—and they were *still* doing it as adults in their fifties. *All* of their acts of betrayal included collusion with my mother.

It was pretty obvious to me that when a mother betrays one child for another, she opens the box that lets out a monster.

In early 2004 when I first began my research into the behavior, I was fortunate to find an online support group that was exceptionally helpful in seeing other members—people like myself— with disturbed families, or seeing family members equally betrayed and many in similar ways.

I felt great compassion, admiration, and understanding for a woman who had a mother much as my own. In fact, the description was so strikingly similar I thought she was actually referring to my own mother.

In her story, a younger brother was told to leave the home at the turn of adulthood and was completely unequipped to do so. An older brother left home for college in a far-away state, and the daughter—that is, the sister—was the target of the mother much like I have reason to believe my sister was as a child. Verbal and psychological abuse were her mother's weapons of choice.

But there were vast differences between this woman and my sister.

My sister feared my mother and complied with all of her demands religiously.

This other woman was made to feel shame and guilt as a small child with the mother secretly proclaiming, "I sacrificed my life for you, you little bitch!" and other shame-causing verbal abuse, causing tremendous guilt in this small and innocent girl. I can comfortably believe my mother did the same to my sister.

It was of no consequence to my sister that my brother was "out there" all alone, if that were true, with no money, no profession and nowhere to go; and my father, I am absolutely certain, had no say in the matter.

Unlike my sister, this woman did not fear her mother. She complied with her mother's demands and tolerated her abuse for the sole purpose of survival. She despised her mother for throwing her brother out with nowhere to go and the treatment she endured as a small child.

Instead of merging with her mother, as my sister did with my mother, she maintained a secret relationship with her brother out of view of their mother, and maintained her sense of self.

She helped him find a place to live and provided money for rent, visited him often, and developed a meaningful sibling relationship comprised of friendship and love as it should have been. Any effort to talk with her mother about bringing her brother home was met with indignant rage. She hated being the personification of her mother's image of a perfect child, while alternatively my sister relished in the glory of such royalty and immunity to do as she pleased.

I recall when the expelled brother was home on visits at holidays and such other times, the sister did her mother's bidding in siding with the cruel demonstrations of devaluing and degrading the son and brother—but this was only in show. The secret pact between the two eventually saved their relationship, and in later years when the mother was old, the brother and sister formed an open alliance in defiance of her. The returning brother was informed, and the three siblings developed a meaningful relationship.

The mother was simply outnumbered, and the tyranny ceased.

My sister could have been the key to stability and survival in the family. She failed herself and failed her family when she accepted the false throne bestowed upon her by my mother.

If my brother was truly evicted by my mother, my sister relished too much the position of her kingdom and her territory, and the superiority and control she was given over the entire family. There was nothing more important than my mother's and sister's relationship, even if it meant destruction of the family unit. The world and everyone in it revolved around them—and only them.

From that, evil took a foothold.

FREE WILL

We are all born with free will. For the most part, people have a choice to be good or to be evildoers. Just as much, people have the free will to be honest or to lie.

My sister had the free will to refuse and resist the temptation of being placed in a position of superiority over the "family," and of refusing the power and specialness my mother erroneously placed upon her, but she did not.

While it was my mother who was responsible initially, there was a threshold and a time when my sister could have refused it. Instead, it was such a thrilling aspect of her life in the home that she kept it with her throughout her adult life.

The problem with that position, however, was that it was not real. It was false. It was fake...an illusion. The only "real" aspect of it was the evil she inflicted on those around her with her grandiosity, control freakery, sense of entitlement, lack of respect for her family, lack of boundaries for other people, and lack of remorse.

My mother achieved her goal of creating the perfect child in my sister. The symbiotic relationship they shared would remain solid as a rock for decades and allow them to wreak havoc and chaos, and to breed despair and hatred in everyone around them.

A CONTRAST OF EVIL

In my view though, there is a dichotomy of evil. The acts on September 11, 2001 were truly evil—the taking of innocent life. School shootings is another act of evil—far too many in civilized society, in my view. Earlier, I discussed my views that there are mentally healthy and mentally ill people; there are good and evil people; and that sometimes, mentally ill and evil people overlap. It would benefit humankind, I feel, if theologians and psychiatrists teamed up to probe the inner dynamics of what the world views mostly as "angry people with psychiatric problems," that I hear so often.

THE LIAR

Everyone lies. I not only agree with this statement but openly include myself in that category. Believe it or not, I lie. I would tell a child of five who draws an ugly picture how beautiful it is. I would promise the world and more to someone attempting to jump off a bridge in utter despair. If I saw a person unquestionably dying in the street, to offer a moment of comfort through love and compassion, I would tell them they would be OK. I would lie through my teeth and say anything if my very survival or that of those I love depended on it in the emotional, psychological, or physical sense.

It would be accurate, then, to say there are good lies and there are bad lies. It is my view that there is only one thing that distinguishes good lies from bad lies, and that is whether a lie is one of treachery, such as betraying trust, evading accountability or to deceive, or one with good intentions. The perpetrating members of my family had one thing in common that has been the hallmark of their existence: their lies were treacherous.

It felt good to lie; they needed to lie; they could not survive without lying.

The extensive, planned, and coordinated attacks from their lies—who would be present, who would launch it, what they would say, how they would lie for each other, who would shift the blame to whom in order to sow confusion, who would put up a decoy, how would they take the focus off themselves—were all created to celebrate and relish in a victory of the lie.

It was at times difficult, at best, to ascertain who was lying and who was offering a semblance of truth, if any. To catch one of them in a lie and confront them with it resulted in rage most of the time, which was often used as a major distraction to throw me completely off balance by providing something else to work through and focus on beyond the lie.

In the case of someone with a high number of narcissistic traits, it is referred to as *narcissistic rage*.

From my experiences, if a person with a severe problem with accountability and credibility is confronted with the truth about their lie, hostility is used as a defensive attempt to turn the tables on you. You discovered the lie and exposed them. How dare you!

Another strategy I observed was the angry and literal "finger pointer in your face" followed with a stern lecture to punctuate their anger at discovery. This lecture usually points to some semblance of a fault within you, or something minute that brought your character or intent into question even years ago, to provide some element of plausibility. The sole purpose of this is to make you back off and stop accusing them, make you doubt yourself, turn the tables on you while taking the focus off themselves, and to thereby take complete power and control over you.

It is also designed to make you fearful to confront them again in the future.

The resulting lack of credibility is so severely harmful and destructive that it permanently destroys trust, love, families, and other people's relationships. In general, it has a negative impact that hurts people—including themselves and for the long term.

To many, the truth about their behavior is so painfully shameful and repulsive, their fractured egos cannot withstand the pain, so they employ all of their resources to expel it.

No matter how strong I thought I was, I had to proceed with extreme caution.

I also learned, from efforts in researching for support, that lies are mutually cooperative. Because someone lies to you does not give power to a lie. A lie only gets its power when you *believe* it.

It is impossible to be lied to unless you are in agreement.

The motivation behind a lie, to me, goes to *intent*. Some lies are innocent and harmless, called white lies. Others are intentionally designed to employ destruction in some form or fashion to achieve a self-serving, self-righteous objective.

People undeservingly die or are put in harm's way by such lies (whether financially, emotionally, psychologically, or physically). Some lies are designed to create chaos and sow division, destroy relationships, destroy families, or change someone's life either in a worse way than it is and sometimes for the long term.

This makes some lies, and the people who delivered them, seriously dangerous.

You have every right to question a lie and the motivation behind it, and you have the right to protect yourself from a liar regardless of what the lie is, or who the liar is—including and especially a family member or someone you are bonded to by emotion. An emotional attachment is the only prerequisite to those who may believe they have power over you, your life, and your decisions. That includes a parent, sibling, lover, partner, husband or wife, and so on.

One who is not bonded to you by emotions and who attempts to chart the course of your life or decisions through lies or force, you can laugh at, or simply tell them not to slam the door on their way out.

So long as you do not hurt anyone in the process, there are no ground rules or limitations for doing what you must to protect yourself and those you love from a liar regardless of who it is.

Document everything— times, dates, places, what was said, record conversations (within legal limits of your state), and get witnesses if you need to, as well as a lawyer or the police when appropriate.

Build a support network.

MEMORY LOSS AND SELECTIVE AMNESIA (THE "I DON'T REMEMBER" STRATEGY)

It seems abundantly clear, based upon documented real-life behavior of people who ridiculously lie and deceive, that selective amnesia is a common defense mechanism designed to feign innocence, evade detection, and project a favorable self-image. Here are four brief examples:

1. In 1973, President Richard Nixon urged his chief of staff to say, "I don't recall," if he was asked to give testimony in the Watergate trial. Chief of Staff H.R. Haldeman was later charged with and convicted of perjury.

2. In February 1990, one year after his presidency ended in 1989, during hearings on the Iran-Contra affair, former President Ronald Reagan said "I *don't* remember" or "I *can't* remember" eighty-eight times in his eight hours of testimony over a secret US arms deal that traded missiles and other arms to free some Americans being held hostage by terrorists in Lebanon. The funds were also used

to support armed conflict in Nicaragua. As president, in November 1986 on national television, Reagan stated the weapons transfers did take place, but the US did not trade arms for hostages. Four months later, in March 1987 again on national television and as President, he took full responsibility.

3. In 2016 during one session of three-plus hours in a Hillary Clinton interview with the FBI over use of her private email server as secretary of state, she said she had "no recollection" over three dozen times.

4. In 2018 during his eight-hour testimony before the House Judiciary Committee on the FISA application process and spying on the Trump campaign, former FBI director James Comey answered more than two hundred questions with some variation of memory loss. He said in a reported total of two-hundred forty-five times either "I don't remember," "I don't recall," or "I don't know."

The inclusion of President Ronald Reagan in the mix is not to deceive you. It is true he said roughly eighty-eight times he could not remember ten months after he left office. In early 1994, five years after he left the White House, he confirmed in a letter to the nation that he was diagnosed with Alzheimer's. The average time for the early, mild stage of this disease to develop is two to four years, so it had developed to a large extent in 1990 at which time he could not remember. While he accepted full responsibility in March of 1987, he could not remember ten months after he left office three years later, in 1990. The moderate, middle stage takes two to ten years. Alzheimer's affects the ability to remember, think, judge, problem solve, find the right words, and express one's self. He died in 2004 ten years after his announcement.

I am making two points here. The first is there are times when someone truly cannot remember. The second is that, by contrast, a conscious lie is a conscious lie. Always consider whether there is a mitigating circumstance when someone says they cannot remember something they did or said. How often have they said it in the past? Have you observed a consistent history or pattern of "forgetfulness" in this one person?

If not, there is usually some sign of a conscious lie, and the "I don't remember" message is often nothing more than an elaborate yet feeble-minded cover-up.

From my experiences, people wedded to dishonesty in the pursuit of self-service at the expense of others (or a particular person) cannot achieve their objective of projecting an image of virtuousness (which is a pretense and thus another lie) without a certain level of deception and self-deception—that is, they lie to everyone, including and especially to themselves.

THE HYPOCRITE

Hypocrites are similar to liars simply because they disavow their own bad behavior. This sends a false signal designed to mislead one into thinking they are virtuous when they are not. The employment of condemnation toward a targeted individual gains reputational benefits while making the perpetrator(s) appear virtuous at the expense of those they condemn.

Misrepresenting one's moral character angers honest people. One study showed that people dislike hypocrites more than liars. This is because what a hypocrite *says* is inconsistent with what they *demonstrate*. The purpose of misrepresenting oneself is always designed to conceal.

Liars and hypocrites both have the potential to cause great damage to others, and interactions with them should be considered only after determining what personal information to share with them.

It has been published by experts, and makes perfect sense, that those emotionally closest to you have the potential to cause the greatest damage.

THE INFAMOUS "SEVEN DEADLY SINS"

My belief that Satan was at work in my family, in some ways, remains foremost in my mind and with good reason. While I could not possibly ascertain whether their evil was human or demonic, I can only describe the look upon my mother's face more than once—the one I have never been able to duplicate.

While I loved her, it was her demons I hated. My love for God, for His knowledge, and my need and fight for truth have equally been my anchors.

A popular book on narcissism by Dr. Sandy Hotchkiss, which I discovered on Amazon and highly recommend, is known by the title *Why Is It Always About You?: The Seven Deadly Sins of Narcissism*. Notwithstanding the Bible, the seven deadly sins—lust, gluttony, greed, sloth, wrath, envy, and pride—are also primary traits of narcissism.

With respect to my family, four out of seven is not a good sign.

GETTING HELP AND FINDING CLOSURE

For me, writing this book has been therapeutic and has offered a measure of closure that I would never have had without reading dozens of books on narcissism, parenting, lie detection, and behavioral science that helped me immensely through the maze of confusion.

My therapeutic sessions were of immense benefit to my understanding, and offered some level of solace that there was absolutely nothing I could do to help my family beyond my extensive attempts year after year.

Through writing and re-reading this book in its entirety, reliving every betrayal, every disappointment, every moment of anguish and frustration, and experiencing again the painfulness of a family that destroyed itself, I can now see I tried to redeem the unredeemable.

It did not work, and it would never work.

The conscienceless are adept at conditioning others to behave as they want them to behave, to manipulate others to achieve their own ends, and ultimately to not only get what they want, but to portray themselves as the victim in the process.

21

Signs of Transformations

2010-2017

"The memory of the just is blessed: but the name of the wicked shall rot."

— PROVERBS 10:7

I was away again for most of 2010 on business. Another year of constant travel had made the decade pass quickly. My profession gave new meaning to the adage "time flies," but time wasn't the only thing that had flown; I had logged more than five hundred thousand sky miles and four trips around the planet.

My visits to my parents in between business trips were largely uneventful, primarily because many of my trips were a month or more in duration by this time, juggling multiple-state locations, so my visits were less frequent.

I recall thinking peace had finally come from my brother.

Until one day in early September.

After a visit to my parents, while walking to my car which was, as usual, parked across the street, my brother yelled out from the house, "Well, well, well, well, well!" five times in rapid succession, yet he was nowhere to be seen. He was obviously lurking in the shadows. His contemptuous tone was similar to the one that had prompted me to dial 911 two years earlier.

I did not respond and continued to my car, climbed in and drove away. A feeling came over me that I dismissed, but to a degree I felt my brother was, and had often, been stalking me.

Later that month, I visited my parents again the day before I departed for North Carolina on another three-week business trip. Standing in the kitchen in my usual position—by the sink in plain view of front and rear entrance doors, I saw my brother walk up the rear deck stairs into his rear house door. Abruptly, he yelled again the same word five times as he had earlier in the month: "Well, well, well, well, well!" He was not as loud as he had been the first time, because our parents were there, I assume, but he said it with the same contempt in his tone.

These were the only two overt acts of vocal aggression that happened in 2010, although I continued to receive occasional aberrant phone calls with hammering sounds followed by an abrupt hang-up. I can only deduce that my frequent business trips and extended absences that year prompted him to be surprised by my presence, and the bizarre "Well, well, well, well, well" was analogous to saying, "Well, looky who's here!"

For the last three months of the year, I continued to visit my parents on my brief returns.

On one visit, it was more pronounced that my father was slowly declining in his health. My parents were both getting older and even more frail, although my father showed deeper and more rapid signs of aging than my mother. He was unable to walk without a cane now, and was also using a walker at this point much like my mother. His steps were short, and he spent most of his days in bed "relaxing."

November was quiet, and my travel was complete for the year in early December. I arranged to have a cocktail and appetizers with my sister at the Harp and Crown near her place of work but unsure why; it was more of the same. You think I would have stopped having faith in her seeing the light by now.

My intent was to suggest the family get together for Christmas in view of our parents' advanced age and health, and try to make at least one Christmas better than the past six, at least for their sake. Our discussion went well up to the point when Kayleigh brought up the current and past family situation.

As always, the diamond stylus was once again dropped on the broken record. I reiterated the dynamics of the family existed long before I came home from military service, and I was drawn into it. Frustrated with that truthful response, she hurriedly gathered her bag and keys and said she was leaving. I changed the topic and she settled back down.

The truth continued to be too painful for her. Nevertheless, this was how she "prevailed" in pathologizing any discussion.

During the course of our conversation, she said bad things went on with my brother and his wife I did not know about. I was never made aware of every specific detail between both sides of the home, but I was surprised when she said the only way the problems might be over was when our parents were either gone and everyone split up, or someone was dead.

This adequately conveyed the severity of the hatred in the family, at least in my view, especially the long-standing hatred between my sister and my brother and his wife. I deduced that Kayleigh was merely making a statement that something drastic, a life crisis of some sort, had to happen before the issues would be resolved.

From my perspective, resolution would only come with acknowledgment of their decades-long behavior and explanations for their treatment, and their objective. At least that was what I would require to resolve anything on a meaningful level.

They had a lot of explaining to do.

The remainder of December was quiet, with the exception that I met a wonderful woman on a dating site. Bianca was vibrant and happy, a hardworking single mother and project management professional who had a daughter in her early twenties. Bianca never married, and I recall thinking, *"Thank God, no ex-husbands to deal with!"*

Bianca was slightly shorter than me at five feet, six inches, with auburn hair she wore in well-placed waves. Her tan skin and dark brown eyes made her appear to be of Italian descent, but she was Irish. She kept herself toned and in good physical condition. Her perfectly applied makeup made her utterly gorgeous.

She had class, and was very feminine.

We dated for many months, and I cringed at the thought of telling her about my family, let alone bringing her to the house to meet my parents. As I gradually made her aware of the situation, she did not seem disturbed by it, I think now because she had never experienced this kind of behavior in her past and had no idea of its severity.

But she was going to find out. That would be inevitable.

I had great hopes that with my parents aging and their deteriorating condition, that the proverbial light would come on in my brother's traitorous mind and he would stop. I also hoped 2011 would be a better year, as I had hoped with past New Year transitions.

In some respects, it would be; something was without question changing in my mother and sister, but the status quo would remain solid as a rock from my brother.

At the end of 2010 my job changed. The program I had worked for in the air force for nine years was winding down and it was time for me to find other work. It was a reprieve of sorts, but because I loved the work, I hoped to get back into the program again one day. I did not mention this change to my family. For one thing, I believed it was of little importance, and for another, I learned from experience that the less they knew about my life, the better for me.

I moved to another defense program with no travel involved—a well-earned reprieve.

PERSONAL TRANSFORMATIONS

During 2011, visits to my family continued to be largely uneventful. In fact, both my mother and my sister showed signs of continued transformation in their behavior. They were essentially behaving as any other mother and sister should—warm, open, communicative, responsive, kind, thoughtful, and exceptionally friendly. I welcomed this change and it brought some level of peace, but from experience I knew that when they were nice, I needed to be more guarded.

Clearly, something was definitely amiss.

In mid-July, my sister informed me that our mother had been diagnosed with cancer—four malignant tumors—and she was placed on medication. Due to her age and health condition, surgery was high risk and out of the question.

My mother and sister continued to show signs of transforming and treated me as a son, a brother and friend, and not as an enemy. I had a sense from occasional comments, that my mother was reluctant to support my brother's behavior and it was pissing him off. For the first time, they were focused on his treatment of *them*.

Ironically, on several visits this year, as I was either arriving or about to depart, my brother happened to be pulling out of his driveway and in his car. It was purely coincidental timing to happen more than once, but looking toward me in my car each time, he would hold up his middle finger.

I never returned the gesture, nor did I permit him to see that I noticed. If it was attention he wanted, he was not getting it from me.

With my relationship between my mother and sister seemingly changing for the better and this pattern being sustained now for some months, I felt confident about visiting my parents without calling in advance as I once did. *If my brother had a problem with it*, I thought, *so what?*

For most of 2011 my father was always cold, even during the searing heat and humidity of summer. Little did I know it was part of the "process" of dying. He continued to spend his days in bed and for some months to come—nearly all day every day. He was shutting down, slowly withering, not eating much, and sleeping most of his days. He could barely walk even with a cane and needed help with basic tasks.

Both of my parents would soon be under hospice care, with nurses coming in several times a week for my father, and a couple of times per week for my mother.

THE HOME FRONT: MORE OF THE SAME

Patrick continued to avoid me so there was no direct conflict, but that was not what the legal agreement was about. The agreement was not about total avoidance; I didn't have a problem interacting with him so long as he behaved himself. *So be it,* I thought.

But it was more of the same from my brother even as my father's health was deteriorating. In late spring 2011, I was parking my car across the street and backing into a space. Coincidentally, it was another of those occasions in which my brother just happened to be pulling out of his driveway as I was arriving and parking across the street.

While he was waiting for passing cars before turning onto the street, we were essentially facing each other. When he did pull out, he turned to look my way, and I saw him again raise his middle finger. I made sure he did not see me notice him. Knowing it must be painful to be denied attention, I was actually enjoying ignoring him.

How infantile, I thought. *Not even as our father is dying can this son of a bitch change.*

My visit was pleasant as were many others that year. Just before I left, I asked Kayleigh about the children and how they were, telling me they were fine and offered the name of the town my niece, Michaela, lived in, which was a couple of towns south of my parents'. Patrick Jr. still lived at home.

She then said, "Patrick has pulled me into this thing between you and him." I was uncertain what she meant or how he had pulled her in, nor did she explain further. Nevertheless, my sister saw this as an opportunity to express her belief that she was "in the middle of it."

She just did not or could not see that she had *always* been in the middle of it.

On a visit one day in August, my sister said she was planning to retire in a few months, and remain home full time to care for our parents. They were certainly declining, and with my mother's cancer and other health issues they required full-time care. They continued to treat me well during my visits and I recall wishing it had been so from the very beginning.

Though I remained extremely cautious, this showed me that it could have been possible for none of the acrimony to have transpired over these past many years.

On a Friday later that month, I received a voice message at home from a county in the southeastern part of the state. The county name appeared on my caller ID; it was the county my niece lived in. I thought she wasn't speaking to me, and I certainly had no enemies down that way (or anywhere for that matter, except of course, at "home.") My internal radar was telling me I should suspect that she or her father had made the call.

This call was significantly different from the others. It was not a person as far as I could tell, or hammering or gunshot sounds as in the several I had received in the past. This one comprised a derogatory phrase in rapid succession: "Eat shit—eat shit—eat shit." It seemed almost like a mechanical voice, like one may find on a device bought from a joke shop. But it could have also been a human voice.

I transferred the message to a microcassette tape and mailed it to my attorney, and added it to my collection. What mattered was not only whether Patrick or my niece made the call, but if they had the capacity to do so.

The answer was obviously yes on both counts.

I decided to perform a reverse phone number lookup online, and discovered the call was made from a pay phone *in* the town my niece lived. I thought, *In this day and age, who makes calls from pay phones? Do they even still have pay phones?* It appeared deliberately targeted to me and, as with the others, was left after my twenty-second voice message greeting. I tried to reject any thought that my niece would do this, but could not have been certain.

After Kayleigh retired, I offered to do what I could to help if she needed it, realizing any support she may have had from my brother and his wife would be limited if any at all. The improvement in my relationship with my mother and sister was such that I was comfortable visiting, although not without the occasional signs of my sister supporting my brother's position and helping keep the children distant from me.

The current environment of seemingly peaceful and stress-free visits would remain so for the rest of 2011 and into 2012.

Until early summer.

I innocently asked my sister how my niece and nephew were as I often did. She responded as she has in the past—they were both doing well, and not offering much beyond that.

The next day following another visit, my sister called saying she was wondering, based on my query, if I had any plans to contact my niece. I told her I was not and that I was just asking how they were, adding that I didn't know how to reach them regardless.

She firmly asked me not to make any effort to contact my niece "because," she said, "there will be hell to pay in this house if you do. We'll answer for it"—meaning her, my mother, and father. She was adamant about this.

I saw nothing changed in all this time, except that I sensed a major rift between my mother and sister, and brother and his wife, and perhaps fear...fear from the certain hell my sister, mother and father would endure should I make an effort to contact my niece or nephew.

So now my brother was into the *sustainment* phase. Sustain the physical and emotional distance between myself and the children, at any cost, to preserve the deception. That required all family members to join in the effort—or else.

In late summer, my father was showing clear signs of deterioration. He was now in bed, not really responsive when awake, asleep most of the time, and perhaps unaware as it seemed. He could only be hand-fed, his breathing was labored, and from lack of nourishment he was little more than skin and bones. It was heartbreaking watching him enter the final stages of his life.

My sister was actually calling me more frequently. On several occasions, she would tell me I should come down—like *now*. One day early in the second week of September, she called and told me the hospice nurse had said "any time". I had a suitcase packed and had arranged reservations at a hotel just minutes from the house. I would stay there when the time came.

Upon my arrival at the house, I laid next to him, holding his hand in hopes he would know it was I who whispered in his ear, "Thank you, Dad. I love you—I've always loved you."

A certified nursing assistant was present helping my sister with my father's needs and tending to him. Later that afternoon while kneeling at my father's side, my niece and brother entered the bedroom. Michaela went to my mother's side of the bed and kissed her goodnight while my brother stood at the threshold of the kitchen and bedroom—just observing.

Was he there to guard his daughter from the big, bad wolf (namely, me), or to ensure there was no contact between us? I doubt a twentysomething niece, kissing her grandmother goodnight, needed a watchdog.

It was the first time I had seen Michaela in seven years. At the moment, though, I stayed focused on my father.

On a Friday I arrived at the house at nearly eight o'clock in the morning and sat on the bed by my father the entire morning. I could look in his eyes and see movement, and I wondered if he could see that I was there. There was no outward indicator of his awareness. Holding his hand, I again whispered in his ear that I loved him. I would often feel his grip, weak as it was, but he was equally holding my hand.

My mother lay with my father into early afternoon. His breathing was more laborious and the entire family was in the house at this time—distant, emotionally cold, but there.

By midafternoon my mother noticed his hand was bluish. She called to my sister who called the hospice nurse and requested someone come right away.

At just about five o'clock in the afternoon, my mother, crying profusely, proclaimed, "He's gone—oh God, why did you take him?"

And he was.

My father was surrounded by his family. Lying quietly on his side facing my mother, he departed peacefully. Representatives from the funeral home arrived two hours later and prepared my father for his final departure from the house. A representative from the church and two hospice nurses were also present.

At the moment of my father's death, as he lay on his side facing my mother, I walked over and touched him. Looking at him, I noticed in the corner of his eye the wetness of a small puddle had formed on the side of his nose. I wondered, at that moment as he departed, whether he knew his family was there with him.

Did he cry because he finally had the one thing he wanted as he soared to heaven, but never received in this life? Or was the puddle a result of some physical process of departing?

I do not know the answer.

What I did know was that any anger I had ever felt was tempered only by my profound sadness that my father was gone.

The next day was no less difficult. We planned to be at the funeral home to discuss arrangements, but my sister called to say that my mother had requested a representative come to the house instead. She was in no physical or emotional condition to go anywhere.

The representative arrived early afternoon, and for the next hour my mother, sister, brother, and I relayed our personal perspectives of my father at the kitchen table, which were essentially the same. The meeting was cordial, but you could have cut the tension with a knife.

Of course, because someone outside of the family was present, Kayleigh, Patrick, and my mother were complete angels. Having completed the initial planning arrangements, the representative departed, as did I. There was more work to be done and information to be provided before the obituary was published and arrangements were finalized, but my sister, brother, niece, and I worked diligently, and separately, to complete them.

My father's obituary appeared in the paper the following day. I notified my attorney and my friends and colleagues.

Monday was a sullen day. I woke up tired and drained of energy. The one-hour private family viewing of my father at the funeral home was later that day. I would meet the family there. My sister called me that morning and offered dinner that night with her and my mother after the viewing. She said she knew I was alone, and if I didn't want to eat by myself at the hotel I could come over. It was a nice gesture. I accepted, and it was a good visit.

My mother was in a confused state I think from the anxiety medication she was taking. Believing my father had died that same day, she wanted to make notification phone calls. My sister repeatedly told her the calls had been made and that Dad had died three days earlier—not today. *She requires constant attention,* I thought.

At the funeral parlor, it was expected that my mother would break down, which she did upon her first look upon the open casket. Tears filled the eyes of some members of the family; I remained alert in case my mother needed swift action or help.

I walked to and kneeled on the pedestal to pray by my father, and I touched him. *The funeral parlor had performed excellent work on him,* I thought, and I expressed my thanks and gratitude to the director.

My niece and nephew brought in the four collages they had made of my father, which were very nicely prepared. I assisted the representatives briefly in arranging room for them, but found myself wandering back to the casket. My son had sent a beautiful arrangement of roses, and sitting on the casket were flowers from my niece and nephew. My father held rosary beads and was dressed in his customary suit and tie, the same dapper outfit he would have worn if he were simply going to the grocery store.

There was a large turnout for my father's wake. I saw many people I had grown up with, old friends I hadn't seen in more than thirty years, as well as colleagues from my current and former jobs.

On one occasion, near the casket, I asked my sister about some of the things positioned on a table that were not familiar to me, and my niece, sitting quietly next to my mother, answered what they were. I acknowledged her response but there was no real conversation between us. I was surprised that she even spoke to or acknowledged me. The loss of a loved one oftentimes is the catalyst that mends broken families, but I did not feel that this was the case with my family.

They would have to come clean, and they were not about to do that.

THE MASS AND FUNERAL

The Mass for my father was incredibly sad. The casket lay in front, near the altar. The priest was an older man, gifted in his presentation, and he paid close attention to my mother. She sat in her wheelchair in the aisle next to a pew where my sister sat on the end. Next to my sister was my brother and his wife, followed by the children and the rest of the family.

My loving partner, Bianca, and I sat in the pew directly behind them.

As part of the ceremony, my brother and I each needed to walk to the pulpit and give a reading. My niece presented the eulogy, and it was apparent she put great thought and emotion into its writing. As part of a Catholic Mass, a point comes where parishioners stand and make a peace offering which is announced by the priest. Normally, people turn and offer a handshake.

Bianca and I stood in the pew as this part of the Mass concluded, expecting my brother and his wife to turn and offer their hands since they were directly in front of us, but that was not to be, nor did they acknowledge either of us as we tried to extend our own greeting.

In the car to the cemetery, Bianca mentioned that in all the years she had been going to church—and she was for many years very active in the church—she never experienced a peace offering not being made to people in front of or directly behind her in the pews.

The motorcade to the cemetery followed a circuitous path through various towns. Waiting at the cemetery were the priest and some others. Following the interment, we went to a restaurant for dinner. Some minutes into the gathering, my brother stood up with his drink and announced a toast to our father; holding up his glass to the group, he capped the toast with a casual "Luv ya, Dad," in contrast to the more respectful "I love you, Dad."

I kept quiet, and certainly kept my thoughts to myself.

For a year before my father's passing, Kayleigh had consistently been thoughtful of me as you've read, and this continued even after his passing. Both she and my mother let me know when my mother had doctor appointments, and generally let me know about her condition without my having to ask. These were all normal aspects of a close family, but sadly it was too late for my father.

I was still curious why they were being so nice to me.

My mother remained in anguish and sadness. After sixty-five years with my father, his absence left a gaping hole in her life. It is said that one cannot be with another that long and survive for very long when their lover departs. I can understand that. She seemed to be holding up, but the fact remained that she was also aging, perhaps faster now that her husband was gone.

I'll be doing this again soon enough, I sometimes thought, and I wondered what would then become of the "family." It would be a good thing if my sister maintained the status quo between us, and helped to restore my relationship with the children. I also hoped that her kindness was through some level of altruism and not because of some pending betrayal based on the deaths of our parents.

I often thought about this, knowing full well, as I had mentioned, that it was when my family was nice that one must be most cautious.

As for my brother, I didn't know how he or Brianna could ever be trusted. I often wondered what would become of my sister, living in the same house with them when my mother was gone. For decades, our mother had been my sister's protector; without her, I imagined Kayleigh would be adrift and wandering aimlessly.

People who demonstrate severe narcissistic traits keep a mental tally and must seek revenge to "even the score." Patrick and Brianna had on several occasions indicated to me to "wait until your parents are gone," when they would be free to seek revenge regarding my sister.

There will be another battle, I was thinking, *one between them and my sister.* Their hatred, justified or not, dated back more than three decades and knowing them as well as I do, I presumed it would be a major battle.

As for my niece and my nephew, I was aware that they may be lost forever from my life and from my son's. This would depend on the degree to which their minds were poisoned, the extent of their need for truth, as well as their growth and development with minds of their own.

Even as late as October 2013, my niece continued to view me as nonexistent. As I sat at the kitchen table on one visit, she walked in. "Hi Michaela!" I proclaimed. She nonchalantly walked to my mother, who also sat at the kitchen table, gave her a hug and kiss, and then kissed my sister's cheek. With that, she walked out the back door calmly without so much as looking toward me. *She turned out just like her parents,* I thought.

The alliance with her father and mother, notwithstanding that they are her parents, will be the determinant as to how she lives her life, and how much pride and admiration she and my nephew have for their parents. If they wanted to love someone in the family, it should have been my father, and me; it was he and I who tried to bring the family together. It was also he, my father, who sustained her and her brother. Indeed, her love for her father and my father would be a dichotomy.

One was good, and one was evil.

A Generation Ends and The Final Blade

"What lies in our power to do, it lies in our power not to do."

— ARISTOTLE

In late summer of 2017, my sister informed me that she had taken my mother to the emergency room, and following a few tests she was admitted for additional testing. I took time off from work and made the round trip every day for a week to visit her.

On Easter Sunday, I visited and in casual conversation, my sister mentioned that neither my niece or nephew, brother or his wife visited my mother, sent her a card or brought her flowers during her hospital stay. Truthful or otherwise, my memory bank recalled the instinctive feeling some time ago that my mother and sister ceased participating in my brother's folly.

By contrast, Bianca and I had been visiting my mother frequently. Driving from New Jersey, we stopped and always bought cakes or chocolates that she liked. Our visits for some time now were meaningful and always loving, peculiar as they were.

My mother's condition in the hospital deteriorated over that week; she could not eat or drink anything without bringing up what she consumed. Her strength was waning and a feeding tube, in her late nineties, was not an option. Ultimately, after a few days of consultations, the doctors said there was nothing they could do but tend to her comfort.

The message was unmistakable.

She remained in good spirits and was alert, but it would be several days before she was sent home. The following day, I stood by my mother's hospital bed with my sister, and my brother and his wife walked in. The doctor and a nurse followed.

Looking upward and pointing her finger toward me, she announced, "He's my backbone;" then she pointed to my brother, standing at the foot of her bed, and said, "He's my bodyguard." It occurred to me that bodyguards have honor; want their own piece of the pie, and want the competition to do their own thing. Bullies, by contrast, are mean-spirited and are relentless looking out for themselves and their own self-interests; they want it all to themselves and want the competition to go away—by any means necessary.

The thought passed quickly as my focus remained on the environment.

Mother was released for home care the next day. It was just a brief time that, while she was comfortable, she became unresponsive. Her eyes remained closed, her breathing was labored, and the unmistakable "death rattle" was prevalent. I thought she might have a few days left, but less than eight hours after being placed in her own bed, she was gone.

The wake some days later reintroduced me to people I had not seen since my father's funeral, both family and old friends. My sister made a collage showcasing my mother's life in photos, from her birth through adulthood and her marriage to my father, and the birth of their three children. My niece, with help from her parents, built two collages showcasing to the audience how special *they* were.

Every photo was of them or their parents with my parents—none with me or with my sister. Off to the side of one collage was my niece's wedding album.

From their perspective, there was no one in my parents' life *but* them.

MOTHER'S FINAL WORDS

Several weeks after the funeral, arrangements were made for my mother's estate attorney to read the will which was read at the house. The attorney shuffled her papers and, between her and my sister, could not find the most current will. I sat quietly and waited.

"Well, I have the 2004, 2006, 2007, 2008, and 2009 versions," my sister said, "but they're copies. I don't have the current one, the 2015 version. I looked everywhere."

The attorney said she did not have it either, but ultimately shuffled through her folder and found it. This was the first time I became aware that there were six versions of the will. I had never seen any of them, and while my sister and brother certainly knew about them and were aware of what they said, they were clearly kept from me.

There was good reason for that.

The 2015 version, the current will, expressed our mother's final words. Patrick received one half of the house while my sister received the other half. At the time of my mother's passing, the house was valued at just over $525,000—more than half a million dollars.

With respect to me, what my mother had told me years earlier on that fateful day in February 2004, was they would buy me out of one third of the home value. Now, my sister and my brother each would provide me with $25,000 ($50,000 total). The lawyer offered suggestions if they did not have the money, for example, taking out a loan or mortgage.

"I'm not doing that!" my brother exclaimed loudly.

"I'm not doing that either!" my sister followed immediately.

It was obvious, despite the intense hatred for each other, that they were still aligned when it came to me. The fifty thousand dollars equated to just under ten percent of the house value.

The attorney continued by stating a provision that anyone contesting the will would only be entitled to receive one dollar.

There was the poison pill...the final blade.

In legal terms, such a provision is called an *in terrorem* clause because its sole intent is to frighten potential heirs from initiating any action to attempt a bigger share of the estate. The literal meaning of *in terrorem* is just that, to strike terror. This is not surprising since my mother had done just that ever since my return from military service.

I doubt any two people receiving $237,000 each (the house value minus $25,000) would feel unfairness and challenge the provisions.

To challenge a will in this state, you must have standing. That means you must have some interest in the outcome of the challenge. This provision often limits challengers to those who were beneficiaries under a prior will that gave them better rights or those who would inherit under state law if there was no will.

For example, if you left one third of your home value to your son in a previous will but considerably less in your most recent will, he would have standing to challenge. This may be worth the risk unless, like myself, the son was not permitted to know what previous wills said while other beneficiaries were aware. This was by design in my case—that is obvious.

If a deceased person (i.e., my mother) was in a weakened state and under pressure from a caregiver (i.e., my sister) to change her will, I could contest the new will based on the undue influence of her caregiver. But that would mean the standard of proof in a will contest is a "preponderance of the evidence," which means that there must be *more* evidence supporting a challenge that there was undue influence than there is evidence not supporting it.

I had no intent to challenge the will, though not because I do not have the evidence. I have years of accumulated media, anonymous letters, outright hate mail, dozens of voice messages from my brother and sister that would lead anyone of sound mind and reasoning ability to conclude, without a single question of doubt, that they unduly influenced my parents when it came to me—and for a very, very long time.

It is not beyond the realm of possibility that my brother and sister tried to make my parents disinherit me entirely. From my years of research, I discovered that a common situation for a sibling with narcissistic tendencies is to ingratiate the parent who holds the wealth, so that they become a confidant and ultimately that sibling becomes the favored and trusted one.

This is testament to the alliance my sister and mother shared from my sister's childhood.

On that day long ago when I saw my mother slapping herself in the face after leaving my sister's room, there was a pathology taking place, some sort of conditioning if you will, to my sister. The absence of real love from my mother to my sister, as far as I can tell from this one incident, may have compelled my sister to self-soothe, to create a substitute—namely, herself.

During the reading, the attorney innocently mentioned that my brother, in his early sixties, would have a long life before he expired with respect to taking out a mortgage to pay me twenty-five thousand dollars. His tone became loud and angry as he described in detail that he had had several strokes and bouts of cancer. "I spent two weeks in the hospital with internal bleeding! I could live for years or I could die tomorrow, so don't tell me I have a long time! We don't know that!" he spat. I sat quietly.

I am no medical expert, but his conditions could have been genetic. My mother had a bad heart for years and a pacemaker like thousands of elderly people, but never a heart attack as far as I know. She also had cancer, but it did not affect her as it has others.

Then again, his strokes, and his wife had one, too, I am told, could have resulted from their normal state of hatefulness and need for "revenge"—day in and day out, week after week, month after month, year after year, decade after decade—every waking hour. The constant negative energy that comes with lying, contriving, formulating constant coverups, planning attacks in some form or other, and maintaining a constant awareness to avoid being revealed was likely also a great challenge.

Living a dark and vile life must certainly take a toll on a healthy body.

As soon as the will was read and he signed a form, my brother went out the door and back to his house without a word—I assume satisfied with his victorious achievement. The attorney left, and I left after a brief discussion with my sister.

The will reading had not sunk in yet, but I felt confused.

During my last fifteen minutes at the house, my sister abruptly stated, "Screw it. If you ever come back down, I will move my car farther back in the driveway and you can park there. Forget that shit about parking your car across the street!"

Having been forced for more than two decades to park my car across the street to keep peace in my life, based in the first place on my sister's hostility over it and my mother's incessant nagging that it was in her way—*now* she would make room for my car?

I realize now this offer was just a means to placate me to help minimize the betrayal of the one-third inheritance—her statement was an attempt to distract me. Now that Kayleigh was victorious, it was time to soothe the intentional wounds after years of abuse. The attorney was just an unwitting tool to employ their betrayal. I'm sure the smear campaign extended to those in power positions who could help them achieve their objective. Had she been made aware of their abuse of me these past decades, she may have been reluctant to be part of the deception.

Nevertheless, it is a common strategy of those targeting someone for betrayal to use anyone, especially someone who has some level of power, to do their bidding. What better way for my siblings to seal their objective of material and financial wealth than to convince the lawyer I was the black sheep—as they did with so many others—the bad son and no-good brother who caused all the problems in the family?

During my drive back to New Jersey my sister sent a text to ask if I was OK. This was just yet another attempt to soothe the wound, and I knew that. I pulled over and called her anyway. It was apparent she was putting out a feeler likely from some level of guilt.

"Well, I'm a bit confused," I said. It was lopsided, and I did not expect it; this was not what had been said in 2004, which, though cruel at the time, felt generous in retrospect. "Mother said I would get one third after she and Dad passed away."

Her response was, "I don't know how, but I'll make it up to you."

"And how do you plan to do that?" I asked.

"Well," she said, "half of the house is mine, and the lawyer *did* say I can do whatever I want with it. I can leave it to *you* in *my* will."

That is just great, I thought to myself. *I have to hope I live longer than you, which might or might not happen in the next twenty years, and I could be eighty years old. What would I do with it then?*

She also said there was $4,500 remaining in a separate account my mother had that were residual funds from the funeral arrangements, and she would send me half, which she did. In the enclosed note explaining the check, she added two keywords, *as promised*. Of course, this was only to emphasize how good she was being to me. It was more of the same old tactic I had seen so many times: grease the knife or slam it in, then soothe the gaping wound.

Their betrayal, I had come to realize for all these years, was always about the inheritance.

I would be remiss if I did not mention a visit in the mid-2000s when my mother and sister demanded to know how much money my monthly military retirement pay was. Red flags warned me not to disclose it, so I did not.

I firmly believe there was good reason for that query; it was part of the consideration as to how much my sister believed my mother and/or father should leave to me. It is not something I believe my mother would think of on her own accord.

Considering the fact that my brother blasted me the day I retired from the armed forces for allegedly not giving him five dollars when we were kids, his blaming me for "making" him spend sixty thousand dollars on cocaine, and the demands from my mother and sister to know how much my military retirement pay brought it all into focus.

There had always been an underlying financial motive to their smear campaign, and it could not have been more precisely connected to their behavior.

Over the coming days, as I was able to think more clearly, I initiated several text message exchanges with my sister that only showed more of her evasiveness. I was certainly curious what each of the wills said, and asked if she could make me a copy of them.

I waited more than ten days with no response. Since she and I had actually had a good relationship for the past five years (or so I thought) and she typically would have responded to my text the same day, it was now obvious it did not benefit her or my brother to let me see the wills. The objective had always been to wait until one of my parents passed, and then manipulate the surviving parent to meet their objective. Being good to me the past five years, in my mind, served only to throw me off the trail; to make me unsuspecting.

She finally responded that she understood my anger, and emphasized she had nothing to do with it, further stating it was my mother's will, not hers, and she felt bad that "you feel this way" about her. As she always did when soothing her willful wounds, she punctuated that she would always be there for me.

She emphasized, "Our parents worked it on their own at the lawyer's office, and the one-dollar provision may have been a recommendation from the lawyer." The truth is, my mother, and more than that my father, would never have thought of it on their own.

This was such a lame lie it was ridiculous. I learned long ago that assuming the opposite of what she said was where the truth would be. The pattern of distancing herself from the success of her betrayals had long been established.

In 2004 my father was in his early nineties. I can assure you, the unbiased reader, he did not drive my ailing mother, unable to walk, two towns away by himself on six occasions from 2004 to 2012—the year of his death, at which time he was nearly one hundred.

A more realistic scenario is that the lawyer came to the house on all six occasions to revise my parent's wills, and without a doubt my brother and/or sister were at the table "helping" them. If that was not the case and my parents went to the lawyer's office, someone drove them.

Wherever the meetings occurred, it would be sheer stupidity for me to believe my sister and brother did not have some part in the process.

My mother had proven many times she would *never* make a decision without my sister's concurrence, insistence, or input. There was never any question about that.

OK, so she claims innocence, I thought. *In that case, she has nothing to hide and has no reason to not provide me a copy of the 2004, 2006, 2007, 2008, and 2009 wills.* I sent another text again asking for a copy of them and waited another five days with no response, but instead received an envelope with a check for $4,500 and a note saying, in part, "There are no copies of past wills. The lawyer asked me to give them to her so she can destroy them."

How convenient, I thought. She had them all these years and no longer had them when I asked for them. Nevertheless, she knew what they said. I thought about asking her, but concluded that surely, she would have developed the standard amnesia (the "I Don't Remember Strategy") that liars employ.

It was not beneficial to put myself through the same deceptive and evasive behavioral responses with which I was all too familiar.

While I had as much right to know what was in them as she did, she always placed herself in a position of power and control—often providing deception by omission as a means of plausible deniability—and always designed to keep the truth of her betrayals at bay.

This recent interaction with my sister also had an effect on Bianca, who shared a meaningful friendship of sorts with my sister on our visits. Bianca has a loving and lasting friendship with her two sisters and brother, and has all of their lives. They would never conceive of this type of betrayal—evidenced by the fact that her parents' wills were divided equally among the children.

Prior to my mother's passing, even knowing well my experiences with my family, Bianca held that my sister was being nice to me and appeared to have changed toward me. She mentioned Kayleigh meeting and becoming part of *her* family after my parents were gone, primarily because she was aware my sister would have no one when my parents passed.

Bianca now had a different view.

"It makes too much sense that their treatment of you was not all about the inheritance—the financial and material gain for them makes it too obvious to deny," she said. She would also eventually tell me, "Neither my brother, my sisters, or myself would ever think of doing that to each other, or treating you like they did. Your sister and I don't really have anything in common, and I'm not going to live in lies."

THE TRUTH ALWAYS COMES OUT IN THE END

As a matter of practice, I have always been aware of my personal information on the internet. Every few months for years I would search my name, locate websites that revealed my personal information, and elect to opt out of them. I simply enjoy my right to privacy.

In early January 2019 I did this again. In a search of my name, I noticed a link with my brother's and sister's names and was curious. I discovered my brother put up for sale his half of the home with an asking price of more than $150,000 above the property value. *Greedy bastard*, I thought. *He'll never get that much.*

The page took several minutes to load. Once it did, I saw that it was a huge spreadsheet of home sales in the area that included the city or town, address of the property, state, names of the seller and buyer, the price and date of the sale, and the residence type.

This public document, readily available on the internet, revealed my sister bought out my brother for his asking price—more than $150,000 above his half of the property value.

Recalling the day my mother's will was read and immediately following the poison pill meant for me, my sister made a complaint, in front of the attorney, about how much property taxes were going up. This also followed both her and my brother's adamancy to the attorney and to me that they were not going to take out a mortgage or loan to pay me twenty-five thousand dollars each.

But in whatever way, she had one hundred and fifty thousand more to give to him.

These were just feeble efforts to make me believe they would face a financial crisis when in fact they were working together to throw me off the scent.

She achieved victory in securing her prize, and he achieved his.

A FINAL PARENTAL LESSON

There is no such thing as a golden child, a queen or a king among siblings. For a parent to make such a designation toward one child is a major failure in parental responsibility, and sows the seeds of betrayal in their children.

Parents who abdicate their power to a child, as my mother did to my sister, in order for that child to rule over the others, or the entire family, reflects an even deeper parental failure, and maps out a lifetime of destructive behavior for the family as a whole.

The one lesson I tried hard and without success to instill in my mother was that parents have siblings so one is not alone when parents pass away. My mother would only look at me with silent indignation. Even though she saw what was happening to the family for decades, she either did not or could not see it, or just did not care.

My mother's passing into the next life left behind the decaying carcasses of my brother, his wife, and my sister. As loving as I had seen my mother at times, and knew was always somewhere in her, she was the model *stage* mother, a one-time super-narcissist who cowrote, coproduced, and codirected decades-long performances of chaos and havoc that could never be reversed. She could not have done it alone, either. She had a willing, fearful fan club.

SIBLING JEALOUSY

From my research, it is not unusual for one sibling to express some level of jealousy toward another sibling—but when they are small children. While this is relatively harmless, it can bring out the worst should it develop into and be compounded with envy later in life.

For many years now, I have enjoyed the meaningfulness of a loving relationship that was only made possible by keeping Bianca away from my family as much as I could with some exceptions. I have learned, through therapy and research, of the concept of "found family." While we don't get to choose our biological families, we do get to choose the members of our found family who might be a mix of blood relatives, friends, and partners, all of whom create a safe and nurturing space for all to grow and to love one another as a "family".

Bianca, her daughter, Nora, and the rest of her family are now my family, and my son has promised he will raise his children, my grandson and granddaughter, in such a manner as to create the family my father deserved as a way to honor his memory and his life. My son and my grandchildren are in the best position to recreate the family in a meaningful way that both my father and I wanted. In these many years since my father died, I still see him in my mind's eye the countless times he approached me; an old, dying, yet loving man, eyes welling with tears, lower lip trembling and pleading with me, begging me to fix the family he wanted.

As I think back to those heartbreaking moments knowing there was nothing I could do, and that I never stood a chance, I still cry for him.

Acknowledgments

"Writing a book is an adventure. To begin with, it is a toy and an amusement; then it becomes a mistress, and then it becomes a master, and then a tyrant. The last phase is that just as you are about to be reconciled to your servitude, you kill the monster, and fling him out to the public."

— SIR WINSTON CHURCHILL

There are many people I wish to thank for helping me decide whether I should proceed with this book or whether it would be a fruitless endeavor. First, I thank my therapist, Jim. I began working with him in 1992, after a few short weeks in my parents' home taught me I would need an anchor in the storm, and without his intent listening, guidance, insight, and understanding for many years, I would never have been able to maintain the emotional and intellectual stability I needed to keep my balance and a clear mind. His knowledge helped to uncover narcissistic behaviors that may have been at work in my mother and my siblings, and, while never validated professionally, this gave me the insight I needed to guard myself. My visits to him were invaluable. I wish to also thank my beloved significant other, Bianca, for her unwavering support. I thank the many doctors and scientists who devoted their lives to the study of human behavior and the depths of one's inner state in hopes of finding a pathway to healing. Thanks to each of the books in the bibliography and those listed for Further Reading I have read based on recommendations by my therapist, as well as those I discovered on the internet and while perusing through the shelves in Barnes & Noble.

The term "narcissism" was first suggested to me by my therapist, Jim. It opened the door to my extensive research into specific narcissistic behaviors. It was through this research that I learned to shield and guard my psychological and emotional self. I express my great personal thanks for the published works psychiatrists, psychologists, and behavioral scientists have contributed to the world; these have benefited me immensely. I'm also grateful for the dozens of long, international business flights that offered me the time to enhance my awareness through their writings. I can only imagine what these scientists endured sitting in the presence of those truly lost and truly evil...trapped in the abyss and glaring stare of nothingness.

Bibliography and Resources

BIBLIOGRAPHY

Brown, Nina W. *The Destructive Narcissistic Pattern.* Westport, CT: Praeger Publishers, 1998.

Golomb, Elan. *Trapped in the Mirror: Adult Children of Narcissists in Their Struggle for Self:* NY, Quill, William Morrow, 1995.

Hotchkiss, Sandy. *Why Is It Always About You?: The Seven Deadly Sins of Narcissism.* New York: Free Press, 2002.

Johnson, Stephen M. *Humanizing the Narcissistic Style.* New York: W.W. Norton Company, 1987.

Peck, M. Scott, *People of the Lie: The Hope for Healing Human Evil.* New York: Simon & Schuster, 1983.

Glimpses of the Devil: A Psychiatrists Personal Accounts of Possession, Exorcism, and Redemption: New York: Simon & Schuster, 2005

Merza, Debbie. *The Covert Passive-Aggressive Narcissist: Recognizing the Traits and Finding Healing After Hidden Emotional and Psychological Abuse.* Oregon, Safe Place Publishing, 2017.

Ronningstam, Elsa F. *Identifying and Understanding the Narcissistic Personality.* New York: Oxford University Press, 2005.

Vaknin, Sam. "The Prodigy as Narcissistic Injury." Talent Development Resources. 2021. https://talentdevelop.com/articles/TPANI.html.

FURTHER READING

Caffaro, John. *Sibling Abuse Trauma: Assessment and Intervention Strategies for Children, Families, and Adults*, 2nd ed. Oxfordshire, UK: Routledge, 2004.

Campbell, Sherri. *But It's Your Family: Cutting Ties with Toxic Family Members and Loving Yourself in the Aftermath.* Morgan James Publishing, 2019

Cloud, Henry, and John Townsend. *Boundaries*. Grand Rapids, MI: Zondervan, 1992.

Donaldson-Pressman, Stephanie, and Robert M. Pressman. *The Narcissistic Family: Diagnosis and Treatment*. San Francisco: Jossey-Bass Inc., 1997.

Glass, Lillian. *The Body Language of Liars: From Little White Lies to Pathological Deception—How to See through the Fibs, Frauds, and Falsehoods People Tell You Every Day*. Franklin Lakes, NJ: Career Press, 2013.

Houston, Philip, Mike Floyd, Susan Carnicero, Don Tennant, and Michael Floyd. *Spy The Lie: Three Former CIA Officers Reveal Their Secrets to Unlocking Deception*. New York: Macmillan, 2012.

Kernberg, Otto F. *Aggressivity, Narcissism, and Self-Destructiveness in the Psychotherapeutic Relationship: New Developments in the Psychopathology and Psychotherapy of Severe Personality Disorders*. New Haven, CT: Yale University Press, 2004.

Meyer, Pamela. *Liespotting: Proven Techniques to Detect Deception*. New York: St. Martin's Press, 2010.

Oakley, Barbara. *Evil Genes: Why Rome Fell, Hitler Rose, Enron Failed, and My Sister Stole My Mother's Boyfriend*. Amherst, NY: Prometheus Books, 2007.

The Social Psychology of Good and Evil, Second Edition. Edited by Arthur G. Miller. New York: The Guilford Press, 2016.

Vaknin, Sam. *Malignant Self Love, Narcissism Revisited*. Prague: Narcissus Publications, 1999.

Wiehe, Vernon R. *The Brother/Sister Hurt: Recognizing Effects of Sibling Abuse*. Brandon, VT: Safer Society Press, 1996.

Sibling Abuse: Hidden Physical, Emotional and Sexual Trauma. Newbury Park, CA: SAGE Publications, 1997.

CPSIA information can be obtained
at www.ICGtesting.com
Printed in the USA
BVHW080953191221
624172BV00001B/8